£22.50

KA 0034844 9

D1433910

UNIVERSITY OF
WINCHESTER

Past and Present Publications

Praise and Paradox

Past and Present Publications

General Editor: T.H. ASTON, *Corpus Christi College, Oxford*

Past and Present Publications comprise books similar in character to the articles in the journal *Past and Present*. Whether the volumes in the series are collections of essays – some previously published, others new studies – or monographs, they encompass a wide variety of scholarly and original works primarily concerned with social, economic and cultural changes, and their causes and consequences. They will appeal to both specialists and non-specialists and will endeavour to communicate the results of historical and allied research in readable and lively form. This series continues and expands in its aims the volumes previously published elsewhere.

For a list of titles in Past and Present Publications, see end of book.

Praise and Paradox

Merchants and craftsmen in Elizabethan popular literature

LAURA CAROLINE STEVENSON

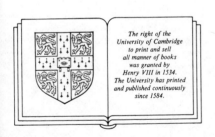

The right of the
University of Cambridge
to print and sell
all manner of books
was granted by
Henry VIII in 1534.
The University has printed
and published continuously
since 1584.

CAMBRIDGE UNIVERSITY PRESS

Cambridge
London   New York   New Rochelle
Melbourne   Sydney

Published by the Press Syndicate of the University of Cambridge
The Pitt Building, Trumpington Street, Cambridge CB2 1RP
32 East 57th Street, New York, NY 10022, USA
296 Beaconsfield Parade, Middle Park, Melbourne 3206, Australia

© Cambridge University Press 1984

First published 1984

Printed in Great Britain at the University Press, Cambridge

Library of Congress catalogue card number: 84–45459

British Library cataloguing in publication data

Stevenson, Laura Caroline
Praise and paradox. – (Past and present
publications)
1. Businessmen in literature
2. English literature – Early modern,
1500–1700 – History and criticism
I. Title II. Series
820.9′352338   PR429.B8

ISBN 0 521 26506 1

KING ALFRED'S COLLEGE
WINCHESTER

820.9
STE   103287

WD

TO THE SAGE PLACE
Georgic farm, pastoral haven

Contents

Acknowledgements

This book began as a doctoral dissertation in History at Yale University. Its final revisions were made at Harvard in 1982–3, when I was an Andrew W. Mellon Faculty Fellow in the Humanities. My primary thanks, then, are due to the Yale University Graduate School and to the Mellon Committee at Harvard for funding a project which took me far longer to complete than I had originally expected.

The American Council of Learned Societies made it possible for me to begin revisions on the book in 1975, by financing day-care for my two children so I could do the necessary research. As a result of their grant-in-aid, I published two earlier forms of parts of this book. 'Anti-Entrepreneurial Attitudes in Elizabethan Sermons and Popular Literature' appeared in *The Journal of British Studies*, 15 (1976), 2–20; 'The Elizabethan Bourgeois Hero-Tale: Aspects of an Adolescent Social Consciousness' appeared in *After the Reformation: Essays in Honor of J.H. Hexter*, ed. Barbara Malament (Philadelphia, 1980). Both articles and the dissertation (Yale, 1974) were written under the name Laura Stevenson O'Connell, which was then mine.

The academic debts above disguise the fact that very little of this book was written in academic circumstances. The chapters here were begun in a study filled with babies, completed in a household of junior high school girls. The research was done in moments snatched between piano lessons given to children too short to reach the pedals; and much of the writing was done in isolation from the scholarly world. These are circumstances in which scholarship can easily fade away, and hence my gratitude to the people who have encouraged and helped me over the past fourteen years is personal as well as professional.

My greatest debts, both personal and professional, are to two scholars whose influence upon this work will be obvious to all who

ix

read it. The late R.S. Sylvester, whose friendship I still mourn, taught me the value of reading literature written by men whose talents did not allow them to explain what they perceived. More than that, however, he taught me, by quiet example, the personal value of literary understanding. Many of the pages that follow may be unworthy of his memory, but every one of them is touched by my reverence for the depth of literary insight and breadth of scholarly commitment which were once his. J.H. Hexter, under whose lash the dissertation was originally written, taught me (by less quiet example) to love controversy, to doubt the obvious, to proceed unabashed in the face of heavy odds, and to hang onto the pigskin until the touchdown is scored. His influence upon my work is spiritual as well as scholarly, and the affection his support has engendered is deep and abiding. In many ways, this book is a tribute to a fifteen-year friendship between two cantankerous people, neither of whom has ever said a harsh word to the other. Miracles occur even in the twentieth century.

I am also indebted to the scholarly friends who have read and criticized my manuscript, particularly to Michael O'Connell, who has read it countless times. Richard Helgerson has discussed Elizabethan authors with me frequently, and the first part of the book has benefited greatly from his criticism. Jonathan Hughes has kept me from misinterpreting economic history out of sheer ignorance. Jo Ann Moran has saved me from making several slips in my discussions of the Elizabethan audience. Norman Jones deserves special thanks for his encouragement and his belief that Elizabethan Englishmen spoke a different language from our own.

Geoffrey Elton has, upon the basis of a very slight acquaintance, read my manuscript and given me suggestions which have greatly improved it. There are not many scholars who would be willing to take time from their own work to further the progress of a person virtually unknown to them, and I deeply appreciate his kindness.

This book could not have been written without the kind and tireless help of Katharine Pantzer, who has allowed me to use the typescript of the unpublished half of the *STC*, and who has also patiently endured my many questions about 'borderline cases' which I have included in or excluded from my canon of popular works. I am very much indebted to both her scholarship and generosity.

My final debt is to my two children, Kate and Meg, who have been lulled to sleep almost every night of their lives by the sound of my typewriter. They have been unfailingly encouraging and under-standing as they have watched the pile of pages grow higher on my desk, and this book, the creation of which has spanned their entire lifetimes, is theirs as much as it is mine.

It is customary to dedicate a book to a person, not to a place. I have broken the custom because there is no single person to whom this book can be dedicated, given its broad range of personal and scholarly debts. I have, therefore, dedicated it to the farm in Vermont where much of it was written – the place where three generations of my family (sage and otherwise) have gathered to learn the lessons of Arcadia, and which I, separated from the academic army by the silence that increasingly surrounds me, have sought as a georgic retreat.

Wilmington, Vermont   LAURA C. STEVENSON
March, 1984

Prefatory note

I have modernized the spelling, but not the capitalization or punctuation, in all quotations. I have not italicized names and nouns, as Elizabethan authors did. I have also modernized all sixteenth- and seventeenth-century titles in the text and in the notes; they appear in their original spelling only in Appendix A.

The following abbreviations are used for works cited frequently.

Annals of English Drama	Harbage, Alfred. *Annals of English Drama, 975–1700*, rev. by S. Schoenbaum (London, 1964).
DNB	*The Dictionary of National Biography*
Dodsley	*A Select Collection of Old English Plays, Originally Published by Robert Dodsley in the Year 1744*, ed. W. Carew Hazlett (15 vols., 1874–6; rpt. New York, 1964).
Greene	*The Life and Complete Works in Prose and Verse of Robert Greene*, ed. Alexander B. Grosart (15 vols., 1881–6; rpt. New York, 1964).
Heywood	*The Dramatic Works of Thomas Heywood*, ed. R.H. Shepherd (6 vols., 1874; rpt. New York, 1964).
Holinshed	Holinshed, Raphael. *Chronicles of England, Scotland, and Ireland*, ed. Henry Ellis (6 vols., London, 1807–8).
Perkins, *Works*	*The Works of That Famous and Worthy Minister of Christ in the University of Cambridge, Mr. William Perkins* (3 vols., 1616–18).

STC

Pollard, A.W. and Redgrave, G.R. *A Short-title Catalogue of Books Printed in England, Scotland, and Ireland, and of English Books Printed Abroad, 1475–1640* (London, 1946; 2nd edn, revised and enlarged, ed. W.A. Jackson, F.S. Ferguson and Katharine Pantzer. Vol. II, London, 1976). References to Vol. I are to the typescript and page proofs of Vol. I, not yet in print.

Simpson

The School of Shakespere, ed. Richard Simpson (2 vols., London, 1878).

Introduction: praise and paradox

The subjects of Elizabeth I witnessed three remarkable intellectual and social changes during their lifetimes: the flowering of English literature, the spread of literacy into the lower ranks of society, and the development and diversification of the English economy. These changes were indirectly related to one another: the prosperity some men gained from economic change was one of the factors that made the spread of literacy possible, and the demands of an increasingly literate audience encouraged Elizabethan authors to expand their literary output. Thus, at one remove, English economic change created circumstances that favoured the burst of literary talent in Elizabeth's reign; and some authors, as if grateful for the favour, returned the compliment by praising the exploits of merchants, industrialists, and craftsmen. The effect of these authors' works on later commercial expansion, exploration and colonization was, of course, indirect; but some secondary, complex connection probably did exist. For the authors who reflected upon men of trade reflected also upon the place they should have in society. They grappled with the problem of fitting men whose money came from commerce into a social structure based on the assumption that status came from land, not capital. In so doing, they pressed against the boundaries of social theory in order to create a place for what, some time later, appeared as commercial self-consciousness.

The works that praised Elizabethan merchants, craftsmen and industrialists have great potential value as guides to the social assumptions, attitudes and ambitions of sixteenth-century Englishmen. Their potential has, however, been neglected in recent years, largely because the works themselves have been thought of as 'middle-class culture' for so long that it is difficult to consider them apart from the Marxist interpretation of social history that dominated scholarship in the first half of the twentieth century.[1] Thus, the

[1] The literature was first analysed in Louis Wright's *Middle-Class Culture in Elizabethan England* (Chapel Hill, 1935). This book remains the only thorough and serious study of the literature on merchants and craftsmen.

1

scholarly generation that has repudiated Marxist ideology has, by association, implicitly denied the value of 'middle-class' literature instead of asking if the literature is necessarily part and parcel of a middle class. And yet, the question is worth asking. The literature, after all, existed without the benefit of Marxist interpretation for over three hundred years before its association with the middle class was noticed; it is possible – even probable – that its essential message has been changed neither by Marxist ideology nor by the attack on the 'myth of the middle class'.[2] And there are compelling reasons for investigating this literature in the light of present scholarship in an effort to find out what its message originally was.

To begin with, the creation of this literature marked a sharp departure from earlier cultural tradition. Before Elizabeth's reign, merchants and craftsmen appeared only in negative literary contexts – in sermons condemning avarice, in estates satires exposing greed and dishonesty, and in chronicles lamenting the fickleness of the commonalty. The development of a new literature that praised the very men earlier works had maligned may have reflected a change in the way these men were viewed in society, and this change deserves investigation. Furthermore, the literature that praised merchants and craftsmen was extremely popular: tales of the heroes of trade went through edition after edition in Elizabeth's reign, and some of them remained popular for years thereafter. It seems, then, that the message of the literature (whatever it may have been) struck a responsive chord in the Elizabethan audience; it would be interesting to know why this was.

Next, the development of the new literature coincided in a suggestive way with the economic events of Elizabeth's reign. The first work in which hyperbolic praise of merchants appeared was published in 1580, a few months before the Turkey Company was formed. This kind of praise developed into a literary vogue between 1592, the year in which the Levant Company was formed, and 1600, the year in which the East India Company received its charter. During this period, 'stock' usurers in drama became benign villains rather than personifications of evil just at the time the elite was depending increasingly on the loans of London financiers. Crafts-

[2]For the attack on Marxist ideology in Tudor and Stuart studies, see J.H. Hexter, 'The Myth of the Middle Class in Tudor England' and 'Storm Over the Gentry', in *Reappraisals in History: New Views on History and Society in Early Modern Europe* (1961; rpt. New York and Evanston, 1963).

men and apprentices emerged as the heroes of plays, poems and tales during the very years the literacy of these men reached the highest point it was to attain for decades to come, and during the years when the wealthier apprentices were embarking on careers in overseas trade that would have been unthinkable two generations earlier. Any one of these incidents alone could be called coincidental, but their aggregate effect suggests there must have been a connection between the economic developments that favoured merchants and craftsmen and the popular literary vogue devoted to their contributions.

The final and most important reason for studying works praising merchants and craftsmen is a theoretical one, based on the comprehension of a much-misunderstood problem – the role of fiction in the interpretation of fact. While many historians and critics insist that fiction presents an utterly distorted portrait of historical fact, a sophisticated understanding of the relationship of the two supplies historians with a methodology that yields insight into the unspoken assumptions of a society in a way other modes of inquiry cannot.[3] The historian, spatially and temporally removed from the society he studies, does not have the anthropologist's opportunity to witness the daily intercourse of his subjects; he is thus in constant danger of missing the nuances of social expression that might reveal aspects of social thought with which he is unfamiliar. Scientific methodology, used by itself, cannot guarantee sensitive understanding of the texture of a society not one's own; demographic studies reveal only the structural patterns of society, and court cases deal principally with extraordinary and deviant social behaviour. Reading fiction, however, permits the historian to see individuals within the society he studies reflecting upon their own experience and trying to make sense of it; any historian who reads literature carefully can gain insight into both the problems that beset society and the way contemporaries viewed them. By thus investigating *how* (as opposed to *what*) people thought about religious, social, psycho-

---

[3] For arguments against the use of fiction in the interpretation of fact, see Lawrence Stone, 'Social Mobility in England, 1500–1700', *Past and Present*, 33 (1966), 22; Peter Laslett, *The World We Have Lost* (New York, 1965), pp. 152–4, and 'The Wrong Way Through the Telescope: a Note on Literary Evidence in Sociology and Social History', *British Journal of Sociology*, 27, 3 (1976), 319–42; Paul Pickrel, 'Childhood and the English Novel', *Smith Alumnae Quarterly* (November 1972), 12.

logical and moral issues, the historian can develop an understanding of the mentality of his subjects.

One of the most valuable ideas structural anthropologists have offered scholars in literature and history is that fiction is not just entertainment, but one of man's oldest ways of reflecting upon the puzzling inequities of everyday life. Given a phenomenon that defies his rational categories of explanation, Claude Lévi-Strauss has pointed out, man makes up a myth – a 'logical model' that helps him reconcile that phenomenon with his cosmology.[4] At its simplest level, a myth creates an explanation for a familiar aspect of man's life; the myth of the Fall, for example, purports to explain why women bear their children in pain and sorrow and men toil for their bread. On a more sophisticated level, however, the myth offers man a means of reconciling himself to the presence of pain in a world God has created; it also provides him with a structure that permits the exploration of the psychology of evil. As such, the myth of the Fall is much more than a primitive explanation for the phenomena of pain and toil; it is a structure for considering complex questions, one that has retained psychological influence long after man has expanded his rational categories of explanation.

Fiction is not identical with myth; a work of fiction is not necessarily written to reconcile unaccountable phenomena with the cosmos. But writing fiction, like myth-making, is a mode of thought – not logical thought that proceeds inductively or deductively to a carefully reasoned conclusion, not discursive analysis that explains events or ideas, but exploratory thought in which a problem is disclosed and considered in time, through the actions of characters. The realm of fiction, unlike that of logical or discursive thought, extends beyond the boundaries of provable truth, and this gives it a great advantage over other means of thought as a way of dealing with certain types of problems. The author who reflects upon the imaginary actions of imaginary characters can isolate various social or psychological issues – love, hate, ambition, social rivalry – from their everyday contexts and consider them without having to deal with their practical consequences. He is free to consider these issues in any frame of reference he chooses, and he can meditate upon their essential nature by imagining their possible effects on human action. Thus, a work of fiction is not just a distorted reflection *of*

[4]*Structural Anthropology*, trans. Claire Jacobson and Brooke G. Schoepf (New York and London, 1963), p. 229.

reality, but a structure that permits reflection *upon* it. It speculates upon what *could* happen if life could be shaped and controlled by ideas, instead of explaining what *does* happen because such shaping is not possible outside the realm of art.[5] This enables fiction to consider problems that may be just beyond the comprehension of men who have hundreds of concrete observations at their disposal, but no way to understand them; it offers a paradigm that may enable them to draw their observations together as parts of a conceptual whole.

Thus, the historian who is alert to the social potential of literary expression can gain insight into the assumptions of the society he studies by examining the artistic paradigms men created in order to make sense of the changes around them. By examining the language in which they formulated their paradigms, he can develop his understanding of the ideological equipment they used to solve day-to-day problems. He can comprehend not only what actions men engaged in, but the imperatives that led to these actions. And in so doing, he can add a dimension to the study of social change.

Study of the Elizabethan literature that praised merchants and craftsmen, then, sheds light upon the imperatives that lay behind Elizabethan reactions to and interpretations of social change. The paradigms created to praise men of trade illuminate the problems that change caused everyday, unspoken assumptions – before these problems were explicitly recognized, and long before they were resolved. The language in this literature shows how great were the limitations of Elizabethan social assumptions, while simultaneously revealing the power these assumptions had to shape the ideology of intelligent men who vaguely sensed their limitations. The literature thus helps historians understand the process of social development by showing them the peculiar state of consciousness that emerges when a society has outgrown an old social ideology, but has not yet formulated a new one.

This study is an exploration of the relationship of language, literary structure and social ideology in the popular Elizabethan literature that praised merchants, industrialists, and craftsmen. Chapter 1 defines a body of 'popular literature' of which the tales of tradesman heroes were a part, and it relates the development of this literature

[5] Clifford Geertz, *The Interpretation of Cultures* (New York, 1973), pp. 443–53.

to the development of the Elizabethan economy. Chapter 2 discusses the social origins and occupations of the popular Elizabethan authors; Chapter 3 relates the development of the literature to the expansion of the Elizabethan audience. The following two sections, using the methodology described above, examine the social assumptions that appeared in the praise of merchants and craftsmen.

The resulting work is far different from the one I originally intended to write, primarily because I had not expected to find that the language Elizabethan authors used to praise commercial men would be foreign to me. Such, however, was the case. For the authors did not praise merchants for their 'diligence', 'thrift', or financial talents; they praised them for being 'magnanimous', 'courtly', 'chivalric', vassals of the king. Similarly, they praised craftsmen not for their 'industry', 'sobriety', and entrepreneurial skill; they praised their 'merriment', 'good housekeeping', 'generosity', and 'obedience'. The labels Elizabethan authors attached to men of trade, in other words, reveal that they never sought to consolidate the social consciousness of these men by appealing to bourgeois values. Elizabethan praise of bourgeois men was expressed in the rhetoric – and by extension, in the terms of social paradigms – of the aristocracy.

This discovery has led me to the unexpected conclusion that social consciousness – the 'cement' that binds a group of men who pursue the same ends together – does not necessarily develop out of a new, separate system of values. In fact, it seems quite possible that a sense of social and economic cohesion precedes the development of an individual value system. I propose, then, through my study of Elizabethan popular literature, that the connection between social values and social cohesion be reconsidered. My research has persuaded me that in times of social and economic change, social fact changes more quickly than vocabulary and ideology, and so men frequently find themselves describing observations of the present in the rhetoric of the past. To dismiss this rhetoric as mere lip-service to tradition is to ignore the pain that attends social change and the confusion that attends formulation of new social ideology. In times of social change, tradition has greater psychological appeal than innovation. Before men abandon old paradigms and develop new ones that accurately describe what they observe, they strain their rhetorical concepts to the snapping point in an attempt to deny the possible ramifications of what they see. The tension between what men really see and what they say they think they see expresses itself in paradox – in terms like 'chivalric merchant', 'gentle craftsman', and 'lordly clothier'. It is this kind of paradoxical thinking that dominates the praise of merchants, craftsmen and clothiers in the latter part of Elizabeth's reign.

In general, if paradoxical language or ideology is left to itself, it will work itself out; what fathers see through the dark glass of oxymoron, sons and grandsons may see face to face in newly formulated paradigms. On the other hand, the development of social ideology is a very delicate process, and it is easily interrupted. If new conditions arise that threaten tentative, paradoxical social observations before they can work themselves out, they simply wither. Sons, instead of (or out of fear of) investigating the potential of new social ideas, justly ridicule the clumsy language of their fathers, point out the flaws in their reasoning, and conclude that the new ideas had nothing in them, after all. This is what happened to the ideas that developed in Elizabethan popular literature. James I's accession and the 'inflation of honours' that followed it did more than devalue peerage. It drove Jacobean writers back to the medieval stereotype of the merchant as grasping usurer and status-seeker, and it encouraged them to ridicule the absurd hybrid merchant-vassals who had been so popular in the 1590s. While the sale of honour in some ways acknowledged the social changes that had occurred in Elizabeth's reign, it had the effect of halting the development of a language that could distinguish class from class and give commercial men an ideological place in the social hierarchy.

Thus the problem of the inter-relationship of money and status, which Elizabethan authors had tentatively begun to consider, did not progress beyond medieval paradigms for many years after the sixteenth-century works on merchants and craftsmen were first published. The paradoxes in Elizabethan social expression were not worked out by the sons or grandsons of the men who originally uttered them; they were resolved by men, born after the Restoration, who wrote in the early eighteenth century. The social ideology of Daniel Defoe and Sir Richard Steele is familiar to modern readers, for they discussed merchants and 'complete tradesmen' in terms of bourgeois values and gentlemen in terms of aristocratic values. They assumed that social conflict between the two groups was fundamentally ideological. Elizabethan authors, however, had only one set of values at their disposal – aristocratic values. To them, the idea that two social groups might conflict with each other on ideological grounds was unthinkable. It is their state of mind, so nearly familiar yet so utterly foreign to the post-industrial world, that is the subject of the coming pages.

Part I

Elizabethan popular literature

1. *Elizabethan popular literature and its economic context*

The first problem that confronts a historian who wishes to examine social perceptions in literature is deciding how to select a canon of works to study. Clearly, it is important that these works have been popular in the age in which they were written. Since literature offers a structure that enables men to reflect upon a variety of problems, works that attain popularity presumably do so because they offer many readers a way of sorting out their ideas on subjects of common interest – even though that structure may later seem simple or inadequate. Conversely, works that appeal to 'fit audience, though few' attain little popularity because they do not offer insights to a wide audience, although the insights they do provide may prove, in retrospect, to have been excellent. Thus, the primary criterion for choosing a work to study must not be its literary excellence or even its social perceptiveness, but its ability to draw an audience to the stage, pulpit, or bookstall.

At the first stages of selecting a canon of literature, it is danger-ous to look for works that were popular with one particular social group. Some of the most popular works in Elizabethan England appealed to people of many social levels; to say that the great dramatists of the stage and pulpit – Shakespeare, Perkins, Dent, Smith – drew only one social group is to distort the depth and breadth of their contemporary impact. Furthermore, selecting literature to read by asserting that it appealed to a certain class leads to circular reasoning. Wright, for example, chose literature that seemed to espouse the values of the bourgeoisie, then concluded that this was 'middle-class literature'. It is no coincidence that the literature, thus chosen, proved there was general interest in the values he was looking for.

In order to avoid circularity and yet read a wide variety of popu-lar books to see if there was indeed literary interest in merchants and craftsmen in Elizabeth's reign, I began this study by selecting a

canon of literature that was available to as large an audience as possible. A perusal of the revised *Short-Title Catalogue of Books Printed
in England* . . . , *1475–1640* suggested that while a great number of
Elizabethan books were printed only once or twice, there were comparatively few that went through three or more editions in a single
decade.[1] These unusually popular works can be said with some confidence to have circulated more widely than any others except the
Bible, text-books and catechisms; they provide a wide selection of
well-read works that can be used to examine the social perceptions
of the period.

Accordingly, the canon of non-dramatic works on which this
study is based comprises all vernacular books first printed in
England between 1558 and 1603 that went through at least three
editions in ten years.[2] There were 189 such books; of these, seventeen went through three editions in three years or less (indicating
faddish popularity of brief duration), twenty-one went through
three editions in four to ten years and then disappeared from the
stalls, and the 151 remaining books (80% of the total) sold steadily
for over a decade. Some of the most popular ones continued to sell
well throughout the seventeenth century.[3]

There are two potential problems with this canon of popular
works. First, little is known about the exact size of Elizabethan
editions, so a book that went through a number of editions may have
sold fewer copies than available publishing statistics indicate. In
1588, a regulation of the Stationers' Company limited the size of
editions of all books but the Bible and text-books to 1250–1500
copies; if this regulation was adhered to, a book that went through
three editions in a decade might have sold as many as 3750–4500
copies, and an extraordinarily popular book like Arthur Dent's

---

[1] Only half of the *Short-Title Catalogue* is currently in print. I am grateful to
Katharine Pantzer of the Houghton Library for letting me examine the typescript
of Vol. I, and to Virginia Renner of the Huntington Library for letting me examine
the page-proofs of Vol. II. The list of popular Elizabethan works appears in
Appendix A.

[2] I have not included translations in the canon. When one approaches a translation,
one has to read the work in the original and compare the perceptions therein with
those the translator inserted; since this takes a thorough knowledge of several cultures, I decided to make this a project of its own. Furthermore, I was most
interested in seeing what Elizabethans themselves wrote about merchants and
craftsmen, and the particular genre of literature most studied here is peculiarly
English.

[3] Charles C. Mish, 'Best Sellers in Seventeenth Century Fiction', *Papers of the Bibliographical Society of America*, 47 (1953), 262–3.

Sermon of Repentance (eighteen editions, 1582–1602) might have sold as many as 27,000 copies in two decades.[4] The printing statistics that exist, however, give no help to the historian who would like to know how strictly this law was followed; they suggest only that the number of copies a printer could run off per edition varied widely.[5] It was most profitable, however, for a printer to print as large an edition as he could if he could be assured of selling all his copies. It cost him as much to have his compositor set one sheet in type as it cost him to have his pressman run of 1500 copies of that sheet; large editions, then, enabled a printer to print a book at the lowest unit cost legally available to him.[6] It is, therefore, difficult to believe that a printer would run off only a few copies of a book that had proven its ability to go through many editions. While a few expensive folio volumes that saw several editions may have been printed in smaller lots because few people could afford them, it is probably safe to assume that most of the popular books circulated as widely as their many printings suggest.[7]

A more serious problem with assembling a canon of popular works is that there may have been more of them than can presently be traced. Bibliographers of the Elizabethan period know that since cheap, popular books were sold unbound, they fell apart easily and were often read to pieces, like the comic-books of the present day. The most popular best-sellers, in fact, are the least likely to have survived; many popular books in the *Short-Title Catalogue* are now available in only one or two copies per edition.[8] There is, then, considerable danger of omitting various popular works from the canon because so many of their early editions have been lost. To deal with this problem, I have included books that went through three editions in *any* decade after their first Elizabethan edition, instead of limiting the study to books that went through three editions in the

---

[4] *A Transcript of the Registers of the Company of Stationers of London, 1554–1640 A.D.*, ed. Edward Arber (5 vols., 1875; rpt. New York, 1950), II, 43.

[5] John Dee's *General and Rare Memorials Pertaining to the Art of Navigation*, for example, went through only 100 copies in its 1577 edition (R.B. McKerrow, *An Introduction to Bibliography for Literary Students* (Oxford, 1927; rpt., 1967), p. 131). On the other hand, when the printers Dunn and Robinson pirated *The ABC and the Little Catechism* in 1585, they ran off an edition of 10,000 copies (Philip Gaskell, *A New Introduction to Bibliography* (New York and Oxford, 1972), p. 162).

[6] Gaskell, *New Introduction*, p. 161.

[7] McKerrow, *Introduction to Bibliography*, p. 133.

[8] H.S. Bennett, *English Books and Readers, 1558–1603* (Cambridge, 1965), p. 300.

first decade after they were printed, on the assumption that there
were more early editions originally printed than those now available. I have also included works whose numerated editions indicate
that they went through more editions than presently exist, and
books whose early editions (usually recorded in the *Stationers'
Register*) are lost, but whose popularity is universally acknowledged.

To complete the canon of popular literature, I have added a list
of popular drama to the 'best-sellers' described above. Drama cannot be selected on the basis of its published circulation, for the
'attached professional' dramatists of this period were under order
(perhaps under contract) not to publish their plays.[9] I have therefore chosen plays that were accessible to large theatre audiences. I
have considered early plays, written between 1558 and the founding
of the London theatres in 1576, that were designed for commercial
itinerant companies that toured fairs, inns and other public places.
I have excluded early plays that required elaborate scenery and
large casts, since these were given by chapel boys, school-boys or
students at the Inns of Court to small audiences at gathering-places
of the elite.[10] I have selected those later plays which, according to
the revised edition of Alfred Harbage's *Annals of English Drama*,
were acted in the public theatres by major companies. The audiences of these plays were large; Bernard Beckerman has estimated
that the average popular play in the 1590s may have been attended
by as many as 15,000 to 20,000 spectators.[11]

My canon of Elizabethan popular literature consists of 296 works
written over a forty-four year period of time. One hundred and
seven of these are plays, seventy-nine are religious books, forty-
eight are works of fiction and poetry, twenty are handbooks of
instruction, sixteen are histories, fourteen are medical and scientific
pamphlets, and twelve are collections of essays and aphorisms.[12]
Amidst this variety of works are books that appeal to all different
tastes. Sermons and treatises sold better, both in number of volumes and in number of editions, than other genres of printed literature, as readers of the research of Edith Klotz and H.S. Bennett

[9] Gerald Bently, *The Profession of Dramatist in Shakespeare's Time, 1590–1642*
(Princeton, 1971), p. 282.

[10] David Begington, *From 'Mankind' to Marlowe: Growth of Structure in the Popular
Drama of Tudor England* (Cambridge, Mass., 1962), pp. 48, 26–7.

[11] *Shakespeare at the Globe, 1599–1609* (New York, 1962), pp. 2, 218.

[12] A topical breakdown of Elizabethan popular literature appears in Appendix C.

would expect.[13] Sir Philip Sidney's *Arcadia*, Edmund Spenser's *Shepherd's Calendar* and William Shakespeare's *Venus and Adonis* appear on the list, which suggests that works of literary quality with aesthetic, rather than practical, appeal could sell extremely well. It would, then, distort the picture of Elizabethan popular literature as a whole to suggest that it reflected only the social and economic interests of the day. Popular literature, then as now, reflected a broad spectrum of moral, aesthetic, social, philosophical – and frivolous – concerns, and while this book will focus on Elizabethan literature that dealt with social ideas, one must always remember that there were many popular works concerned with different subjects.

Among the 296 popular works, however, there were eighty that were concerned with merchants, clothiers, craftsmen and the economic and moral context of their lives. These works together made up 27% of the canon of popular literature – a sizeable percentage, though by no means a large body of 'middle-class culture'. These works were, moreover, clearly influenced by works that had little to say about social and economic questions. The moral views of the preachers appeared in Deloney's novels and apprentice ballads. The pastoralism of Sidney and Spenser appeared in the works of third-rate authors who competed for an audience. The Euphuism of Lyly, popular with the intelligentsia in the 1580s, appeared in the 1590s in works like Deloney's novels that were concerned with social subjects.[14] Thus, the most prominent Elizabethan authors, whether or not they wrote about social subjects, gave the hack-writers of what I have called 'the bourgeois hero-tale' literary structures to use for their considerations of society; it was up to the lesser writers to turn these structures to their purposes.[15]

It is also worth noticing that many of the works with which this study is primarily concerned were among the most popular books published in Elizabethan England. The three preachers who had the most to say on social and economic subjects, for example, were the

---

[13] Klotz, 'A Subject Analysis of English Imprints for Every Tenth Year from 1480 to 1640', *Huntington Library Quarterly*, 1 (1937–8), 419–19; Bennett, *Books and Readers*, pp. 112–13.

[14] For the spread of the appeal of *Euphues*, see G.K. Hunter, *John Lyly: The Humanist as Courtier* (Cambridge, Mass., 1962), pp. 279–88.

[15] L. Stevenson O'Connell, 'The Elizabethan Bourgeois Hero-Tale: Aspects of an Adolescent Social Consciousness', in *After The Reformation: Essays in Honor of J.H. Hexter* (Philadelphia, 1980), pp. 267–90.

most popular authors of their day. Arthur Dent, the most rhetorical of these, had tremendous contemporary appeal. His *Sermon of Repentance* went through eighteen editions between 1582 and 1602, and nineteen between 1602 and 1638; and his *Plain Man's Pathway to Heaven* went through at least twenty editions between 1601 and 1640. Dent drew his audiences with what can only be called racy descriptions of sin and hell-fire condemnations of corruption, greed, and social ambition. In a milder vein, there was Henry Smith, nicknamed 'Silver-Tongued Smith' by his many London followers, some of whom took down his sermons short-hand and rushed them to the press – with resulting confusions of text. His *Sermon of the Benefit of Contentation* (thirty-seven editions, 1592–1637) rivalled Dent's penitential sermon in popularity; and seven of his other sermons went through twenty or more editions between 1590 and 1640. The third of these preachers, Wright's 'apostle of practical divinity', William Perkins, gave Puritan theology its most systematic treatment.[16] The shortest, least-complicated treatise in which he presented his explanations, *The Foundation of the Christian Religion*, went through twenty-six editions between 1590 and 1638. Nine of his individual treatises and sermons, in which he dealt with themes of grace and damnation, conscience, usury and charity, went through ten to twenty editions apiece.

Turning from religion to fiction and poetry, one finds that the most popular work printed in Elizabeth's reign was Thomas Tusser's *Five Hundred Points of Good Husbandry, United to as Many of Good Housewivery*, which went through twenty editions between 1573 and 1638. This work was a georgic poem written in doggerel verse, filled with practical advice and many moral sayings that encouraged diligence and thrift. Robert Greene's estates satire, *A Quip for an Upstart Courtier*, which went through six editions in 1596 alone, compared values of flashy courtiers and ancient gentlemen in a lively dialogue that also included many remarks on the duties of craftsmen and a tale about the fellowship of shoemakers. Most influential of all works of fiction about social and economic subjects were Thomas Deloney's novels. *Jack of Newbury*, the first of these, concerned the exploits of a worthy apprentice who became a fabulously wealthy clothier without sacrificing his soul to success. The two parts of *The Gentle Craft*

[16]Louis B. Wright, 'William Perkins: Elizabethan Apostle of "Practical Divinity" ', *HLQ*, 3 (1940), 171–96.

presented a fictionalized history of the shoemaking trade; stories drawn from it inspired Thomas Dekker's play *The Shoemakers' Holiday* and William Rowley's *A Shoemaker, A Gentleman*. Finally, *Thomas of Reading*, in which Deloney turned again to the clothing trade, inspired four plays (all of which have been lost) and Henry Robarts' unsuccessful imitation, *Haigh for Devonshire*. There is no doubting the influence and popularity of Deloney's works, though many of their early editions have been lost. He combined the popular heroics of apprentice ballads with the cheerful bawdiness of jest-books; he mingled moments of pastoral romance and Euphuistic language with serious consideration of the place of wealthy men of trade in the social hierarchy; and finally, he wrote with a wonderful ear for dialogue and an unfailing instinct for telling a good yarn. The vigour with which he praised men of trade apparently caught the interest of an audience already used to hearing such praise in the shortened chronicles of John Stow and a few London plays and apprentice ballads, and other hack-writers quickly imitated his works in their efforts to attain popularity.

The most popular works of non-fiction in the period all appealed to a large audience by offering a great deal of information in comparatively few pages. Some of these works were of obvious use to men of trade, although they also appealed to a general audience. *The Writing Tables* of Frank Adams or Richard Grafton's *Little Treatise, Containing Many Tables and Rules*, for example, attracted readers who needed to remember how to convert weights and measures, wanted a calendar of feast-days, or needed miscellaneous bits of information, such as the distances between English towns. Men who needed legal information could turn to William West's *Symbolaeographia*, which taught them how to draw up contracts – a skill increasingly useful in an age in which trade was becoming complex and oral contracts between neighbours were no longer sufficient for the way business was done. Finally, men who had climbed the social ladder and needed learning to go with their clothes could find plenty of aphorisms in Nicholas Ling's *Politeuphia* which would enable them to be eloquent at short notice. These works, all of which went through ten to nineteen editions between their first appearance and 1640, obviously supplied a need in a society whose changing economic procedures brought some men considerable wealth and an ambivalent social position; like the works of fiction that considered the relationship of wealth and 'genteel' behaviour, these handbooks reflected upon the social and educational pressures success put upon its recipients. In this context, the popularity of John Stow's *Summary of English Chronicles* takes on particular interest; each of its successive editions contained more London history than its predecessors, and offered detailed portraits of eminent Londoners to men interested in the city's traditions. In an obvious attempt to give London's wealthiest and most important citizens a dignified history, Stow uncovered a great deal of material about merchants that other chroniclers left untouched, and he influenced both the tone and the content of the fiction and drama written about London's leading citizens.

While one can say confidently that many of the books dealing with social and economic topics were the most popular ones in Elizabethan England, when one turns to the stage it is more difficult to assess relative popularity. There are no records of the attendance of the majority of Elizabethan plays; the only plays for which an estimate of audience size is possible are those produced at the Rose between 1592 and 1597 – plays for which Philip Henslowe noted 'box-office' returns in his diary.[17] Unfortunately, these plays were produced just before the vogue of citizen drama became popular, so one cannot determine whether a play like Heywood's *Four Prentices of London* achieved the popularity of Marlowe's *The Jew of Malta*, an 'old favourite' that the Henslowe companies produced thirty-six times between 1592 and 1596. One can, however, make a few observations about popular drama that help to establish it in its context and go on from there to make an educated guess about the popularity of a few plays that dealt with merchants and craftsmen.

Traditionally, the acting companies did not, as acting companies do today, produce a play for as many consecutive performances as they could without losing money. Instead, they kept ten to fifteen plays in their repertory, producing new ones as they were written, dropping old ones when they stopped drawing an audience, and reviving old favourites several times over a period of years. A new play might be given once a week for a few performances; then, if it failed, it could be dropped entirely, and if it lost its audience slowly, it could be produced again in a month or so.[18] This system allowed the actors to draw an audience of regular playgoers who did not object to seeing a play several times, provided there were a variety

[17] Walter W. Greg, ed., *Henslowe's Diary* (2 vols., London, 1904–8), II, 338–41.
[18] Beckerman, *Shakespeare at the Globe*, Chapter I.

of plays to view. It also allowed them to draw comparatively infrequent playgoers, some of whom may have had little time and money for luxuries, to plays with an assured reputation. Finally, it enabled them to cater to London's floating population of non-residents, men who came to the city on business (of trade, or law, of the court, or of Parliament) and wanted amusement during their stays.

Given this scheme of things, an extremely popular play like *The Jew of Malta* probably owed its box-office success to its ability to bring back a certain percentage of loyal fans several times; it also profited from its reputation with a core of loyal viewers and drew a portion of new viewers each time it was produced. Alfred Harbage has suggested that the average attendance of such a play was 1250 people per performance (in a theatre that held some 2000 if filled to capacity), many of whom had seen the play before.[19] This means that if the *Jew of Malta* drew between 1250 and 2000 people to each of its thirty-six performances as an 'old' play, it attracted some 28,000 to 45,000 men and women to the Rose in the 1590s – even if three-quarters of the audience saw the play twice. This is an audience that compares favourably with that of the very most popular books in the London bookstalls.

Henslowe's records suggest that during the mid-nineties, the plays that drew large audiences were those that were in the easiest sense theatrical, with gloriously wicked villains, beautiful maidens, and attractive heroes. Wicked usurers (the antithesis of later citizen heroes) like those in *The Jew of Malta* or *A Knack to Know An Honest Man* (twenty-one performances, 1594–6) could be counted upon to draw a crowd. Blood-and-thunder plays like Kyd's *The Spanish Tragedy* (sixteen performances as an 'old' play in 1592, thirteen performances in 1597) also attracted many people, and the melodramatic plot and theme of Marlowe's *Doctor Faustus* (twenty-five performances as an 'old' play, 1594–7) did very well too. Extravagant theatricality went out of date as acting styles changed and audiences became accustomed to the subtleties of Shakespeare and Jonson, but the enduring popularity of these old plays, some of which did as well in print as on the stage, suggests that blood and thunder gradually became 'high camp' to audiences that had developed more sophisticated taste. Furthermore, melodrama, like

[19] *Shakespeare's Audience* (New York, 1941), p. 33.

the prose of *Euphues*, seems to have attracted unsophisticated audiences after it had exhausted the serious literary interest of the elite. The 'rant' that originally brought onlookers to *The Spanish Tragedy* lived on in plays that appealed to citizen audiences, like Heywood's *Four Prentices of London* and *1 Edward IV*.

Unfortunately, an assessment of plays that appealed to a citizen audience has to rely on printed popularity. This is not terribly satisfactory, since theoretically the dramatic companies printed a play only if they were in financial difficulties – the managers assumed that an audience that could buy a play would not return for a second or third viewing, and they feared that a printed play would be available for rival companies to act.[20] Nevertheless, popular plays did come into print (with or without the consent of their authors) and for lack of better indications of popularity, it is to these plays one must turn to estimate how well drama with civic heroes attracted audiences.

Generally, plays with a London setting seem to have done fairly well. There is no record of the popularity of one of the most interesting of these – *A Warning for Fair Women*, in which a London merchant's wife murders her husband to marry a gentleman. But a play of the same moral nature, *How to Choose a Good Wife From a Bad*, went through seven editions between 1602 and 1634 – one edition less than Shakespeare's *Richard II*. Two of the plays which receive a great deal of attention in this work also did well in print. Heywood's *1 Edward IV*, which, despite its title, is primarily concerned with London citizens and a country tanner, went through six editions (two less than *Doctor Faustus*) before 1640. Thomas Dekker's *The Shoemakers' Holiday*, which centred upon Simon Eyre, a shoemaker who became Lord Mayor of London in Deloney's fictitious history of the Cordwainers' Company, went through five editions at this time. Despite the lack of evidence about dramatic audiences, then, one can at least conclude that the citizen drama produced in the last four or five years of Elizabeth's reign compared respectably in printed popularity with the much greater plays of Shakespeare and the earlier, melodramatic plays of Marlowe. They were outsold in editions (and probably on the stage, since the old favourites stood the test of constant revivals) by Kyd's *Spanish Tragedy*, which was printed ten times between 1592 and

[20] E.K. Chambers, *The Elizabethan Stage* (4 vols., Oxford, 1923) II, 183–4.

1631, and by *Richard III* and *1 Henry IV*, which also went through ten editions apiece. Still, the Dekker and Heywood plays were well known in the period in which they were written, and while they did not compete with the works of Shakespeare in literary excellence, they were certainly superior in quality to a great number of lesser Elizabethan plays. At the end of Elizabeth's reign, citizen comedy and London history attracted the best of the second-string playwrights in London; it seems probable that the plays also drew a good-sized audience.

It can be safely asserted, then, that the works about merchants, clothiers and craftsmen published and produced during Elizabeth's reign were far more popular than most Elizabethan works. The most popular of these works, as we have seen, were the very most popular books in their day, and even those which went through only five or six editions were among the 189 printed books which sold that many editions out of the thousands of volumes printed during the reign. The best of the citizen plays also seem to have attracted large audiences, though it would be unsafe to estimate how large these audiences were, given the scanty evidence available. While we cannot say that there was a 'great body' of 'middle-class literature' that appealed to Elizabethan audiences, we can at least say that works on merchants and craftsmen were attractive to a substantial portion of the Elizabethan reading public. When the authors of the books and plays in the canon of Elizabethan popular literature expressed their social views, they affected the opinions of the largest audience of their day, and they gave that audience a way of thinking about the social hierarchy, its values, and the place of merchants, clothiers, and craftsmen in Elizabethan society.

The emergence and unquestionable popularity of books and plays considering economic questions and celebrating the achievements of merchants and craftsmen brings up the problem of the commercial context of popular Elizabethan literature. Historians of an earlier generation, relying on published statistics and influenced by the Whig belief in English history's progressive development to imperial greatness, believed that this context was one of steady commercial and industrial expansion.[21] In the 1930s, this belief was corroborated by John Nef, whose work on the English coal industry convinced him that the country had experienced a 'first industrial

---

[21] See W.E. Minchinton, ed., *The Growth of English Overseas Trade in the Seventeenth and Eighteenth Centuries* (London, 1969), p. 5.

revolution' between 1540 and 1640, and had enjoyed a period of substantial growth in capital investment, technological develop-ments, increased production, and urbanization.[22] Such a context provided a perfect atmosphere for the sudden development of a literature that praised men of trade. In recent years, however, his-torians have re-examined Tudor and Stuart economics in great detail, relying on unpublished sources and using sophisticated techniques of measuring economic growth. The revised picture of the Elizabethan economy that has emerged from their works is one of a pre-industrialized country, characterized by primitive tech-nology, with a slow rate of technological advance, an abundance of inefficient and unskilled labour, and a limited market economy that sustained stagnation rather than growth.[23] This is hardly an economy which warrants the growth of a middle class that seeks literary fare, as it seeks money, omniverously and greedily. Thus, the economic context of popular literature requires a brief re-examination.

A 'brief re-examination', however, is bound to be controversial, for current scholars disagree markedly in their interpretations of the Elizabethan economic scene. Some, having studied the reverses of the mid-sixteenth century, refer to the age as one of economic deso-lation or plunder.[24] Others, examining the work of Tudor adminis-trators who strove to increase England's prosperity, have suggested that the increase of domestic industry and the increased demand for consumer products enabled wage-earners to keep up with inflation by seeking new forms of employment.[25] The disagreement lies partly in emphasis: does one wish to accentuate the poverty of a pre-industrial society in which power and influence belonged to the rich alone, or does one wish to look at the advances which enabled men who took social injustice as the divine scheme of things to work as they could to achieve what few rewards were available? Disagree-ment lies also in the nature of local evidence, for some areas in

[22] *The Rise of the British Coal Industry* (2 vols., London, 1932). A useful discussion of Nef's thesis and its various refutations appears in Sybil M. Jack, *Trade and Industry in Tudor and Stuart England* (London, 1977).
[23] This definition of the pre-industrial economy appears in L.A. Clarkson, *The Pre-Industrial Economy of England 1500–1700* (London, 1971), p. 22.
[24] See Charles Pythian-Adams, *Desolation of a City: Coventry and the Urban Crisis of the Late Middle Ages* (Cambridge, 1979); W.G. Hoskins, *The Age of Plunder: King Henry's England, 1500–1547* (London and New York, 1976).
[25] See Joan Thirsk, *Economic Policy and Projects: The Development of a Consumer Society in Early Modern England* (Oxford, 1978).

Elizabethan England prospered while others suffered; local studies, then, emphasize strengths and weaknesses on a geographic basis. What follows is an attempt to walk a precarious middle line between theories of 'poverty' and theories of 'economic growth'. This attempt is based upon the belief that the Elizabethan economic atmosphere combined stagnation and development, poverty and prosperity, personal opportunity and corporate conservatism in a puzzling mixture, and that Elizabethans reacted to this atmosphere (according to their temperaments, ranks, and opportunities) with aggression, complacency, indifference, confusion, dissatisfaction, anxiety, anger, or despair.

By modern standards, making a living in Tudor England was difficult and precarious; by contemporary European standards, however, it was comparatively easy. Social and economic difficulties there certainly were, but they were not worsened by taxes arbitrarily imposed by a foreign emperor, brutal inquisition and thousands of heretic burnings, mass murder in a capital city, and unremitting religious war that extinguished the trade of a great commercial centre. Elizabethan England was blessed with internal peace, if not with universal concord; with the possibility of economic development, if not the consistent fact of it; and with monarchical stability, if not with security on the scores of marriage and succession. Elizabethan popular literature emerged in a country that enjoyed what, by European standards, can be described only as domestic bliss.

When Elizabeth came to the throne, however, English commerce was backward by European standards; and, despite its progress, it was still working to catch up with European economic developments in 1603. The country had only a small merchant marine, only one large-scale industry, and limited trade routes on which it was dependent for a large number of essential imports. Internally, the prospect of significant economic growth – rising per capita income – was severely limited by two related rises, one of population, which doubled between 1500 and 1700 (with the bulk of the increase between 1550 and 1650), and the other of prices, particularly those of grain, which outstripped the rise in wages during the last half of the sixteenth century by a ratio of roughly 7:3.[26]

[26]D.C. Coleman, *The Economy of England 1450–1750* (London and New York, 1977), pp. 18–19, 29; Peter Clark and Paul Slack, *English Towns in Transition 1500–1700* (London and New York, 1976), p. 83.

These two increases put a severe strain on English agriculture and industry, for if the excess population were not to starve, the economy had to expand enough to provide growing numbers of people with employment and food. The economy does seem to have absorbed its extra population (the increase in population suggests, at the very least, that most people were getting enough to eat); but that absorption was always precarious, and a great many wage-earners lived a hand-to-mouth existence even in good years. In times of trade slump, poor harvest, or disease, the poor starved, if not everywhere, at least in locations that could not support extra mouths; and the problem of 'sturdy rogues and vagabonds' was caused in part by the expansion of the population beyond the economy's saturation point.[27] The grim possibility that many harvests would fail in a row (as happened in the 1590s) and that starvation would become a permanent resident in the lower orders was never far off in this fragile economy; but it never came to pass. The period did not witness economic growth, but it did see economic change that enabled wage-earners to stay marginally employed most of the time and permitted agricultural labourers to produce enough food to feed the growing population.

Above the level of wage-earners, there were men in a position to take advantage of the comparative cheapness of labour, exploit new patterns of demand, seek new markets for wares both in and out of England, and bring more land under cultivation. Among these men were merchants who traded wares overseas or internally, clothiers who took advantage of changing patterns of demand for English products by diversifying their output, and craftsmen who supplied wares for a growing population and who, sometimes, were able to move from manufacture into the more lucrative business of wholesale trade. These men's successful manipulation of economic trends kept the economy from unbroken stagnation; it also brought them economic well-being. But their ability to take advantage of the developments that impoverished their neighbours aroused mixed feelings in a conservative society, and their wealth raised serious questions about the place of rich businessmen in the social hier-

[27] Andrew B. Appleby, 'Disease or Famine? Mortality in Cumberland and Westmorland, 1580–1640', in *PP*, 26, 2 (1973), 403–41; David Palliser, 'Dearth and Disease in Staffordshire, 1540–1670', in C.W. Chalklin and M.A. Havinden, eds., *Rural Change and Urban Growth, 1500–1800: Essays in English Regional History in Honour of W.G. Hoskins* (London, 1974), pp. 54–75.

archy. It was economic change, not economic growth, that brought
these men to the attention of the popular authors – change that left
thoughtful men with many questions and few answers.

Among the richest and most prominent men who profited from
the changing English economy were the London merchants connected with the export of cloth. During the early sixteenth century,
as trade in wool decreased and trade in cloth increased, the export
of cloth had become increasingly under the domination of London;
by 1550, the city was exporting 90% of England's cloth, whereas a
century earlier, she had exported barely half of it.[28] By the time
Elizabeth ascended the throne, English merchants were also ship-
ping the bulk of the cloth they exported themselves, instead of relying on foreign merchants as they had earlier in the century. This
economic development was very profitable to the small group of
London merchants who had a monopoly on the marketing of cloth
– the merchant adventurers. The Fellowship of Merchant Adventurers, formally recognized in 1486 and 1502, was technically a
fellowship of all merchants connected with the cloth trade, not just
London merchants. As the primary route for the cloth trade became
that between London and Antwerp and the profitable export trade
was sucked away from provincial ports, however, few provincial
merchants could afford to make the large trading investments that
London merchants could – in fact, few of them could even afford the
high entry fee the adventurers set as the price of admission to their
ranks.[29] Thus, the profits from some half of England's total export
trade fell into the hands of these few London merchants; and more
than half these profits accrued to the elite of the Fellowship (consist-
ing of some 11–12% of its total membership) which by itself controlled half the trade on which the company had its monopoly.
Clothiers, provincial merchants, and lesser London merchants all
deeply resented the adventurers' monopoly on the cloth trade, but
their complaints to the government fell on deaf ears; Elizabeth had
a quick eye for men wealthy enough to lend her money, and she
used the adventurers' substance repeatedly in return for protecting
their rights.[30]

[28] Coleman, *Economy of England*, pp. 51–2.
[29] G.D. Ramsay, *The City of London in International Politics at the Accession of Elizabeth Tudor* (Manchester, 1975), pp. 46–50.
[30] In 1535, seventeen out of 131 active Adventurers engaged in Antwerp trade owned half the cloth of the Fellowship; between 1606 and 1618, twenty-six of the 219 active Adventurers owned half the cloth. See Peter Ramsey, *Tudor Economic Problems*

The power of the merchant adventurers was not limited to overseas trade. Wealth paved the path from private life to public office in London, and so bright young merchants who joined the Adventurers eventually rose to become mayors and aldermen of the city. In the first half of Elizabeth's reign, the great majority of city rulers were the most prosperous members of the adventurers, with the result that the period 1550–80 saw a succession of mayors and aldermen whose wealth was of a scale never seen before in those positions, although London's leaders had always been rich.[31] The wealth of these men, exhibited in the pageantry of civic government, Lord Mayor's Shows, and spectacular charities, was as visible (though not necessarily as great) as that of the aristocracy. Thus, ironically, while the commercial and political monopolies of the merchant adventurers aroused hostility among lesser merchants and craftsmen in London, the wealth and charity of the great tycoons in city government were also sources of civic pride – a pride to which the popular authors who depended on London's presses and theatres for their livings could appeal.

The merchant adventurers were not the only merchants in London – though no doubt they would have been happy to have enjoyed that position. In fact, commercial trends of which they failed to take advantage gradually led to their decline, and they lost place as commercial and political leaders of the city in the early decades of the seventeenth century. The merchants who replaced them were members of the new trading companies founded during Elizabeth's reign.[32] These companies were created after the London–Antwerp commercial axis on which the adventurers' trade was founded was upset by trade stoppages in the 1560s, then permanently destroyed by the Spanish repression of the rebellion of the Netherlands in the late 1560s and early 1570s. The merchant adventurers managed to survive the upset by re-establishing themselves successively at Emden, Middelburg and Stadt; but other merchants, possibly worried about England's total dependence on one trade route and certainly eager to find lucrative trade not covered by the

(London, 1963), p. 64; Richard Grassby, 'The Personal Wealth of the Business Community in Seventeenth-Century England', *Economic History Review*, Series 2, 23 (1970), 229. On Elizabeth's use of these wealthy merchants, see Ramsay, *City of London*, p. 50.

[31] Ramsay, *City of London*, pp. 41–3.

[32] Robert Brenner, 'The Civil War Politics of London's Merchant Community', *PP*, 58 (1973), 53–107.

adventurers' monopoly, began to revive old trade routes and set up new ones with countries newly discovered by English explorers. Elizabeth and her councillors encouraged this enterprise, for they had begun to realize that commercial expansion and political power went hand in hand, and they were ready to give official backing to businessmen who wished to open negotiations with rulers of distant countries. Thus, Elizabeth's reign saw the creation of the Spanish and Eastland Companies in the 1570s, the Turkey, Barbary, and Africa Companies in the 1580s, the amalgamation of the Turkey and Venice Companies into the Levant Company in 1592, and the founding of the East India Company in 1600. These companies were not all enduring or immediately successful on a large scale; their foundations did not constitute a commercial boom. They did, however, expand the horizons of English trade, provide new markets for English cloth, provide a new emphasis on trade for re-export, and establish mechanisms for long-term capital investments necessary in commerce with distant countries. Furthermore, the geographic expansion of trade, along with the semi-piratical missions of the British sea-dogs with which this expansion was contemporary, created a demand for more and larger ships that resulted in the employment of hundreds of men (from thirty different crafts) in London shipyards.[33] Thus, while the new trading companies did not affect commercial growth immediately, they did improve employment opportunities for some men and – because of the wealth of the merchants in the new companies and the majesty of the new ships used in trade – their development was a visible one to which Londoners could point with pride.

The third group of London merchants that profited from the economic changes in Elizabeth's reign was that of wealthy retailers – grocers, mercers, drapers, merchant taylors, goldsmiths, and members of the other great companies. Barred from overseas trade by the ordinances in trading companies that limited their membership to 'mere' merchants (as opposed to retailers with a few foreign investments on the side) these men put their energies into domestic trade; they sold textiles, marketed imports in London and the provinces, provided the city with food and fuel, and supplied the increasingly showy court with luxuries and loans. There was a fortune to be made in domestic trade, and as London's population

---

[33] Jack, *Trade and Industry*, pp. 99–101.

grew (from about 60,000 in 1520 to 80,000 in the mid-1560s, to some 200,000 in 1603 before the plague), an increasing number of retailers profited from the dependency of city dwellers on their services. Thus, retailers by the end of the reign had come to be able to share the joys and sorrows of public office with merchant adventurers in London; by James I's reign, approximately half the aldermen of London were primarily concerned with domestic trade rather than foreign.[34]

Below the merchant adventurers, 'new' overseas merchants and principal retailers in wealth and political power in London, there were many merchants who were extraordinarily prosperous but operated at a more modest level than the civic elite. There were many more of these relatively wealthy merchants than there were fabulously rich tycoons. Richard Grassby's study of the net assets of a sample of London freemen at their deaths between 1586 and 1614 indicates that 15.9% of the 1581 freemen were 'middling merchants' worth between £1000 and £5000 in personal (not real) property; only 3.2% of the freemen were worth between £5000 and £10,000, and only twenty merchants out of the total were worth more than £10,000 – less than 1%.[35] Famous London merchants like Sir William White or Sir Thomas Gresham were not typical sixteenth-century capitalists; they were the Rockefellers and Carnegies of their age, men whose wealth gave their class a reputation for wealth out of proportion to the actual number and riches of its members.

In provincial towns, as in London, there existed elites of wealthy merchants who dominated city companies and politics. These men were prominent and well off, but they operated on a much smaller scale than the great merchants of London. In Exeter, the cargoes of merchants' ships were usually owned by groups of two to twelve merchants – and the ships that sailed from Exeter were twenty- to thirty-ton vessels, not the hundred-ton ships that sailed out of the Thames after the 1580s. The range of trade done from provincial ports was not great. Half of Exeter's fleet, for example, was concerned with domestic coastal trade; most of the other half traded with France.[36] The division between 'mere merchants' and retailers,

---

[34] Robert Ashton, *The City and the Court, 1603–1643* (Cambridge, 1979), p. 15. The population figures are drawn from Clark and Slack, *English Towns*, p. 83, and Ramsay, *City of London*, p. 33.
[35] Grassby, 'Personal Wealth', pp. 229, 224.
[36] W.G. Hoskins, 'The Elizabethan Merchants of Exeter', in S.T. Bindoff, *et al.*,

moreover, was far less common in provincial ports than in London. Provincial merchants were generally both wholesalers and retailers; a vintner who imported wine, for example, might sell some to private customers as well as distributing it to other retailers. Some merchants even picked up a variety of interesting commodities in their overseas voyages and then sold them to customers when they got back to their shops.[37]

The lack of division of labour (and of capital) between wholesale and retail trade in provincial cities, the short range of trade to which merchants confined themselves, and the comparatively small local markets with which they dealt limited the wealth of provincial merchants. While the richest of them may have been worth as much as the middling London merchants in the £1000–£5000 category, there were none whose wealth competed with that of the extraordinarily rich merchants of London.[38] Money was not everything, of course; a man worth £4000 in a provincial port was at the very top of the social ladder, one of the most prominent members of the most prestigious companies in his town, and no doubt a mayor or alderman. His counterpart in London was a lesser member of a larger company, closed out of the ruling elite by his richer brethren, and a man of limited social prestige and political power. A moderately prosperous merchant who liked the excitements of city government and the respect due to a local elite was probably happier in the small ports of the counties than in the increasingly complex sea of London.

The merchants portrayed in Elizabethan popular literature were, for the most part, not provincial magnates or middling London merchants, but the great London merchants whose wealth reached fairy-tale proportions. This is not altogether surprising; the leaders of a social group are more visible than the rank and file of its members, and wealth beyond the common man's wildest dreams tends to gather legends unto itself. One of the most appealing legends that attaches itself to wealth is that the fabulously rich man used to be poor like everybody else. The story of Dick Whittington and his cat, for instance, stresses Whittington's early poverty and misfortune, thus linking him with the large body of poor labourers and appren-

eds., *Elizabethan Government and Society: Essays presented to Sir John Neale* (London, 1961), p. 170.
[37] *Ibid.*, p. 171.
[38] *Ibid.*, pp. 172–3; Grassby, 'Personal Wealth', pp. 230–3.

tices who came to London to seek a fortune in Elizabeth's reign; Whittington's success is an obvious expression of these men's hopes to attain prosperity and rule the city to which they have come as poor and bewildered workmen from provincial England. Another appealing legend that accompanies great wealth is that it can be obtained without sullying the character of the man who has it. In a Heywood play produced in the same year as the first version of the Dick Whittington tale (1605), the hero, Sir Thomas Gresham, buys a pearl so expensive that even princes balk at its price, grinds it up, pours it into his wine, and drinks it to pledge the health of Queen Elizabeth. This episode is generated partly by nostalgia, for Elizabeth had died two years earlier, and the scene certainly reflects as much on the worth of the queen as on the wealth of the merchant; but it takes its tone from the glitter that surrounds great wealth and from the glory that such wealth, spent thus loyally (if vulgarly), brings to England's greatest city. Gresham in this play is not just a great merchant; he is a great patriot, and his wealth enables him to express his love of his monarch and his city. He has become rich to serve his queen, not to serve himself.[39]

Thus, to explain the literary interest in merchants during Elizabeth's reign, one does not have to postulate the existence of a commercial boom. One has instead to recall the spectacular growth of London in the period, and reflect that this growth was generated by her domination of England's export trade and made possible by the efforts of the retailers who fed and clothed the city. The growth of London was accompanied by the growth in wealth of a few spectacularly successful merchants who, as civic leaders, were friends of privy councillors, sometimes even friends of the queen, financiers and attirers of courtiers, and Members of Parliament. Their activities brought glory to London and, by extension, to all of England. But London was the home of the theatres and bookstalls, and London was the city to which an increasing number of people flocked from the countryside, drawn by the lure of prosperity at a time in which poverty was the lot of so much of the population. By creating and perpetuating tales of London's most prestigious citizens, the popular authors could attract audiences by expressing in exaggerated fashion the small man's hopes of becoming so rich he would never have to face want again, or by assuring the moderately

[39] The play is *2 If You Know Not Me, You Know Nobody*. The episode appears in Heywood, I, 301.

prosperous man that money, properly spent, was a symbol of patriotism, charity and civic pride, not just of hard-earned personal success. At the same time, the authors could praise the virtues of London, which was becoming the commercial and cultural centre of England, by praising the virtues of its rulers.

It would be a mistake, however, to think that the literary interest in commercial wealth was purely a London phenomenon. There was more substance in the popular literature about merchants and industrialists than the familiar Whittington story might lead one to think. In addition to focussing the dreams of men who desired prosperity for themselves, these stories allowed authors to ponder the connection between money and social status. This connection was an extremely important one in which power and privilege went to the social elite and the principal social division lay between the gentry and everybody else.[40] Could phenomenal wealth (not just prosperity) leap over social boundaries and make one man as good as another? Could dreams of commercial success be accompanied by dreams of becoming part of the social elite? These questions could be answered only by analysing the effect of phenomenal wealth wherever it occurred. In Elizabethan England, it occurred in London merchants and also in country clothiers, the men responsible for the continued success of England's most important export.

England's clothiers, of course, were not all wealthy men. At the top of the scale of clothiers were men whose wealth (and the legends surrounding it) was as great as that of the merchant adventurers with whom they traded at Blackwell Hall. Peter Blundell, for example, was worth £40,000 at his death, a figure that put him in the same income bracket as the two or three wealthiest London merchants; William Stumpe of Malmesbury and John Winchcombe (Jack of Newbury) had wealth in similar proportions.[41] Like their counterparts in the London mercantile elite, these men were exceptional; many clothiers were merely prosperous, and others, whose total output might be only seven or eight cloths a year, were indistinguishable in income and status from independent weavers and small yeomen.[42]

Sixteenth-century labour conditions favoured the prosperity of

---

[40] See below, Chapter 2, n. 2.
[41] Grassby, 'Personal Wealth', p. 231; G.D. Ramsay, *The Wiltshire Woollen Industry in the Sixteenth and Seventeenth Centuries*, 2nd edn (London, 1965), pp. 31–6.
[42] Jack, *Trade and Industry*, p. 102.

clothiers. Clothing depended on the rural division of labour known as the 'putting-out' system, in which clothiers distributed wool and yarn to spinsters, weavers, and finishers (fullers, dyers, shearers) in their homes, passing material on to the next stage of production when it was ready. As population and prices rose, more and more men and women who lived in pastoral farming areas found it necessary to supplement their agricultural incomes by taking in work from clothiers.[43] Since the price of cloth rose faster than the wages the clothier paid his employees, the clothier was in the happy position of hiring an increasingly large labour force and still seeing his expenses grow more slowly than his profits – if he could sell all his cloth. The danger of hiring a growing labour force was that the Antwerp market could purchase, dye, and re-sell only a certain amount of English cloth. This essential fact had been ignored until 1550, for the industry was booming and profits seemed endless; but the limits of expansion became apparent in that year, when Antwerp merchants bought less cloth than England produced. The result was a depression in the clothing trade, which, though temporary as a nation-wide disaster, marked the permanent end of the clothing industry's initial phase of expansion.

In Elizabeth's reign, the industry was forced to change from one which produced pure wool cloth of different kinds under the pressure of expanding demand to one which, faced with the threat of stagnation, diversified and produced a variety of different products. After the break-up of the London–Antwerp axis in the 1560s and the expansion of English trade into the Mediterranean, demand for heavy cloth dropped, and demand for lighter, cheaper, more colourful fabrics increased. Clothiers had either to supervise the making of new kinds of cloth or lose their market; not surprisingly they chose the first alternative. One of the most important changes that resulted from this diversification was the creation of the 'new draperies' – worsted, woollen-and-worsted, or worsted-and-silk cloth – the techniques for which were supplied by Protestant refugees from the Netherlands who came to England in the 1560s and 1570s. The chief centres of production for these new cloths were East Anglia (with flourishing centres at Norwich and Colchester) and parts of Somerset and Devon. Clothiers in other

[43] Joan Thirsk, 'Industries in the Countryside', in *Essays in the Economic and Social History of Tudor and Stuart England in Honour of R.H. Tawney*, ed. R.J. Fisher (Cambridge, 1961), pp. 70–88.

parts of the country developed different cloths; thus, the West Riding of Yorkshire became the centre for the manufacture of cheap, high-quality kerseys, and Lancashire became the centre for the linen industry. As luxury cloth became increasingly popular at court, silk-weaving began to become a prosperous trade; the raw silk imported in increasing quantities (12,000 pounds in 1563; 51,697 pounds in 1593) was made into cloth at Canterbury, Sandwich and London.[44]

Thus diversified, the clothing industry made the fortunes of many clothiers in Elizabeth's reign. The depression of the 1550s, however, had marked the end of the big, boom-time fortunes of men like John Winchcombe or William Stumpe. Furthermore, although Elizabethan clothiers were extremely important to the crown because of the aulnage duties they paid, the tax on the export of cloth their business brought to the queen, and the loans clothiers frequently made the government in times of need, clothiers lost local power that had accrued to the clothing giants of the first half of the century. Wiltshire clothiers, for example, ceased to sit in the Commons after Elizabeth's accession (with only two exceptions), and a herald's visitation of the county in 1565 resulted in several clothiers 'disclaiming the name of gentleman' (a distinction which had presumably been given them because of their wealth and local stature). One of the most prestigious clothiers in Wiltshire, in fact, was even 'disgraded' from gentility.[45] The country gentry, who had rubbed shoulders with Stumpe and his contemporaries as they had all reaped the benefits of the sale of monastic land, had apparently grown disturbed by the power wealthy clothiers were gaining in the county; there is some evidence of a conscious movement on their part, through the distribution of taxes and the preservation of social snobbery, to keep the rich industrialists in their places. Thus, while Elizabethan clothiers had to cope with changes in demand and diversification of their products, they had also to face a loss of social and political power in their localities. The social tensions generated by their success aroused considerable contemporary interest, if the popularity of Deloney's novels is any indication of concern with the problem. For Deloney placed the tension between money and status at the very centre of his first book, *Jack of Newbury*, and the

[44] Coleman, *Economy of England*, pp. 81–2; Jack, *Trade and Industry*, pp. 102, 106.
[45] Ramsay, *Wiltshire Woollen Industry*, pp. 46–7.

result was one of the most daring and penetrating analyses of the relationship between money and status written during the period.

The third commercial group popular authors considered in their works was composed of craftsmen and the apprentices and journeymen who worked in their shops. To Elizabethans who lived in London and provincial towns, craftsmen were an everyday sight, for they supplied nearly all familiar goods made in England – pots, pans, knives, tools, harnesses, shoes – in this pre-industrialized society in which everything was made literally by hand. Though craftsmen could be found in tiny villages, most of them lived in towns; and the larger the town, the more craftsmen of different types it tended to have.[46] The extent to which craftsmen dominated the free (non-labouring) citizenry of towns is apparent in freemen's registers, which indicate that six different basic crafts groups (textiles, clothing, leather, metal, building and victualling trades) employed three-quarters of these men.[47] Craftsmen, then, were far more numerous than merchants. They were also far less wealthy: 58.63% of the London freemen in Grassby's study had net personal assets of under £500 at their deaths, and the great majority of these men were worth less than £250.[48]

In Elizabeth's reign, the organizational structure on which crafts had historically been based was changing, with resulting tension between old ideals of fellowship and carefully controlled absence of competition and new capitalistic opportunities. Since the middle ages, English crafts had been organized into units of association and control called gilds, whose purposes were promoting the welfare of their members by keeping the trade of each particular craft in the hands of craftsmen who worked in that town, maintaining standards of work, enforcing apprenticeship, and keeping up a just level of wages. Behind this organization was the medieval assumption that town dwellers and men in the immediate vicinity of towns depended on local craftsmen for all their wares and that towns were relatively isolated from each other. In these circumstances, only the very

[46] For example, Sudbury (Suffolk) had 1200 inhabitants and forty-nine trades; Norwich, with a population twice as large, had eighty; London had some 160. The figures are from 1520, but it is the proportions that are important. Coleman, *Economy of England*, p. 72.

[47] Clarkson, *Pre-Industrial Economy*, p. 80. Students will find Clarkson's summary of the recent scholarship on the distribution of the urban work force, which appears on pp. 88–92, extremely useful.

[48] Grassby, 'Personal Wealth', p.224.

wealthy could afford to 'import' goods from larger towns on a regular basis; the rest of the community depended on local craftsmen and took care of extraordinary needs at large biannual fairs.

As early as 1500, however, this simple, locally organized economy was breaking down, and by the time Elizabeth ascended the throne gilds found themselves confronted by a relatively complex social and commercial network with which their ideals were not equipped to deal. To begin with, as the number of people in England increased, growing numbers of rural men migrated to towns in search of work, with the result that the proportion of the population living in towns rose perhaps twice as fast as the population as a whole.[49] The increasing labour supply and the demands of growing towns put pressure on the gilds to admit more men to membership; if they refused, craftsmen moved outside city walls into the suburbs (where gilds had no power), thus threatening the gilds with the loss of their historical monopolies on local trade. Furthermore, the increasing size of towns made it necessary to go farther afield to obtain raw materials enough to supply urban crafts; thus some craftsmen went mainly into trade and supplied their less enterprising or lucky colleagues with wholesale goods. In the course of time, the men who had gone into trade became wealthier than the manufacturers and dominated both gilds and city government. Thus, the master craftsmen who had formerly been able to regulate their own trade found themselves subordinate to men whose interests lay in the expansion of trade rather than in the creation of local monopolies traditional gild philosophy considered to be best suited to craftsmen's interests.[50] This development did not necessarily hamper the business of a skilled craftsman with an eye for demand; in fact, it gave him possibilities to expand his trade. But the breakdown of the ideal was disturbing to many craftsmen, and their irritation at being controlled by men who had little concern for the welfare of their aspect of trade was understandable, especially since that control was gained through manipulation of the institution that was supposed to insure the well-being of all its members.

Finally, the increasing complexity of trade and the opportunities

---

[49] The increase, of course, was not evenly distributed; some towns actually lost population because of the plague or adverse economic trends. See Clark and Slack, *English Towns*, p. 83.

[50] Clarkson, *Pre-Industrial Economy*, p. 104; D.C. Coleman, *Industry in Tudor and Stuart England* (London, 1975), pp. 20–1; George Unwin, *Industrial Organization in the Sixteenth and Seventeenth Centuries* (2nd edn, London, 1957), pp. 70–1.

for advancement that accompanied it led to a breakdown in the carefully guarded demarcations between craft and craft that had once been an essential feature of the gild system. Once the powers of gilds weakened, a glover might buy a little extra leather and sell it to other men in the leather trade, a tanner might become a butcher by selling the meat of cattle he slaughtered for their hides. Gradually, this sort of moonlighting became the norm in some towns, with the result that the name of a man's craft might have very little to do with what he did for a living. In London, this process was accelerated by the 'custom of London', which enabled any freeman to become a member of another company once his apprenticeship was served. Because of this custom, official company membership had come to have almost nothing to do with the realities of trade in Elizabeth's reign. A survey of the yeomanry of the Drapers' Company, for example, reveals that only twenty-five of the 528 members were actually drapers: 116 of the others were tailors, eight were haberdashers, sixteen were upholsterers, and there were also cutlers, grocers, vintners, a goldsmith and a bowyer among them.[51]

By the end of Elizabeth's reign, craft gilds were in a state of change, confusion and decline in many (though not all) of the towns in England. This does not mean that crafts were decaying or that individual craftsmen were turning out fewer wares than before. Many skilled craftsmen, in fact, were prospering as increased freedom from gild restrictions, increased demand for their products, and the opportunity for doing a little side investment enabled them to maximize their profits. The development of English 'projects', made possible by the immigration of foreign craftsmen and the skills they taught their English counterparts, also enabled artisans to prosper by making consumer goods which had hitherto been imported.[52] As we shall see in Chapter 3, the rise in the size of towns and the new opportunities for craftsmen made it possible for many of them to educate their sons between the 1560s and 1580s.

The breakdown in gild organization, however, was a change that created tensions and arguments in towns and cities – tensions that have been amply documented by George Unwin and Robert Ashton.[53] One of the issues that caused friction was that of political

[51] Ashton, *City and Court*, p. 49.
[52] Joan Thirsk, *Economic Policy and Projects*, Chapters I and II.
[53] Unwin, *Industrial Organization*, Chapter III; *The Gilds and Companies of London* (3rd edn, London, 1938), Chapter XV; Ashton, *City and Court*, Chapter II.

power; men who did well in trade tended to take power in both the gilds and the towns away from men who manufactured goods. Another issue, however (and one that is much harder to document), was that of belief in tradition against the belief in flexible manipulation of economic trends; and it was this tension that appeared in the literature written about craftsmen. On the one hand, the literature praised men who had a quick eye for profit; on the other hand, it praised craftsmen by celebrating the traditions of their gilds. Greene, Deloney and Dekker drew heavily on the traditions of the Cordwainers' Company (nicknamed, with what significance we shall see presently, the gentle craft) in their works on shoemakers. Heywood drew upon the ballad of 'Edward IV and the Merry Tanner of Tamworth' in his *1 Edward IV*. The authors who glorified apprentices drew famous figures from various companies and gave them a fictitious history. Behind these stories were gild traditions, amplified and embellished, and untouched by the idea that a man might be a vintner in the Drapers' Company or a tanner that made shoes. All the craftsman stories are set in a 'golden age' past, and they celebrate with a certain sense of nostalgia a spirit of equality that reigns among master craftsmen, journeymen, and apprentices. Yet Simon Eyre becomes a draper and Lord Mayor of London; Richard Casteler becomes a wealthy citizen – the 'egalitarian' craftsmen rise to wealth and prosperity. Which are the popular authors to celebrate, the intelligence and skill with which lowly craftsmen climb the economic ladder to fame and fortune, or the spirit of fellowship that dominates the gild ideal? The works on craftsmen and apprentices meditate upon this question, but they come to no clear conclusion.

The inspiration behind popular literature on merchants, clothiers and craftsmen, then, was not economic growth that generated a large middle class, but economic change that called older social assumptions into question. In one sense, change brought opportunity, if one could only take it – and the Winchcombes, Greshams and Whites who managed to bend economic trends to their own well-being gained the admiration of men and boys who came to towns in hopes of finding a prosperous alternative to rural poverty, even as they aroused the jealousy of other men in trade whose gilds and companies they dominated. If great merchants and clothiers aroused mixed feelings in the small, they aroused the hostility of the gentry, who had been brought up to think that manipulation of the economy was demeaning and that trade kept a man from joining the social elite, no matter how rich he might be. Thus, the success of the men who profited from changing economic conditions was upsetting in a society whose social hierarchy and industrial organizations were both founded in increasingly anachronistic medieval assumptions. The understandable temptation to admire business success and still cling to old values, thus reaching a psychological compromise between new and old, forced men to deny the social change that inevitably followed economic development and population growth. This was the problem the popular authors unwittingly confronted; they found themselves running into clashes between theory and reality time after time as their fiction explored economic and social ideas they could not quite articulate.

Why, if popular literature on merchants and craftsmen raised more problems than it solved, did Elizabethan authors try to write it at all? The easiest answer is simply that it sold well and was thus profitable to write. There was a place in Elizabethan culture for literature that appealed to civic traditions; as the religious and civic festivals that had been part of the yearly routine of medieval cities were suppressed in Elizabeth's reign, other, more-secular pageants replaced them. In London, for example, the Lord Mayor's Show, with its allegorical praise of monarch and city and its re-enactments of great episodes in London history, became the one great civic pageant of the year; after Elizabeth's death, when the popular literature about men of trade went out of date, some of its principal authors – Munday, Dekker and Heywood – wrote civic pageants that kept up the praise of London's great citizens.[54]

There was more to the popular literature about merchants, clothiers, and craftsmen than there was to the civic pageants, however, and their substance accounts both for their popularity and for their demise. In addition to praising civic traditions, these works articulated men's desires to become prosperous in an age in which two-thirds of the population was poor. They expressed admiration for men who controlled economic developments that baffled their neighbours. Finally, they attacked (however obliquely) the problem of the inter-relationship of money and status; and this was a central problem that confronted all Elizabethans in a thousand daily

[54] See Pythian-Adams, 'Ceremony and the Citizen', pp. 57–85; Unwin, *Gilds and Companies*, Chapter XVI.

episodes, a problem for which they needed some structure that organized their ideas. The popular authors failed to provide that structure; as the troubles they repeatedly encountered indicate, their social assumptions could not be stretched far enough to postulate the necessity of forming a new scheme of values on which social thinking should be based. But they came very close to seeing what was needed, and their conclusions, it seems, aroused the interest of a large and sympathetic audience.

2. The popular Elizabethan authors

Looking across the spectrum of prominent Elizabethan authors, one can see that several of them were the sons of merchants or craftsmen. Marlowe, for example, was the son of a shoemaker; Ben Jonson, the stepson of a brick-layer; Shakespeare, the son of a glover; Lodge, the son of a grocer who became lord mayor of London; and Munday, Chettle and Peele were, respectively, the sons of a draper, a dyer, and a salter. The familiarity of the backgrounds of these men led Louis Wright to imply that the majority of Elizabethan authors came from middle-class families; and his word on the subject has been accepted as gospel in later works on literary history, for the simple reason that it is the only word.[1] This interpretation is, however, a by-product of the Marxist model of pre-industrial society – a model long since proved to be inaccurate.[2] It is, furthermore, extremely misleading, for it encourages scholars to assume that Elizabethan authors came from like backgrounds, received roughly comparable educations, and adopted one profession – writing. No assumption could be further from the truth. Elizabethan popular authors emerged from a wide variety of backgrounds and adopted a wide variety of professions. While their educations were alike in some respects (for after a Tudor youth learned to read English, he embarked on a study of the classics that lasted until he left school), they differed greatly in thoroughness and in length. In many cases, indeed, the popular authors of Elizabeth's reign had in common only the fact that, at one point in their busy lives, they set pen to paper long enough to produce a book. The

[1] *Middle-Class Culture*, pp. 17–18; Edwin H. Miller, *The Professional Writer in Elizabethan England: A Study in Nondramatic Literature* (Cambridge, Mass., 1959), pp. 7–9; Altick, *English Common Reader*, p. 17.
[2] Laslett, *World We Have Lost*, p. 38; Stone, 'Social Mobility', pp. 18–20; David Cressy, 'Describing the Social Order in Elizabethan and Stuart England', in *Literature and History*, 3 (1976), 35.

careers of Elizabethan popular authors, then, need to be re-investigated in the light of new knowledge and recent research. The following sketch will serve that purpose, and it will also introduce the popular authors whose works are the subjects of this book.

Any discussion of Elizabethan authors is necessarily a sketch, not a painting, for the evidence concerning many authors is sparse. To begin with, one cannot ascertain the exact number of authors responsible for the 296 popular works under consideration, for twenty-nine works are anonymous. This does not necessarily mean that there are twenty-nine authors about whom nothing can be said; twenty-three of the anonymous works are plays, many of which were probably collaborative efforts of dramatists who can be 'counted' as authors of other plays. It does mean, however, that though there may have been as many as 150 or 160 popular authors in Elizabethan England, we know the names of only 142. Nine of these 142 authors are known only because their names appear on their works; there is no other information about them. The total number of Elizabethan authors about whom something can be said, then, is 133.[3]

The family origins of 106 of the 133 authors can be traced with a fair degree of accuracy. Seventy-seven authors came from families whose status was recorded: eight from clerical families, thirty-six from gentle families, and thirty-three from non-gentle families. Of the thirty-three authors from non-gentle families, twenty-two were sons of merchants or craftsmen; three were sons of yeomen, and four were the sons of, respectively, a scrivener, a parish clerk, a mariner, and a master gunner. The four remaining sons of non-gentle men were of indeterminable occupation: three were listed 'pleb.' in Oxford or Cambridge matriculation records, and the last (Gosson) is known only to have been poor. Twenty other authors, whose familial status is not recorded, almost certainly came from non-gentle backgrounds; nine others came from families that may have been gentle.[4] Thus, of the 106 authors whose backgrounds can

---

[3] A complete summary of the backgrounds, education and careers of the popular authors appears in Appendix B.

[4] In designating authors gentle or non-gentle, I have decided to say all authors who were sizars at Cambridge were non-gentle. This may be arbitrary, but all the other sizars among the popular authors whose parental social stations are known were non-gentle. I have marked those authors who were sizars with an asterisk. The following, judging from their careers, were probably non-gentle: H. Baker, J. Baker,* Bacon, Bourne, Bradshaw,* Dekker, Deloney, Forde,* Gee,*

be traced, at most 42.05% (36 + 9 = 45) were gentle, while 50.4% (33 + 20 = 53) were non-gentle, and 7.48% (8) were clerical. One should add that the sons of clerical families were not from the ranks of the distinguished clergy; with the exception of Richard Rice (the son of Cardinal Wolsey's chaplain), they seem to have come from the families of parish priests or minor ecclesiastical officials. Clearly, while the sons of merchants and craftsmen did not dominate the popular literary profession in Elizabethan England, the elite did not have a monopoly on literary talent, whatever its power in other endeavours.

As a rule, the education of the popular authors led them not to the world of trade but to the worlds of the court, pulpit or stage. While as many as fifteen of the authors were connected with trade (probably as apprentices) in their youth, few of them liked it well enough to embrace it as a means of livelihood.[5] Anthony Munday and Ben Jonson rebelled against such imprisonment of their talents; both ran away to the Continent. Others, like Angel Day, Nicholas Ling and Henry Chettle, were lucky enough to be apprenticed in the printing trade; they took the opportunity to meet literary men. Still others, more docile than Munday and Jonson, served out their terms but turned to literature in later life; John Stow and Richard Johnson were the best known of these, and it is possible that Thomas Deloney (about whose early years nothing is known) should be added to the list.

In contrast to the few authors who were trained in trade, sixty-eight got degrees from Cambridge or Oxford, fifteen more studied

---

Grafton, Greenham,* Harrison,* Johnson, Ling, Shelford,* Timberlake, Udall,* Weever,* Wilson,* Woodes.*

It is harder to decide which authors may have been gentle, since positions and patrons were open to those with money and talent, not just those with breeding. Thus, Dent, Drant, Perkins, Playfere and Robson were all pensioners at Cambridge, but so were Harvey and Marlowe, sons of men of trade; Dowland and Bullein studied on the Continent, but this may indicate the presence of money or patronage; and Cancellar and Edwards may have had connections at court from gentle families – but they may also have been lucky in finding patrons.

[5] Armin was a goldsmith's apprentice (Jane Belfield, 'Robert Armin, Citizen and Goldsmith of London', *Notes and Queries*, 27 (April 1980), 158–9). H. Baker, who dedicated *The Well-Spring of Sciences* to the merchant adventurers, may have been apprenticed to them earlier. Bourne was free of the Gravesend Mercers' Company and may have been an apprentice; but he was also a mathematician and an inkeeeper, so his membership may have been honorary. Ten others were almost certainly apprentices: Browne, Chettle, Cotton, Day, Deloney, Grafton, Johnson, Ling, Stow, Timberlake.

at a university without getting a degree, six studied at the Inns of Court, and three studied abroad. Thus, ninety-two (69%) of the 133 authors about whom there is information had at least a taste of the education that in social theory made any man a gentleman.[6] A few authors received their educations in private households. Gervase Markham was one of these; Michael Drayton, who was a page at the house of Sir Henry Goodere, was another; and Leonard Mascal, who spent his later life in the household of Matthew Parker, may have been a third.

A final group of authors who were not apprenticed, educated privately or sent to university were (as far as one can tell) the products of grammar schools. Sir Nicholas Malbie and Edmund Tilney (later Master of the Revels) were two of these, though they may have had access to private tutoring. Most of the others were playwrights; and the most famous of them were Shakespeare, Dekker and Kyd. Kyd was educated at the Merchant Taylors' School, Shakespeare at King Edward's Grammar School in Stratford-upon-Avon, but little is known about the education of the other playwrights except that it was obviously solid enough to allow them to enter the literary profession through the stage door.

In their later years, six of the authors were members of major London companies or were practising merchants. Three of them (Roger Cotton, John Browne, and Henry Timberlake) were actively engaged in trade; as a consequence of this activity, they were not prolific authors. Timberlake, a merchant adventurer, wrote a record of his pilgrimage to Jerusalem, and nothing else. Roger Cotton, one of five sons of a Shropshire gentleman, was a draper with deep religious interests. He was a friend and patron of Hugh Broughton (the divine satirized in Jonson's *Alchemist*); as a consequence of his patronage, he wrote three religious books, only one of which was popular.[7] John Browne, a Bristol merchant, was a man of one book; but his *Merchant's Avizo* (1589) was the first practical manual for merchants to be written in English. Aimed at young merchants on their first trips abroad, it taught them to write

---

[6]In 1577, William Harrison said the word 'gentleman' applied to 'who soever studieth the laws of the realm, who so abideth in the university giving his mind to his book, or professeth physic and the liberal sciences' – so long as he could maintain the 'port, charge, and countenance of a gentleman'. *The Historical Description of the Island of Britain*, in Holinshed, I, 273.

[7]*DNB*, *sub.* Roger Cotton; and Cotton, *A Direction to the Waters of Life* (London, 1590), Dedication (to Hugh Broughton) and Epistle to the Reader.

informative letters to their masters, keep simple accounts, convert currency, and listen attentively to the more experienced merchants who were trading around them. It was the only one of the best-sellers to be written specifically for merchants by a merchant.[8]

In addition to these three merchants, there were three others who may have practised trade but were chiefly interested in other pursuits. William Bourne was one of these; he was free of the Mercers' Company in Gravesend (and seems to have been an innkeeper on the side), but his chief passion was applied mathematics. Richard Grafton signed himself 'grocer' in 1537 and was a warden of the Grocers' Company in 1555 and 1556; but in the intervening years he was instrumental in printing both the Matthew's Bible and the Great Bible, and during the reign of Edward VI he was the king's printer. He lost that position when he printed a proclamation for Lady Jane Grey; thereafter he returned to the Grocers' Company and became an MP for London. He did not begin his career as a chronicler until the 1560s.[9] John Stow was a tailor, but he never rose higher than the position of yeoman in the Merchant Taylors' Company. He was, before everything else, an antiquarian and a man well known in London's antiquarian circles.[10] In a different category from these three men of trade were Anthony Munday and William Hunnis. Munday, after a long career as an author of romances and plays, became a draper and wrote many pageants for the city of London. Hunnis, Master of the Boys in the Chapel Royal, was made an honorary member of the Grocers' Company because of a judicious marriage.[11] Neither man was trained for trade.

Of the three writers connected with the printing trade, Henry

[8] *The Merchants Avizo, by I[ohn] B[rowne], Marchant, 1589*, Patrick McGrath, ed. (Boston, 1957), Introduction, p. xxx. Baker's *Well-Spring of Sciences* may fall into this category; it is an arithmetic manual, dedicated to the merchant adventurers, and it claims to be 'not only profitable for Merchants, but also for all Artificers'. It is not altogether certain, however, that Baker was a merchant.

[9] *DNB*, *sub*. William Bourne and Richard Grafton. Charles Kingsford touches upon Grafton's career as a chronicler and his rivalry with Stow in his edition of Stow's *Survey of London* (2 vols., Oxford, 1908), I, ix–xiii.

[10] Stow was a tailor for at least a decade before he became a scholar; he was admitted to the freedom of the Merchant Taylors' Company in 1647. He was at work on a copy of Lydgate's poems as early as 1558, but his first publication (an edition of Chaucer's works) did not appear until 1561. See Stow, *Survey*, I, viii–xi.

[11] Julia C. Turner, *Anthony Mundy: An Elizabethan Man of Letters* (Berkeley, 1928), p. 143; M.C. Bradbrook, *The Rise of the Common Player: A Study of Actor and Society in Shakespeare's England* (Cambridge, Mass., 1962), pp. 225–7.

Chettle was the most interested in literary pursuits. After his first year or two as a printer, he supported himself (if such a phrase can be used for a man perpetually in debt) by his playwriting, and he appears to have given up printing.[12] The other two were printers first, writers second. Angel Day, stationer, wrote *An English Secretary* (1586); it appealed primarily to the growing number of men who were interested in becoming secretaries to noble families.[13] Nicholas Ling, printer, compiled *Politeuphia* (1597), which also was written for men who needed to appear well educated and eloquent. It was a collection of aphorisms, labelled 'God', 'Love', 'Wealth', 'Poverty', 'Folly', 'Blessedness', so a man could find them quickly if he needed an idea; it was a commonplace book for scores of men too unintellectual to keep their own. Day and Ling knew their trade; they wrote what they knew would sell.

The one craftsman who can be said to have written for craftsmen was Thomas Deloney, a silk-weaver by trade and a balladeer and novelist by vocation. Very little is known about his life; the existing evidence reveals a man occasionally in trouble for expressing his social views too freely and a ballad-monger whose interest in appealing to men of simple taste won him the scorn of his more particular colleagues. Deloney took up the cause of the Elizabethan poor in the late 1590s, when a series of bad harvests had led to a period of dearth and high prices. In 1596 the lord mayor was looking for him because he had written one 'Ballad on the Want of Corn' in 'that Vain and indiscreet manner, as that thereby the Poor might aggravate their Grief, and take occasion of some Discontent'. Furthermore, it had come to light that this same 'idle Fellow' had written a book for silk-weavers, 'wherein was found some such like foolish and disorderly matter'.[14] The mayor did not find Deloney, but the near-scrape with the law apparently turned the weaver from writing social pamphlets to the composition of prose fiction. The four novels he wrote between 1596 and his death in 1600 contained nothing explicitly subversive, but they did take up the cause of the poor, and they looked searchingly at the place of craftsmen in the social hierarchy.

---

[12] Harold Jenkins, *The Life and Work of Henry Chettle* (London, 1934), pp. 5–17. Chettle was a printer until 1596, but after 1591 he seems to have worked as a journeyman, not a master printer.

[13] The long title of *The English Secretary* promises that it contains 'the parts and Office of a Secretary, in like manner, amply discoursed'.

[14] *The Works of Thomas Deloney*, ed. Francis O. Mann (Oxford, 1912), p. ix.

There was, then, some connection between trade and literary endeavour in Elizabethan England – especially Elizabethan London. But the men who straddled the literary and mercantile worlds were only thirteen out of 133 authors, and their impact, however interesting it may be, should not be exaggerated. There were, for example, more courtiers who wrote best-sellers than there were merchants and craftsmen: nineteen popular authors were connected with the government or court in some fashion. Burleigh, Bacon, Raleigh and Sidney were the most successful of these. Spenser, Conway and Davies held official posts in Ireland or the Low Countries. Lyly, Tilney, Edwards and Hunnis all held literary positions at Elizabeth's court; Lewkenor was master of ceremonies to James I. As one would expect, none of these concerned themselves with the social consciousness of merchants or craftsmen; they wrote for the sophisticated circles in which they moved.

By far the largest group of popular authors was that of divines – fifty-five of them, most of whom were supported by livings or lectureships. Among these, eight were bishops, and they were not particularly interested in the social consciousness of the commonalty. Babington, the only one who concerned himself with the social aspects of religion, wrote his pamphlets before he became a bishop. Whitgift, Jewel and Cooper were engaged as heavy artillery in the crossfire of Anglican controversy with Puritans and Catholics. Abbot wrote a brief history of the world; King, a very dull series of lectures. Hall, a bishop in James' reign, was known in Elizabeth's chiefly for writing his best-seller, a satire that Whitgift ordered to be burnt.

A second group of divines wrote prose or poetry that was designed to comfort sad souls. The most familiar of these today is the Jesuit martyr, Robert Southwell, whose *Saint Peter's Complaint* was published anonymously in 1595 and went through eight more editions by 1615. At the opposite end of the religious spectrum, William Fulke, a wealthy London citizen's son, who became a Puritan who lived most of his life on the Continent, appealed to *able Sermon of Faith*. In the same vein, Andrew Kingsmill, a puritan who lived most of his life on the Continent, appealed to afflicted men with his *Most Excellent Treatise for all Such as are Troubled in Mind*. These works and the many devotional books like them were aimed purely at the souls of their readers; the authors took little interest in social problems.

There is much more of social interest in the works of a third group of divines, most of whom were Puritans. Two of them, Thomas Brasbridge and William Bullein, were divines who were also doctors; both of them wrote medical treatises which promised to help city dwellers against epidemics of plague or sweating sickness.[15] The others were the most eminent Puritans of the last third of the sixteenth century – John Foxe, Laurence Chaderton, Richard Greenham, Arthur Dent, Henry Smith and William Perkins. These men were not directly concerned with the social consciousness of merchants and craftsmen; all of them insisted that they were interested in the souls of all Christians, of whatever status. They had a great deal to say, however, about social duties and obligations, and their works reveal the moral framework which surrounded Elizabethan social consciousness.

So much has been made of the Puritans' links with capitalism and the bourgeois work ethic that one might expect these Puritan preachers to be from bourgeois backgrounds. In fact, however, this was not the case. Henry Smith's father was a gentleman sufficiently distinguished to marry Burleigh's sister after the death of his first wife; Chaderton's father was a gentleman; both Dent and Perkins were pensioners at Cambridge, which suggests that they came from wealthy (and possibly gentle) families. The other two were of humbler origins; Foxe's father was a citizen of Boston, Lincolnshire, and Richard Greenham was a sizar at Cambridge. The poverty of Foxe and Greenham followed both of them for the remainder of their lives. Foxe, whose Puritan sympathies made him decline the possibilities of livings, had prestigious friends in Burleigh, Walsingham, the Duke of Norfolk and the Earls of Bedford and Warwick, but he apparently gave a great deal of the money he got from his patrons to the poor and was frequently insolvent.[16] Greenham spent most of his life as pastor of Dry Drayton, Cambridgeshire, where he rose at four in the morning to

---

[15] Brasbridge, *The Poor Man's Jewel, That is to Say, A Treatise of the Pestilence* (London, 1578); Bullein, *A Dialogue Against the Fever Pestilence*, ed. Mark W. and A.H. Bullen (Early English Texts Society, extra series, no. 52, 1888, rpt., London, 1931). Bullein's *Dialogue* is one of the few neglected popular works which does not deserve its fate; it is an interesting combination of a colloquy, a morality play and a medical manual which contains several jest-book stories, remedies for disease, and a treatise on the art of dying. A.H. Bullen has written a brief study of the work in *Elizabethans* (1924, rpt., New York, 1962), pp. 155–81.

[16] J.F. Mosley, *John Foxe and His Book* (London, 1940), pp. 12–16, 102–4.

preach to his parishioners, catechized the village children himself, and preached twice on Sundays for twenty years. But his parishioners were unmoved by his devotion to their souls, and he left Dry Drayton, poor and discouraged, in 1591. He died in London in 1594; his sermons, published posthumously, did not even bring him a few pence from a printer.[17]

Most like Greenham in situation was Arthur Dent, as far as one can tell. Upon graduating from Cambridge, he was presented with the living of South Shoebury, Essex, by Richard, Lord Rich; he preached there for twenty years. His existence was probably more comfortable than Greenham's because of Rich's patronage and because of Dent's marriage into the Culverwell family, in which there was some money. In spite of his popularity, however, Dent did not seek greener pastures in later life.[18]

Two of the other Puritans were academics. Chaderton, disinherited by his father for becoming a Protestant in the 1560s, studied at Cambridge and got his BD in 1578. When Emmanuel College was founded in 1584, he became its first master, and he retained the post until he was eighty-six. During his tenure of office, he made Emmanuel the most prominent of the Puritan colleges; after his retirement, he lived on for eighteen years among the Puritans he had trained.[19] William Perkins, like Chaderton, lived in Cambridge after he got his degree; he was elected a fellow of Christ's College and appointed lecturer at Great St Andrew's, just across the road, in 1584. Despite many offers of preferment, he kept his two positions until he resigned his fellowship to marry in 1595. He supported his family on his lectureship; his wife was not a member of the gentle families with whom Perkins was popular, and she seems to have brought him little more than a baby each year of their seven-year marriage.[20]

Henry Smith declined to take a living because of his Puritan sympathies and preached in London after 1582. In 1587 he became

[17] The best short life of Greenham appears in H.C. Porter, *Reformation and Reaction in Tudor Cambridge* (Cambridge, 1958), pp. 216–18. Margaret Spufford, having examined the wills of Greenham's parishioners, has concluded that the pastor's despair over their hardness of heart was probably warranted, and not just 'a subjective judgement on his labours, made in a fit of depression'. See *Contrasting Communities*, p. 328.

[18] *DNB*, *sub.* Arthur Dent; Porter, *Reformation and Reaction*, pp. 239–40.

[19] *DNB*, *sub.* Laurence Chaderton; Porter, *Reformation and Reaction*, pp. 239–40.

[20] *The Work of William Perkins*, ed. Ian Breward, The Courtenay Library of Reformation Classics (Abingdon, Berkshire, 1970), III.

lecturer in the parish of St Clement Danes, probably through Burleigh's influence. Here he gained a large following and the nickname 'Silver-tongued Smith' in the three years he preached before his death.[21] He is an interesting example of a man of superior birth and education who had a genuine touch with the populace; his sermons were taken down in shorthand by his followers and sometimes published in the resulting garbled forms.

The remaining group of popular authors can best be called professional writers. Some, like Breton, Davison, Hayward, Harman, Markham, Stubbes and West, were gentlemen who dabbled (with varying degrees of seriousness) in poetry and pamphlets. Others, like Harvey and Warner, had professional careers to support their literary endeavours. But eighteen of them (nineteen if Chettle is included), made their livings with their pens. All of them wrote for the stage at one point in their careers, though several of them also wrote poetry or pamphlets. Among these professionals, the men most concerned with merchants and craftsmen were William Haughton, Thomas Heywood and Thomas Dekker. Almost nothing is known about Haughton except that he was one of Henslowe's most prolific playwrights in the 1590s.[22] Heywood was a preacher's son, and he was sent to Emmanuel College in 1591, which suggests a Puritan background. He left Cambridge for London and the stage, however, and in the twenty-five years after 1596 he wrote for the popular acting companies: for Derby, Oxford and Worcester's Men at the Boar's Head and the Rose from 1599 to 1603, and for the Queen's Men (as Worcester's men became at Elizabeth's death) thereafter. The Queen's Men moved to the Red Bull, notable for its citizen audiences, in 1605; many of Heywood's plays were written with an eye to pleasing this popular crowd. After 1620, Heywood turned to the writing of pamphlets and pageants for the London Lord Mayor's Shows.[23] He supported himself to a large extent by appealing to the taste of London citizens.

Thomas Dekker was born in London (almost certainly to a non-gentle family) and began to write plays for the Admiral's Men about 1595; during the next eight years he was one of the most reliable

[21] *DNB, sub.* Henry Smith; Thomas Fuller, *The Church History of Britain*, ed. James Nichols (3 vols., London, 1842), III, 33–4.

[22] Chambers, *Elizabethan Stage*, III, 334.

[23] Arthur M. Clark, *Thomas Heywood, Playwright and Miscellanist* (1958, rpt., New York, 1967), Chapters I–VII.

playwrights of the Henslowe companies. Like Heywood, he wrote
for the Queen's Men after Elizabeth's death, and most of his plays
were put on at the Red Bull, though he occasionally wrote plays for
the coterie theatres, collaborating with Webster in *Westward Ho*
and *Northward Ho* for Paul's Boys in 1605.[24] Like Heywood too,
Dekker wrote pamphlets, many of which portrayed aspects of
London life, and he also wrote city pageants for London. Dekker
and Heywood were not the only playwrights who wrote for London
audiences. Of the eighty plays extant from the period between 1580
and 1603, thirty-four contain merchants or craftsmen as characters.
Most of them are anonymous and few of them are, by any literary
standard, good. But they are mostly works designed to play upon
the reactions of a popular audience. Dekker, Heywood and
Haughton (most of whose plays have been lost) were merely the
best known of the popular playwrights.

The Elizabethan popular authors could be called professionally
articulate men – poets, preachers, pamphleteers and playwrights
whose vocation was to amuse and instruct a large audience. On the
whole, they were not men of trade, either by birth or training; certainly, they were not middle-class men who wrote for the middle
class. But while this is true, a fair number of the popular authors,
whatever their rank, were interested in recording or romanticizing
the history of the trading citizens in London. And while there were
bishops, courtiers and scholars among the popular authors who
wrote for a sophisticated audience, there were many others who
were concerned to attract an audience that was not primarily that of
the university or court. The popularity of their works suggests that
their attempts to reach a great number of people were successful –
and it is to this body of readers and listeners that we must now turn
our attention.

[24]M.T. Jones-Davies, *Un Peintre De La Vie Londonienne: Thomas Dekker* (2 vols.,
Paris, 1958), I, 28–39, 50–7.

3. *The popular Elizabethan audience*

Literary historians have long assumed that the Elizabethan audience was composed of people with an exceptionally high rate of literacy and an extraordinary interest in the stage and the printed word. R.K. Webb, for example, has estimated that 'Tudor England may have known a literacy rate of forty or fifty per cent', and Richard Altick, while more cautious, has also suggested that a great number of Elizabethans could read. Wright has said that many of these literate Elizabethans were tradesmen and their families who 'pored' over books; others, Elizabethan apprentices, spoke with more 'clerkly wisdom' than scholars of earlier centuries.[1]

These descriptions are more impressionistic than factual, though there is no doubt that the Elizabethan audience was larger than any earlier English audience and that some portion of it was composed of men of moderate income. It is difficult to avoid impression in any study of audience, for audiences leave few traces after they disperse; frequently the only evidence available to historians who wish to study an audience are the portraits drawn by the authors who wished to appeal to it. Elizabethan authors portrayed their audiences as eager, intelligent men who were deeply interested in the written word; they courted this audience in their prefaces and titles. But such courtship, of course, was written specifically to create the impression that there was a wide audience for Elizabethan books that every literate man would do well to join. The prefaces say nothing about the possibility of reading in a predominantly rural society in which only a fraction of the population was literate.

Authorial prefaces should not, however, be dismissed entirely, for they frequently suggest that popular authors were interested in attracting men below gentle status who might desire instruction or

---

[1] R. Webb, *The British Working Class Reader 1790–1848: Literacy and Social Tension* (London, 1955), p. 14; Altick, *English Common Reader*, pp. 15–18; Wright, *Middle-Class Culture*, pp. 17–18.

entertainment. Medical authors, for example, were eager to make their works available to men of limited income and education. Thus, William Bullein's pamphlet *The Government of Health* (1558) announced on its title page that it was 'reduced into the form of a dialogue, for the better understanding of the unlearned'. Twenty years later, Thomas Brasbridge entitled his pamphlet *The Poor Man's Jewel*, informing his readers that his remedies for the plague were briefly described because long books were 'more costly, than that every man could buy them'. In the same tradition, the printer of the anonymous *Rich Storehouse or Treasury for the Diseased* (1596) advertised that it was written for 'the great benefit and comfort of the poorest sort of people that are not of ability to go to the Physicians'.[2]

Religious authors of the period also appealed to unlearned men, emphasizing the importance of instructing all people in the fundamentals of Protestantism. William Perkins, for example, dedicated his *Foundation of Christian Religion* to 'all ignorant people that desire to be instructed'. And Arthur Dent opened his *Sermon of Repentance* by asserting that he eschewed learned rhetoric because it was the 'froth of man's wisdom', blowing up 'the bladder of vanity, till it burst with swelling'. As for himself, 'I seek especially the salvation of the simple and ignorant, and therefore stoop down to reach their capacity'.[3] The statement need not be taken entirely at face value (Dent was the most rhetorical of Puritan preachers), but the advertisement for the 'plain style' did assure potential readers that this was not a sermon larded with Latin phrases and difficult syntax. And since the work was one of the two most popular books in Elizabethan England, one can assume that the advertisement, at the very least, did no harm.

There were also books whose prefatory material appealed directly to the men this study concerns. Humphrey Baker's *Well-Spring of Sciences* claimed to be 'not only profitable for Merchants, but also for all Artificers'. Bourne's *Regiment for the Sea* claimed to be useful to all seafarers, 'Pilots, Mariners, Merchants, etc.'.

---

[2] Bullein, *A New Book Entitled the Government of Health* (London, 1558), title page; Brasbridge, *The Poor Man's Jewel*, sigs. A3$_v$–A4; A.T., *A Rich Store-House or Treasury for the Diseased* (London, 1596), title page.

[3] Perkins, *The Foundation of the Christian Religion, Works, I*, sig. A2. The epigraph (Psalm 119: 130) is 'The entrance to thy words showeth light, and giveth understanding to the simple.' Dent, *A Sermon of Repentance* (London, 1583), sigs. A2–A2$_v$.

Deloney dedicated *Jack of Newbury* to 'all famous Clothworkers', *The Gentle Craft, Part I* to the 'Yeomen of the Gentle Craft', and *The Gentle Craft, Part II* to the wardens of the Cordwainers' Company.

In all, twenty-nine of the 189 popular non-dramatic works conspicuously announced that they were written for the 'common sort of men'. Of course, they might also have appealed to gentlemen as well, but many authors apparently felt, as Thomas Lupton did, that it was better 'to profit a great sort, than to feed the fancies of a few, well assured, that the learned eloquent, can better perceive plain speeches than the slenderly learned and common sort can understand eloquent discourses'.[4]

Introductions like Lupton's certainly indicate that some popular authors sensed there was an audience for plain fare. They are, however, chiefly informative about the audience to which these authors did *not* confine their appeals; 'the learned eloquent', men schooled in Latin, men of literary tastes, probably gentlemen. But who were the 'unlearned'? Obviously they could read – a fact that distinguished them from most of their brethren. The 'common sort of person' could be anybody below gentle rank; a 'poor man' could be anybody from the lower ranks of the great London companies to a destitute wage-earner.[5] The sales pitches of authors and printers indicate men of this type may have read books, but they give no exact information about the dimensions of the Elizabethan audience. These dimensions can be studied only by evaluating the social, economic and intellectual changes that worked together to create the expansion of literacy that occurred during Elizabeth's reign.

Assessing the literacy of Elizabethan Englishmen has been made far easier for historians by the appearance of David Cressy's thorough and energetic study of the subject, and what follows leans heavily on his work. It must be remembered, however, that the study of literacy is not identical with the study of a literate audience in this period, for the nature of the evidence obscures reading skills at the very point one would like to know most about them. The most 'standard and direct' method of measuring literacy is to ascertain how many men could sign their names on legal documents when

<hr />

[4] *A Thousand notable Things of Sundry Sorts* (London, 1595), Preface of the Author to the Reader.
[5] David Cressy, 'Educational Opportunity in Tudor and Stuart England', *History of Education Quarterly*, 16 (1976), p. 309.

required to do so, and to compare the resulting number with the number of men who could not sign in identical circumstances.[6] This method is open to distortion, not because men signed their names on documents they could not read, but because more Elizabethans could read than could write. Reading and writing were taught separately in Tudor England (and long afterwards), and reading was taught before writing. This system was practical in a society in which education was not the norm and tended to be intermittent for all but the fortunate few who could afford to go to school for a number of years. A man who had learned a little reading as a boy could read the Bible (perhaps only his own copy, in which his visual memory could be triggered by the location of the words on the page); a man who could read a little better could read contracts and indentures well enough to avoid being cheated by the men with whom he dealt. But writing, which took longer to learn and required fine motor coordination totally unfamiliar to many men in menial, agricultural, and even some skilled trades, was a skill that had no intrinsic merit if one did not need it to keep accounts and business journals. There was no social stigma against men who, like Shakespeare's father, signed documents with their marks; in a practical world in which so few men were able to read, it was reading, not writing, that gave a man a business edge over his neighbours and a first-hand knowledge of the Bible.[7]

Literacy statistics, then, force us to ignore the people who could read but not write, and these people may form a larger group than Cressy would like to admit. His argument that only those who had learned both reading and writing were 'functionally literate by the standards of the seventeenth century' sounds suspiciously circular – as if only those people whose literacy can be measured were 'really' literate.[8] This, however, was not uniformly the case; it is more realistic to admit that despite the scientific appearance of the statistics we now have available on Elizabethan literacy, we do not and cannot know how many men and women there were at the end of the sixteenth century who could read the works of the popular authors.

Be this as it may, the statistics do shed considerable light on the distribution of minimal education during Elizabeth's reign. The best

[6] Cressy, *Literacy and the Social Order: Reading and Writing in Tudor and Stuart England* (Cambridge, 1980), pp. 53–4.
[7] *Ibid.*, pp. 10–25.   [8] *Ibid.*, p. 55.

sources presently available for the study of general distribution of literacy in this period are collections of signatures from three oaths and vows taken and signed by every man in England over eighteen years of age in 1642–4. The returns from these, sampled in 40,000 signatures from 400 parishes in twenty-five counties, indicate that adult male literacy in these two years was a little over 30% in rural areas, with a slightly higher average in towns.[9] This does not mean, however, that one-third of the men in each parish could sign their names; in fact, averages fluctuated widely from parish to parish. In Cornwall, for example, one parish had a literacy rate of only 8%, while another had a rate of 53%; in Nottinghamshire parishes, literacy ranged from 7 to 73%; and in London, as one might expect, the average literacy was 78%. Despite these wide local variations, however, the average literacy did not change greatly from county to county, and it stayed consistently in a range of 20 to 40%.[10]

The oaths on which these statistics are based were, of course, signed some forty years after Elizabeth died, and it is dangerous to project them backwards. But Cressy's study of ecclesiastical court depositions from the dioceses of Exeter, Durham, Norwich and London indicate that adult male literacy rose sharply during Elizabeth's reign but reached a plateau in the early seventeenth century, even declining in some social groups. It seems safe to suggest, then, that in 1603 adult male literacy was in the vicinity of 28% – a rise of about 8% from the 20% Cressy estimates was the figure at the beginning of the reign.[11] The geographical pattern of literacy, with wide local variations but overall consistency, was probably much the same as that of the 1640s.

Cressy's work reveals a fact of exceptional interest to the study of popular audiences: the rise in Elizabethan literacy was due almost entirely to the increase in the writing abilities of men below gentle rank. Except in the far north, where standards of living, gentility and education were lower than they were in the south, gentlemen were almost universally literate by the time Elizabeth came to the throne; thus, increased literacy can be attributed to the gentry only

---

[9] *Ibid.*, pp. 65–72. The oaths were the Protestant Oath of 1642, the Vow and Covenant of 1643, and the Solemn League and Covenant of 1644. Cressy gives statistics for *il*literacy, as is the common statistical practice. I have reversed his percentages (70% illiteracy = 30% literacy) in my own analysis. A reader unversed in statistics may find it confusing to contemplate rises and declines in illiteracy; and I prefer to discuss changes in audience in terms of men who *were* literate.

[10] *Ibid.*, pp. 73, 76–7. [11] *Ibid.*, pp. 168–71, 176.

insofar as the number of gentlemen increased. Down the social scale, there was a surge in yeoman literacy early in the reign which stagnated as yeomen in different parts of the country reached a literacy rate of about 60%; yeomen made no further spectacular gains until the 1620s and 1630s.[12] Among husbandmen, literacy rose from a mere 6% in the 1560s to 13% in the 1600s in Durham and from 7% to 21% in Norfolk and Suffolk. In Essex, where literacy was generally higher in all social groups, they maintained a plateau of 19% during the last twenty years of the reign.[13]

While some of the gains in general male literacy can be attributed to the educational gains of yeomen and husbandmen, tradesmen had the greatest and most consistent gains of the period. In Durham, the least literate of the dioceses for which records have been studied, tradesman literacy rose from 16% in the 1560s to 45% in the 1600s. In the southern counties under consideration, tradesman literacy jumped from 33% in the 1580s to 51% in the 1600s; during the same period, it rose from 54% to 80% in London and Middlesex. While the literacy rate of tradesmen was highest in the environs of London, the gains were by no means limited to cities and towns. In rural England, all of the tailors and weavers sampled for literacy in the 1560s were unable to write their names; but in the 1600s 47% of the tailors and 38% of the weavers could sign. The most solid and substantial gains in Elizabethan literacy, then, were those of the men whose achievements were first praised in print during the 1580s and 1590s.[14]

In every social group, the increase in literacy follows the same pattern, although that pattern occurs over different periods of time. Some time during Elizabeth's reign or shortly before it began, each of the social groups studied reached a plateau of literacy: a rate of total literacy for the gentry (once the gentlemen in the north caught up with those in the south during Elizabeth's reign); of about 60% for yeomen relatively early in the reign; of about 50% for craftsmen and 19% for husbandmen by the end of the reign. Beyond this level of literacy there was little rise; yeomen gained in literacy during the reigns of James and Charles, but the literacy of tradesmen stabilized and even declined a little, while the literacy of husbandmen also fell off slightly. The statistics point to a great increase in literacy of men below gentle rank who were schooled during the early years of

[12] *Ibid.*, pp. 150, 155–6.   [13] *Ibid.*, p. 153.   [14] *Ibid.*, pp. 146, 148–54.

Elizabeth's reign – the generation of Shakespeare, Heywood, Dekker, Deloney, and the many obscurer writers whose works appealed to merchants and craftsmen. Once literacy reached a certain point, it could expand no further without a change in economic and cultural conditions; further dramatic rises in literacy did not occur until the end of the seventeenth century (when, perhaps not entirely by chance, a new kind of literature appealing to tradesmen began to appear).

What, then, can we say about the gains in literacy during Elizabeth's reign, even after we have admitted that the statistics do not reflect the total number of people who could read? Most simply: the assumption that in pre-industrial England 'literacy [was] a characteristic of the members of the dominant elite, and of them alone' is fundamentally incorrect.[15] It may appear superficially that if all the gentlemen and professionals in England were literate by 1600, while only three-fifths of the yeomen, half the tradesmen and one-fifth of the husbandmen could sign their names, the *number* of literate men diminished as one descended the social scale. But this was not the case; the status groups in the lower levels of society were larger than those at the top. The elite formed only about 5 to 10% of the Tudor population – at a generous estimate, perhaps 7% of the entire adult male population was composed of completely literate gentle and professional men in 1600.[16] Assuming an adult male literacy rate of 28%, then only 7% of the literate men in England could have been members of the elite; the remaining 21% must have been non-gentle. The elite, then, were certainly the best-educated men in Elizabethan England, with a knowledge of the classics, the law, and theology that far surpassed that of men of lower rank. In terms of mere literacy, however, they were outnumbered approximately three to one.

Potentially, then, the audience for Elizabethan popular literature was composed not just partly, but primarily of men of lower status. There are several reasons for this development. First, in the wake of the Reformation, England saw a burst of school foundations: eighty-six new grammar schools appeared in Edward's reign, and seventy-two more in the first twenty years of Elizabeth's. Grammar schools were beyond the needs and the means of yeomen

[15] Laslett, 'The Wrong Way Through The Telescope', p. 329.
[16] On the proportion of the elite in the total population, see Laslett, *World We Have Lost*, p. 26; Stone, 'Social Mobility', p. 20.

and craftsmen, but the wave of educational enthusiasm that produced them also produced hundreds of new petty schools, in which
local children were taught to read and (if they could afford to stay
long enough) to write and do easy sums. Grammar-school and university graduates, of whom there were an increasing number, found
it lucrative to teach petty school while looking for more prestigious
positions; as a result, good-quality basic education was available to
an increasing number of men of lower status.[17]

The development and improvement of petty schools would not
have been necessary, however, if there had been no demand for
basic education among yeomen, craftsmen and husbandmen. That
demand was present, and sometimes even extraordinary. For
example, in the Cambridgeshire village of Willingham, only thirty
of 102 men who subscribed money to found a petty school in 1593
could give as much as a pound. The others contributed pennies and
shillings as they had them, and were rewarded by seeing the foundation of a school that taught the sons of all subscribers. The school
was a testimony to parental desire to give their children advantages
they had not had themselves, for over three-quarters of the subscribers to the school could not sign their names.[18]

Why did these parents make such a financial sacrifice to educate
their children when they had received so little education themselves? One reason was that since they had been children, the Bible
had appeared in English; the excitement of being able to read it, at
a time of religious confusion, moved many people to educate themselves and their children. There were, however, other reasons for
learning to read, and these became increasingly evident at the very
time the Bible became generally, cheaply, and legally available. For
many schoolboys struggling with their letters, the immediate, practical reason for becoming literate was that minimal education was
becoming a useful business tool in an increasingly complex, commercial society.

For example, a yeoman whose father or grandfather had bought
land after the Dissolution of the Monasteries simply used his land to
feed his own family at the beginning of Elizabeth's reign. As the
population increase of the last half of the century increased the

[17] Cressy, *Literacy and the Social Order*, pp. 167–9; Peter Clark, *English Provincial
Society from the Reformation to the Revolution* (Hassocks, Sussex, 1977),
pp. 188–92.
[18] Spufford, *Contrasting Communities*, pp. 193–5.

demand for grain and pushed up its price, however, that yeoman found it profitable to increase the amount of land he cultivated and grow more grain. If he had the good fortune to live near a market town, port, or manufacturing centre, he found that his market grew faster than his increasing harvest, for the growing number of town dwellers produced no food of their own and relied entirely upon the agriculture of its outlying areas. Thus assured an expanding market for his produce, the yeoman began to invest most of his profits in the production of his most lucrative crop, and it soon became his primary source of income. As he specialized his farming efforts, more of his business became bound up with trade; he had to market the grain, purchase commodities with the money he earned from trade, keep track of fluctuating prices, and (sometimes) even find a reliable middleman to sell his crop. As trade increased, so did the necessity of keeping records, reading contracts, writing letters and doing the 'paper work' connected with business. A literate man could take advantage of these trends, and if his business prospered, the literacy that had helped its progress lent an aura of near-gentility to the successful man. The period in which yeoman literacy rose and demands for agricultural expansion increased coincided with the 'rebuilding of rural England'. The yeoman who could afford a large house with glass windows found literacy an ornament as well as a tool of trade.[19]

The necessity of bringing more land under cultivation affected men whose farms were too small to permit specialization negatively. Many husbandmen during this era, unable to take advantage of rising grain prices because they had to concentrate upon feeding their families, frequently found themselves unable to keep up their land without falling hopelessly into debt. Some of them sold their land to yeomen and became agricultural wage-earners; others scraped along as best they could. The increasing complexity of the economy tended to widen the difference in prosperity between husbandmen and yeomen, and the difference in their degrees of literacy accentuated the social difference between them.[20] If a husbandman squeezed out pennies to educate his son, it was out of

[19] D.C. Coleman, *The Economy of England 1450–1750* (London, 1977), pp. 44–5; W.G. Hoskins, 'The Rebuilding of Rural England, 1570–1640', in *Provincial England: Essays in Social and Economic History* (London, 1963), pp. 131, 140.

[20] Coleman, *Economy of England*, pp. 46–7; Spufford, *Contrasting Communities*, pp. 165–7. See also Keith Wrightson, 'Aspects of Social Differentiation in Rural England, c. 1580–1660', *The Journal of Peasant Studies*, 5 (October, 1977), 33–47.

the hope that the boy might have some prospect in life other than that of hard and mindless toil.

Another economic trend affecting the rise of literacy in Elizabeth's reign was the diversification of English manufacture that resulted from the 'projects' first advocated by the Commonwealth Men of the 1540s and 1550s. Projects were investments designed to expand in number and increase in quality the goods manufactured in England by training English artisans to make wares hitherto imported from the Continent, thus increasing employment at home and lessening England's dependence on expensive imports. With this in mind, the Commonwealth Men encouraged foreign tradesmen to come to England and train craftsmen in different English towns. Their efforts were successful: French tradesmen taught the ironworkers of Sussex new techniques of ironfounding; Bretons improved the techniques of sailmaking at Ipswich; and Flemings began processing worsted cloth at Glastonbury, a technique that soon spread to Norwich and other provincial towns. Projects that had seen a temporary lull in Mary's reign started up again vigorously in Elizabeth's. The introduction of techniques of growing woad and collecting alum made it possible to dye wool in England, instead of sending it to the Continent to be dyed and re-importing it to be finished. At the same time, Dutch immigrants to East Anglia and Kent brought with them the techniques of making the famous 'new draperies'; they also brought new techniques for the production of luxury goods and everyday necessities. Thus Norwich became the centre for knitting English stockings and lace (just as these items became fashionable), and Maidstone became the centre for the production of linen thread, which was soon used all over the country.[21] The populations of these towns and others like them grew in size and in prosperity because of the number of skilled craftsmen they could attract – literacy prospered in such situations.

The results of specialized manufacture in different towns were several. As we have seen, towns ceased to be self-sufficient; they relied increasingly on food grown in the areas surrounding them and upon the men who brought that food to market. Moreover, as English goods became cheaper and better made, they began to compete in price with Continental goods; hence English wares had to be

[21] Thirsk, *Economic Policy and Projects*, pp. 26–9, 35, 40–8.

shipped to London or provincial ports to be sold overseas. Towns traded specialized goods with each other, thus becoming dependent on internal merchants, carters, and the fluctuations of prices.

The growth of internal trade greatly increased the complexity of business; it also increased the demand for education among trades-men, who soon learned that a man who could keep his own records had a distinct advantage over one who could not. The need for education was particularly felt in towns, in which the bulk of complex trading took place. Accordingly, tradesman literacy rose substantially faster in towns than in the country. In Norwich, for example, 68% of the tradesmen who testified in the diocesan court between 1580 and 1640 were literate, and 67.7% of the tradesmen from Maidstone, Faversham and Canterbury who testified between 1629 and 1640 were also literate. At this time, only 45% of the tradesmen in rural East Anglia could sign their names – a difference of some 23%.[22]

Among tradesmen, as among yeomen and husbandmen, the increased need for literacy affected the most prosperous men more than the members of the poorer trades. Dealers and superior retailers, whose business involved a great deal of paperwork, were almost entirely literate from 1580 on. By contrast, men whose work was menial and done locally were unaffected by the growing complexity of trade, had no need for literacy, and few achieved it: thatchers and miners, for example, had literacy rates of only 9% and 4% respectively. In the middle ranges of rural trade, tanners had a rate of 63%, fullers of 50%, cordwainers of 48%, and simple shoemakers (the heroes of craftsman literature) of 35%.[23] Within each craft, there was another gradation of literacy; master craftsmen, the most prosperous and prestigious members of their companies, were most likely to be literate, and the company average depended upon the extent of literacy in the less-prosperous members of the craft.

The concentration of literacy present in large provincial towns by the time of Elizabeth's death existed to an even greater degree in metropolitan London. The city of London had long had a good proportion of literate tradesmen; already in the 1580s, 72% of them

[22] David Cressy, 'Education and Literacy in London and East Anglia, 1580–1700', Unpublished Ph.D. thesis, Cambridge, 1972, pp. 328–9; Clark, *English Provincial Society*, p. 213.

[23] Cressy, *Literacy and the Social Order*, pp. 132–3. The figures are for the period 1580–1700.

could sign their names, and by 1603 that figure had risen to 83%. It is safe to say that only the men in the most menial crafts and the least-prosperous members of the poorer trades were likely to be illiterate within the city walls. The greatest rise in tradesman literacy that took place during Elizabeth's reign, however, appeared in suburban London. In Middlesex, for example, tradesman literacy rose from 23% in the 1580s to 69% in the 1600s.[24] A growth in literacy this sudden could not have been caused solely by an increased demand for education and a rise in the number of suburban petty schools any more than the increase in London's metropolitan population could have been caused by a rise in the proportion of births over deaths in an age when thousands of citizens could be killed by the plague in a single summer. The rise in suburban literacy was due rather to the immigration to London that raised its metropolitan population from 60,000 in 1520 to 200,000 in 1603.[25] Granted, this immigration brought many impoverished people to the city who lived in filthy lean-tos that horrified the City Fathers – but the literacy figures of the area tell another, happier story. London and its environs attracted an increasing number of literate tradesmen during Elizabeth's reign, men who had the tools to handle the complexities of London market for food, clothes, shelter, and luxury items, and who had come to the city to better their economic positions.

Because of London's growing tradition as a centre of literacy and the growing requirement for literacy among its more-prosperous inhabitants, the ability to sign extended with comparative breadth across the whole spectrum of tradesmen and the men who served them. Some of the men counted as 'tradesmen' in Cressy's studies were great merchants, men of wealth and sophistication who handled two-thirds of England's overseas trade and distributed foreign and domestic goods throughout London and England. These men were more than literate, although not all of them were educated beyond their practical needs; many of them gave their sons the best education England could offer, encouraged the increase of education by endowing grammar schools and colleges, gave generously to scholarships, and acted as patrons for scholars

[24]Cressy, 'Literacy in Pre-Industrial Society', *Societas*, 4 (1974), 235.
[25]John Patten, *English Towns 1500–1700* (Dawson, 1978), pp. 88–9, 133–4. On the effects of fire, plague and other disasters on urban population growth, see pp. 56–76, 135–9.

and scientists, either individually or as company members. These were the men who financed the operations of the Merchant Taylors' School, St John's College, Oxford, and Gresham College. And they also encouraged what Christopher Hill has called 'adult education' in London by endowing public lectures in mathematics and navigation (given in English, not Latin) and maintaining Puritan lectureships.[26] It was partly through the efforts of these men that education became increasingly available as the demand for it grew.

Below the level of these great merchants, there was a group of non-producing retailers – fishmongers, fruiterers, poulterers, cheesemongers – who were also completely literate. These were the men who bought agricultural goods and distributed them throughout the city; they grew increasingly prosperous as the food market in London grew so enormous that it was no longer practical for farmers to sell their own produce in the city. As London grew, it became necessary to import food from farther and farther away, and record-keeping became more and more essential; hence the prosperity and the business of the major retailers required them to be literate.[27]

Throughout all the ranks of trade – through shoemakers, tailors, thatchers, bricklayers, glaziers, carters – the average literacy, craft for craft, was considerably higher in London than it was in rural areas.[28] Furthermore, the apprentices who came to London were either required or expected to be as literate as the men they served; 82% of the apprentices from London and Middlesex in Cressy's

[26] On English grammar schools founded by London merchants, see W.K. Jordan, *The Charities of London, 1480–1660: The Aspirations and the Achievements of the Urban Society* (New York, 1960), pp. 226–35. On the merchant taylors' connection with St John's, Oxford, see pp. 258–9. The merchant taylors also paid John Stow a pension of £6 *per annum* for his work on English chronicles (Stow, *Survey*, I, xxiv–xxv). On the foundation and operation of Gresham College, see Jordan, *Charities of London*, p. 253; Christopher Hill, *Intellectual Origins of the English Revolution* (Oxford, 1962), Chapter II. Hill's association of Puritanism, capitalism, the scientific revolution and the Civil War has been hotly contested in *PP*, nos. 28, 29 and 31. His argument that London merchants subsidized scientific 'adult education' in London, both independently and through Gresham College, however, is unrefuted and extremely interesting. Gresham particularly desired scientific lectures to be given in English, so that they could be understood by men whose education included no Latin – that is, craftsmen, sailors and ordinary citizens as well as the learned (p. 35).

[27] F.J. Fisher, 'The Development of the London Food Market, 1540–1640', *Essays in Economic History*, ed. E.M. Carus-Wilson (1954; rpt. London, 1961), I, 146.

[28] Cressy, *Literacy and the Social Order*, pp. 132–5.

study could sign their names. Servants in London were also exceptionally literate: 69% of the servants studied in London and Middlesex could sign their names, as compared with only 24% in the dioceses of Norwich, Exeter and Durham.[29] In London, at least, servants and apprentices were a potential part of the Elizabethan audience.

The problem of female participation in this audience is a vexed one, for all the evidence that allows female literacy to be studied is inconclusive. There were certainly Elizabethan women who could read and write; some women of gentle rank were very well educated indeed and became patrons of several authors. On the other hand, there may have been a number of women who were able to read but not to write, and are therefore inaccessible to statistical study. If women were taught to read and sew (since sewing was a necessary feminine accomplishment and writing was not), there may have been many more readers than writers among the female population. Some of these women apparently taught their children to read before (or instead of) sending them to school; others taught petty schools to which a writing master came occasionally to teach writing to the more advanced children. Did these women teach girls as well as boys? Did they learn from their own petty-school experience? There is some pictorial evidence that this may have been the case, but it is far from conclusive.[30] It is possible, in any case, that the statistics that show only 18% of the women in Canterbury and less than 10% of the women in London and East Anglia could sign their names greatly underestimate the number of female readers in Elizabethan England.[31]

On the other hand, there is little evidence that authors and printers in Elizabethan England thought there was a large group of literate women who would read books that appealed to them alone. A study of books for women between 1475 and 1640 has identified only 163 such books for the whole period, and some of these books

[29] *Ibid.*, p. 129.
[30] Margaret Spufford, 'First Steps in Literacy: The Reading and Writing Experiences of the Humblest Seventeenth Century Spiritual Biographers', in Harvey J. Graff, ed., *Literacy and Social Development in the West* (Cambridge, 1981), pp. 127–8, 134, 149; J.W. Adamson, 'The Extent of Literacy in England in the Fifteenth and Sixteenth Centuries: Notes and Conjectures', *The Library*, series 4, 10 (1929–30), 163.
[31] Cressy, *Literacy and the Social Order*, pp. 144–9; Clark, *English Provincial Society*, p. 213.

were certainly not published only for a feminine audience – Spenser's *Faerie Queene* and Montaigne's *Essays*, for example, which were included because of their dedications.[32] While the existence of books written for women certainly argues for a literate clientele, the presence of these books argues mainly for a gentle clientele. Among the women's books were three books in the popular canon; two of these were definitely written for women who had to manage servants and run large households, and the third concerned the death of Philip Stubbes' (literate) wife, who died shortly after giving birth to her first child. Of these three books, only the third had any universality; its extreme popularity may indicate that it reached more women than most books did. Death in childbirth was a subject that invoked fear and sympathy not limited to any social rank. From the 'market' standpoint, however, this book was exceptional. It seems that while women could join the popular audience by reading to themselves or by being read to by men, they were not perceived as a separate, lucrative literary audience until the eighteenth century. By this time, the measurable literacy of women had increased greatly, at least in London; so it may be that the literacy statistics available for women in the sixteenth century yield an accurate portrait of the women who had the leisure, education and inclination to do more with their skill than read the Bible and teach little children the rudiments of learning.[33]

Among the literate, reading was not equally easy for all. A dedicated reader without much money to spare would have to do some planning if he wanted to read. He did not necessarily have to buy books; they could always be shared: a Yorkshire yeoman named Adam Eyre lent Foxe's *Acts and Monuments* and several contemporary sermons to his neighbours between 1646 and 1649, and probably many of his Elizabethan contemporaries did the same. In cathedrals, the Bible and Foxe's *Acts and Monuments* were placed near the altar so all men could read them.[34] In Kent, many parish churches had one or more books so their parishioners could practise reading, and this may have been true in other counties too; there are

[32] Suzanne Hull, *Chaste, Silent and Obedient: English Books for Women, 1475–1640* (San Marino, California, 1982), pp. 144–217.

[33] On the place of women readers in the eighteenth-century audience, see Ian Watt, *The Rise of the Novel: Studies in Defoe, Richardson and Fielding* (Berkeley and Los Angeles, 1957), pp. 43–5.

[34] Mildred Campbell, *The English Yeoman under Elizabeth and the Early Stuarts* (1942; rpt. New York, 1960), pp. 266–7; Mozley, *John Foxe*, p. 147.

several wills extant that leave money to the parish church to buy books, indicating that there was some lay interest in making books available to many readers. Possibly some citizens had access to school libraries in their areas, as may have been the case in Faversham, Sandwich and Tonbridge.[35] And while there is no 'hard' evidence that men could pool their pennies and buy a book to share or read aloud, common sense suggests that this was one easy way men could enjoy popular pamphlets and jest books without worrying about the cost. The poor survival rate of jest books certainly suggests that their dubious wit brought pleasure to a number of readers before they finally fell apart.

The expense of reading, however, was not overwhelming unless one bought large books that needed to be bound. A jest book or a medical pamphlet could be had for the price of two quarts of small beer – 2d. Grafton's *Tables and Rules*, a pamphlet by Greene or a single sermon cost about the same as a quart of a more luxurious drink, ale (4d.) – but it lasted longer. A quarto of a popular play like Heywood's *1 Edward IV* was a small extravagance, costing as much as a cheap dinner for two (6d.). An edition of the psalms cost as much as a quart of sack (8d.) – a drink, as John Stow sadly remarked, 'above the reach' of many.[36] But sack was not beyond the means of a reasonably prosperous craftsman or yeoman, though he might have thought twice about the expense. Larger works were more of a financial sacrifice: Babington's treatises *Of the Commandments* and *Frailty and Faith*, with their comforting words on the holiness of poverty, cost nearly half a year's rent on a one-room weaver's cottage (2s.). Such a cottage, in fact, could have been built for the same price as three copies of Perkins' collected *Works* (£5).[37] A man who lived in a one-room cottage, however,

---

[35] In 1575 a yeoman left money for a copy of Calvin's *Institutes* for his church at Maidstone, Kent (Campbell, *English Yeoman*, p. 268). At about this time, a widow left money to buy a Bible for the church in Twyford, Leicestershire, and a servant left 20s. to buy Foxe's *Acts and Monuments* for his church. (Leicester County Record Office, Probate Inventories for the Archdeaconry of Leicester: Record of Book-owning compiled for the Cambridge Group for the History of Population and Social Structure by Miss W. Herrington of Leicester. Wills from the period 1575–99. I am grateful to Roger Schofield for making Miss Herrington's study available to me.) See also Clark, *English Provincial Society*, p. 209.

[36] Book prices (all for unbound volumes): Francis R. Johnson, 'Notes on English Retail Book-prices, 1550–1640', *The Library*, 5th series, 5, 97–108; commodity prices: Harbage, *Shakespeare's Audience*, pp. 57–9.

[37] Robert Jahn, 'Letters and Booklists of Thomas Chard (or Chare) of London, 1583–4', *The Library*, 4th series, 4 (1923–4), 224 (Babington). Rent on a cottage

was unlikely to be a reader; the more prosperous men of his trade could have saved up money to buy Babington's pamphlets, though they would probably have chosen to buy Perkins' sermons in cheap, separate editions. There is certainly evidence that craftsmen did buy expensive books, particularly the Bible; and the printers encouraged this tendency by making the Bible more cheaply available. For example, a master carpenter who accumulated an estate of some £27 on his shilling-a-day wages would have had to save a month's pay for a folio Bible (six weeks, if he had it bound). But the Bible was also printed in quarto for 9s., and, after 1582, in octavo for 5s.[38] Just at the time when more craftsmen and yeomen were becoming literate, the Bible appeared in their price-range and many other cheap, vernacular books appeared in print. This could not have been an accident. The changing composition of the Elizabethan audience created a demand for vernacular works at a reasonable price.

Once a man decided to buy books, it was not too difficult to get them. Londoners, of course, had the easiest access to bookstalls and the greatest selection of books, but books were available in provincial towns as well. Canterbury, for example, was an active bookselling city; books were sold at fairs by London book-sellers who came to do business directly, by resident book-sellers, and also by merchants who kept a side-stock of texts and a few religious books. The last group is of interest to historians, for it explains why some cities mention book-binders among their freemen, but no booksellers: reading material could be sold by any retailer who wanted a relatively inexpensive side-line in his shop, and in many towns the book trade may have been carried on chiefly in this manner.[39] In Cambridge, of course, there were bookstalls; in the 1580s such best-sellers as *Euphues*, Lambard's *Duties of Constables*, Edwards' *Paradise of Dainty Devices*, and *Remedies for Diseases in Horses* were available there.[40] In Shrewsbury at this time, one Roger Ward,

---

varied from 4 to 7s. a year (Hoskins, 'Leicester', pp. 56–7); Perkins' *Works*, unbound, cost 33s. (Johnson, 'Book-prices', p. 108).

[38] On carpenters' wages, see J.E.T. Rogers, *A History of Agriculture and Prices in England* (7 vols., 1886–1902, rpt. Vaduz, 1963), V, 672. On a carpenter's estate, see Hoskins, 'Leicester', p. 65. The folio Bible for which the price is given is a King James, available in 1616 or 1617 at 25s., unbound, or 40s. bound (Johnson, 'Book-prices', p. 97). An unbound quarto Bible cost 9s. in 1584 and an octavo Bible cost 5s. (Jahn, 'Letters and Booklists', p. 230).

[39] Clark, *English Provincial Society*, p. 210.

[40] Jahn, 'Letters and Booklists', pp. 219–37.

who had incurred some difficulties after printing illegally in London and decided that it would be wise to change locations, set up a large shop (2500 volumes). Most of his books were devotional manuals and grammar-school texts, but he had multiple copies of works in the popular canon which he thought he could sell quickly. Among these were eighteen copies of Wilson's play *The Three Ladies of London*, nineteen copies of a 1584 edition of Greene's *Pandosto* (no longer extant), forty-two copies of Dent's *Sermon of Repentance* (probably his pirated edition), fifteen copies of Lambard's *Duties of Constables*, and a few copies of *Seven Sobs of a Sorrowful Soul for Sin*, Becon's *Sick Man's Salve*, *Euphues*, and several others.[41] This stock may have been too large for a small provincial town in the 1580s – Ward's bookstore is known to historians because it failed. We do not, however, know the whole story; Ward's business practices had been shady in London, and his ruin may have been partly of his own making. If he had opened his shop a decade later, however, when literacy was higher than it had been in the 1580s and book-owning more common, he might have survived in spite of himself.

Book-ownership, a nearly non-existent phenomenon at the beginning of Elizabeth's reign, except among scholars and the gentry, became more common as the reign progressed. To a certain extent, the rise in book-owning can be studied by examining probate records at the diocesan level, which contain the inventories of every man worth more than £5 at his death, whether he left a will or not. Very few of these records mention book-ownership in the 1560s: in Canterbury, for example, only 8% of the probate surveys available mention books, and all those surveys concern the property of the top third of the town's citizens. By the 1600s, however, one-third of these well-established citizens had books, and the figure had risen to 45% by the 1620s.[42]

Records from the county of Leicestershire, taken from a larger and broader sample, also illustrate an increase in book-owning. In the early years of Elizabeth's reign, from 1550 to 1574, only fifteen out of the 1749 men whose estates were surveyed owned books – less than 1%. By 1600 to 1624, the years in which men educated between

[41] Rodger, 'Roger Ward's Shrewsbury Stock', pp. 250–2.
[42] Peter Clark, 'The Ownership of Books in England,1560–1640: TheExample of Some Kentish Townsfolk', in L. Stone, ed., *Schooling and Society: Studies in the History of Education* (Baltimore and London, 1976), p. 99.

1565 and 1589 would have died, book-owning had increased to 7.8% (out of a sample of 1844), indicating that one out of every 12.7 men whose estates came to probate had literature of some sort in his household.[43] The records suggest that a number of yeomen, craftsmen and husbandmen began to buy books after 1575. In 1575 to 1599 (years for which probate records no longer exist and one has to rely on wills), two grocers, two woollen drapers, an ironmonger, a tailor, a mason and a bellfounder had books, and one husbandman (out of 773 surveyed) had a Bible. Ten clerics and two gentlemen also owned books at this time.[44] The social distribution of books in the next generation (1600–24) is obscured by the vagueness of the records; sixty-five of the 145 men owning books were of unspecified status. The inventories that do mention status, however, suggest that there were more books at all levels of society: books appeared in the households of twenty-four gentlemen, eighteen clerics, fourteen yeomen, ten craftsmen, and twelve husbandmen. Unquestionably, as book-owning grew more popular, books were not bought exclusively by the gentry.

As sources for measuring book-ownership, however, probate records are finally disappointing; they do little more than confirm the commonsense assumption that as literacy increased, more people bought books. The records, which frequently omit the status of the man whose estate was surveyed, also tend to refer to the man's books as 'his books', or 'sundry books'. One might hope that the few books that are mentioned by title might give insight into Elizabethan taste at different social ranks, but they do not. Most of the books whose titles are recorded are large, devotional works; almost none of the books in the popular canon appear. This fact has led some scholars to suggest that popular literature in Elizabeth's reign was not so popular as the number of its editions makes it seem, but the conclusion is unwarranted.[45] Books that are mentioned in probate inventories are without exception those of a size and

---

[43] All references are to the Leicester Probate Inventories, as stated above, note 35. The statute requiring that the property of every person be inventoried immediately upon his death (21 Henry VIII, c. 5) also said the Archdeacon and other officials could not charge a probate fee when the estate was not clearly worth more than £5. In practice, probate officials simply did not survey his estate unless he left a will. In Leicester, the officials were relatively careful about the estates they examined; many of the men whose estate appear are husbandmen, labourers and servants.

[44] The records of 1575 are drawn from wills, since probate records for this period do not exist.

[45] Clark, 'Ownership of Books', p. 109.

importance to be bound; and a bound book was an item of taxable worth that could conceivably be sold second-hand if the deceased left considerable debts. Cheap, unbound books, however, deteriorated quickly, had no resale value, and frequently pre-deceased their owners.[46] In records which recorded books at best in a cavalier fashion, these tattered, stitched-together quires were simply not worth mentioning. Thus, the absence of all books in the popular canon but Foxe's *Acts and Monuments*, Pettie's *Palace of Pleasure* and Henry Smith's complete *Sermons* should not make one doubt the popularity of cheaper books that went through many more editions; it should make one doubt the value of probate records as indicators of popular Elizabethan taste.

It is safe to conclude on the basis of probate evidence, however, that by the time 28% of Elizabethan adult males could read, a fair number of them did so. If one out of every three well-to-do citizens in Canterbury owned books that required binding and one out of every twelve or thirteen men above the rank of husbandman in Leicestershire owned such books, there was a fair amount of reading being done by the end of Elizabeth's reign. The men who owned books were not exclusively gentle or professional; yeomen, craftsmen and husbandmen bought relatively expensive books for their amusement or instruction.

One did not, of course, have to be literate to be a member of the Elizabethan audience. In any community, it was possible for the literate to read aloud to their illiterate neighbours, wives, servants or families.[47] Furthermore, most popular literary genres of the period were sermons and plays, and these were available to the illiterate as well as to the educated.

The man who lived in London, of course, whether literate or illiterate, had a tremendous advantage over his provincial counterparts. If he wanted to hear a sermon he could go to Paul's Cross or to St Clement Danes to hear Henry Smith. On other days of the week and on holidays, he could see a play for a penny. To many men of limited income, the literary opportunities London offered must have been welcome indeed. But men in provincial areas had access

[46] Oliver Willard, 'The Survival of Some English Books Published Before 1640: A Theory and Some Illustrations', *The Library*, series 4, 23 (1942–3), p. 173.

[47] See Elizabeth Eisenstein, 'Some Conjectures About the Impact of Printing Upon Western Society and Thought: a Preliminary Report'; Natatlie Z. Davis, 'Printing and the People: Early Modern France', in Graff, *Literacy and Social Development*, pp. 53–95.

to some oral culture. Both Greenham and Dent preached in rural parishes, though they were of a different order of magnitude from most country pastors. Before the founding of the London theatres in 1576, groups of itinerate actors gave plays in towns and villages; some companies continued to travel after the theatres settled in London, and occasionally the plague drove London companies to the road.[48] Men in county towns were probably not cut off from oral culture, and even villagers could hear a sermon or see a play at country fairs.

The problem with an audience of spoken literature is that it is very difficult to determine its social composition. There is little direct commentary on the audiences in London, and most of what there is is negative. The City Fathers protested against the founding of the theatres because they drew crowds (and the attendant problems of fire, filth and possible social unrest); they disliked large gatherings at sermons for the same reason.[49] These protests made much of the fact that sermons and plays were attended by the dregs of society, and though they almost certainly overstated the case, it is true that there was a strong element of humble men in the audiences of both entertainments. In religious matters, there was a strong current of potentially sectarian belief among men of low status in London as early as the 1560s, and later, even more 'orthodox' preachers drew men of craftsman status.[50] When the parishioners of St Clement Danes presented a petition to Lord Burleigh in favour of giving that living to Henry Smith, for example, it was discovered that the men who signed it included a grocer, a locksmith, and a 'good number of ordinary tradesmen, as smiths, tailors, saddlers, hosiers, haberdashers, glaziers, cutters, and the like'. Some of them signed the petition with their marks.[51]

There were merchants and craftsmen at the London theatres, of course, though historians of theatre disagree about their proportion in the total audience. In the halcyon days of the middle class, the

[48] On itinerate actors, see Alfred Harbage, *Shakespeare and the Rival Traditions* (1952; rpt. New York, 1968), pp. 3–28.

[49] Valerie Pearl, *London and the Outbreak of the Puritan Revolution: City Government and National Politics, 1625–43* (London, 1961), pp. 40–1; Harbage, *Shakespeare's Audience*, pp. 6–7. Harbage points out that the complaints of the City Fathers had little to do with the plays being produced.

[50] Patrick Collinson, *The Elizabethan Puritan Movement* (Berkeley and Los Angeles, 1967), p. 94.

[51] William Haller, *The Rise of Puritanism* (1937; rpt. New York, 1957), p. 29.

rowdy, cheerful citizen audience of Shakespeare's plays got perhaps more attention than it deserved; in the wake of the attack on Marxist interpretations of social history, one is now asked to believe that the bulk of the audience was composed of 'privileged playgoers' – gentlemen, professionals, students, merchants, skilled craftsmen and wealthy apprentices.[52] Like the old middle class, the group of 'privileged' men expands and contracts easily at the whim of the historian who uses it, as it appears that any person who patronized the theatre was *ipso facto* privileged. Nevertheless, the point that steady playgoers had to have both ample cash and ample leisure is well taken, and it tallies accurately with what is known about the practices of theatre managers.

The theatre owners made the bulk of their profits from the seats they sold in the galleries, which cost 2d. or 3d. apiece, depending on the view they afforded of the stage and the padding on the bench. These seats, which protected the audience from rain and wind, were more expensive than standing places in the theatre yard, which (if one could endure rain, squalor, and the discomfort of standing for two hours) could be had for merely a penny. Penny customers were, perforce, less numerous than those who paid 2d. or a groat; measurements of the Fortune Theatre suggest that the galleries held more people than the yard.[53] The construction of the theatres, then, suggests that the managers bargained on attracting an audience that preferred, for the most part, comfort to economy when spending an afternoon at the theatre. They provided that comfort at double or triple the price of the minimum fare, apparently confident that they could thus increase their profits without losing a substantial part of their audience.

On the mere evidence of theatre prices, however, one cannot assume that gentlemen filled the galleries while craftsmen filled the yard. The plain fact of the matter is that the theatres provided the cheapest entertainment in London short of a walk in Finsbury Fields with a pretty girl or (to those with a less-secular outlook) an open-air sermon. A craftsman who saved two pennies could choose between standing through two plays, sitting through one play, or drinking two quarts of small beer with his friends. For the price of a quart of

[52] Alfred Harbage, *Shakespeare's Audience*, *passim*; Ann Jennalie Cook, *The Privileged Playgoers of Shakespeare's London, 1576–1642* (Princeton, 1981), especially pp. 11–51.
[53] Cook, *Privileged Playgoers*, pp. 185–95.

ale, he could choose between seeing four plays in the yard, two plays in the galleries, or combining one or two afternoons at the theatre with buying a jest-book. It was not the price of the theatre that kept a man with limited income away from it; it was the time. Here, gentlemen had an undeniable advantage over men of trade; they were, for the most part, masters of their own time, and they could arrange their business in town in such a way to leave their afternoons free. A craftsman, whose hours were set by statute and the necessities of earning a living, was less free to plan his day as he wanted; whether he could afford it or not, he could not go to the theatre two or three afternoons a week.[54]

Nevertheless, there were a great many craftsmen in London, and though any one of them might have had difficulty finding the time and the money to go to the theatre on a regular basis, as a group there were probably a number of them in any specific audience. Gentlemen may very well have provided the staple audience the theatre managers needed in order to maintain a profit, but there were certainly enough craftsmen, merchants, journeymen and apprentices in London to fill many seats at a popular performance. The theatre was accessible six days a week. For a penny, a man could see a play which would have cost him 6d. to buy – a clear saving of 5d. and a clear gain of an enjoyable afternoon. Seeing a play was effortless, once one had arranged to get to the theatre: one did not have to find a light by which to read it, one did not have to puzzle over difficult works, one did not have to cope with a poor text – one had merely to watch. Is it possible that these facts, familiar in a city filled with men of minimal education, could have been lost upon the trading population of London?

Finally, the popularity of plays with citizen heroes – *Jack Straw, 1 Edward IV, The Four Prentices of London, The Shoemakers' Holiday* and many others – suggests that the playwrights and managers did not cater exclusively to an audience of courtiers, gentlemen and students. The theatre managers knew their business; none of them died poor. They knew that men who attended plays were not just men who could afford to go to the theatre without counting the time and the money, but those who liked plays well enough to find time and money to go. Finally, an historian of theatre must trust the entrepreneurial instincts of Philip Henslowe and his contemporaries. These men had to build up a clientele; to do so,

[54] *Ibid.*, pp. 224–8.

they produced plays that appealed to citizen audiences as well as plays that appealed to gentlemen with advanced educations and intellectual tastes.

It seems, then, that all merchants and many craftsmen were in a position to enjoy the Elizabethan works discussed in this study. Merchants were committed to education and made it available to young men who grew up in London and country towns; they endowed libraries, founded grammar schools and colleges, and gave financial assistance to scholars. Minimal education, partly as a result of their efforts, reached beyond the ranks of the wealthiest traders and retailers; in London, some form of learning extended well into the ranks of poor freemen who were worth under £250 at their deaths.

Given the information we have about the Elizabethan audience, the popular authors' assumption that a fair number of their readers were 'unlearned' but literate seems to have been fundamentally accurate. The readers to whom they appealed were not the intelligentsia who enjoyed university education, a grand tour, and a serious interest in sophisticated literature, though these men wrote and inspired some of the finest literature of their time. Many of the readers to whom the popular authors appealed in their introductions were simply literate; their learning was a tool of trade and a path to first-hand cultural or religious experience. This was the audience the popular authors coaxed to read other works in their introductions, and the audience for whom some of them wrote books and plays about merchants, clothiers and craftsmen. Great dramatists could write for the intellectual and the humble playgoer; great preachers could attract the gentleman and the small London radical. But some popular authors were content to write second-rate literature that reflected upon the problems and desires of 'the unlearned' – or, as we would say, the unsophisticated. That a good portion of this 'unlearned' audience was composed of merchants, craftsmen, and apprentices is an inescapable conclusion.

Part II

The businessman in armour

4. *Principal citizens and chief yeomen*

When Elizabeth I became Queen of England, English merchants were figures of great importance in London and provincial towns, but in literature they were familiar only in two of Chaucer's *Canterbury Tales*, in London chronicles, and in the works of preachers and satirists who portrayed them as grasping misers.[1] By the end of Elizabeth's reign, however, merchants had become familiar literary figures, and they had acquired a new cultural image as men whose exploits served England well.[2]

The original image of the merchant as usurer did not die out entirely as the more positive portraits of merchants became popular; to morality-play writers, the figure of greed was too interesting to ignore, and so merchants appeared as usurers in such plays as *The Tide Tarrieth No Man* (1576), *The Three Ladies of London* (1581) and in Lodge and Greene's late morality play *A Looking Glass for London and England* (c. 1590). In the hands of Marlowe and Shakespeare, however, the usurer took on sins beyond greed; and in the hands of Heywood and Haughton, usurers became 'stock' villains and outraged fathers. By the end of our period, the usurer had ceased to be criticized merely for lending at interest and was given a new list of characteristics.

As the usurer became increasingly weak and silly on the stage, some popular authors experimented with the flexibility of the medieval merchant stereotypes. Grafton's *Abridgment of the*

---

[1]See F.J. Levy, *Tudor Historical Thought* (San Marino, California, 1967), pp. 17–26; C.L. Kingsford, *English Historical Literature in the Fifteenth Century* (1913; rpt. New York, 1962), Chapter IV; G.R. Owst, *Literature and Pulpit in Medieval England* (2nd edn, Cambridge, 1961), pp. 352–8. For the treatment of merchants in estates satires, see Ruth Mohl, *The Three Estates in Medieval and Renaissance Literature* (1933; rpt. New York, 1962). The two *Canterbury Tales* in which merchants appear are *The Merchant's Tale* and *The Shipman's Tale*.

[2]A list of the popular works in which merchants are portrayed appears in Appendix D.

Chronicles of England (1563) and the first edition of its rival, *Stow's Summary of English Chronicles* (1565) were little different from earlier city chronicles; but by 1580, Stow had developed the old format into a vehicle for celebrating the great deeds of London's leading citizens.[3] John Foxe, writing in another historical tradition, praised the faith and bravery of merchants who had been martyred in Mary's reign; his portraits, in time, mitigated the standard moral stereotype of the merchant as a worshipper of Mammon.

In the last half of the reign the merchant took on a truly positive image. The image had its roots chiefly in the historical research of John Stow, but it was probably also influenced by the chivalric codes that appeared in London's trained bands. As early as the reign of Henry VII, a band under the patronage of Prince Arthur had made the most of obvious references to the heroic past; its members took on the characters of Lancelot and other knights of the round table and developed passionate interest in heraldry. In 1583, just three years after Stow's research was first printed in large-scale form, Richard Robinson published *The Ancient Order . . . of Prince Arthur . . . With a Threefold Assertion Friendly in Favour and Furtherance of English Archery at this Day*, in which he explained (with pictures less than illuminating) the heraldry of the band. To it he appended a treatise on the history of British shooting, obviously hoping the chivalric material in the front of the book would disguise the fact that the long-bow was not the weapon of the feudal aristocracy. But the pamphlet did not sell (there was only one edition), and although the authors who praised merchants in chivalric terms were undoubtedly influenced by the traditions of the trained bands, they did not glorify archery. Like Stow, they turned to a civic past, finding (or creating) heroes who acted like gentlemen and lords, not like hearty yeomen. The merchants they praised needed a new tradition; apparently, the authors felt no urge to associate them with a group below them on the social scale.

Thus Stow, Deloney, Dekker, Haughton, Heywood and other popular authors strove to combine research with chivalric tradition, knowledge of merchants' economic contributions with prose romance. Deloney, for example, used gild legends to reflect upon the economic usefulness of his subjects, attempts that frequently led him into interesting sociological tangles. Dekker and Heywood

---

[3] See below, Chapter 6.

combined scenes of chivalric heroism with London street-scenes, with the same puzzling outcome. These paradoxical portraits suggest that the desire to praise merchants, instead of villifying them as earlier writers had, brought Elizabethan writers face to face with a problem they could not understand. Why should this have been so?

One cause of the author's dilemma was that while literary portraits of merchants changed, definitions of merchant status remained constant throughout Elizabeth's reign. The economic and political descriptions of merchants that were published early in the reign had at their base the assumption that merchants were inferior to gentlemen in both status and social worth, though their wealth enabled them to deal with great sums of money. This was essentially a negative definition of a social group that needed a positive image – yet to change the definition of the group would have required a set of values Elizabethan authors did not have at their disposal. Why this was the case can be seen if one looks carefully at definitions of merchant status and the everyday usage of the social terms in which merchants were described.

The economic definition of merchant status was articulated by Richard Mulcaster in 1581 and by the anonymous author of 'An Apology of the City of London' (later published by Stow in his *Survey of London*) in approximately the same year. Mulcaster divided the realm into two groups: gentlemen and commonalty. The commonalty he further divided into 'merchants and manuaries generally', merchants being those who earned their livings in trade, manuaries being those who lived by 'handiwork' and 'labour'. The distinction between them, he said, was 'by wealth'.[4] The absence of agricultural men from this division suggests that Mulcaster thought of England in terms of London; the apologist clarified his definition by saying it related only to London. He divided Londoners into 'Merchants, Handicraftsmen, and Labourers'. Merchants and retailers formed the smallest, richest group; handicraftsmen were skilled workmen; and labourers were those whose work required no 'cunning'.[5] According to both these definitions, a merchant was a wealthy man engaged in commerce and retail who did not have to labour for his living, but who nevertheless was not a gentleman.

[4] Richard Mulcaster, *Positions*, ed. R.H. Quick (London, 1888), p. 197.
[5] Stow, *Survey*, II, 207–8.

The political definition of merchant status was first made by William Harrison in 1577. Harrison divided the population into four 'sorts' of men: gentlemen, 'citizens or burgesses', yeomen, and 'artificers or labourers'.[6] Citizens were those men who had 'next place to gentlemen' and were not only 'free within the cities', but of 'some likely substance to bear office in the same'. He added: 'In this place also are our merchants to be installed, as amongst the citizens (although they often change estate with gentlemen, as gentlemen do with them, by a mutual conversion of the one into the other).'[7] Merchants, while 'next place' to gentlemen, were not gentlemen; they were above yeomen in status and differentiated from 'artificers or labourers' by their stature in cities.

Sir Thomas Smith adopted Harrison's description of the social hierarchy almost *verbatim*: in his *De Republica Anglorum* (completed in 1577 but not published until 1583), he divided the kingdom into four groups: 'gentlemen, citizens, yeomen, artificers, and labourers'.[8] Citizens, he said, were next after gentlemen in political matters, but they served the commonwealth only in towns, for 'generally in the shires they be of none account'. Smith did not include all merchants among citizens; he placed 'merchants and retailers which have no free land' among the 'fourth sort of people which do not rule'.[9] To be a citizen in Smith's definition, a man had to be more than a buyer and seller; he had to be wealthy enough to own property. Harrison's definition of the four 'sorts' of people, slightly clarified by Smith, remained acceptable for at least thirty years after it was made. In 1607, William Camden divided the estates of the realm into five groups ('a king or monarch, nobles, citizens, freemen whom we call yeomen, and artisans'), adding that

---

[6] Holinshed, I, 263. Harrison's *Historical description* was published in the first volume of Holinshed's *Chronicles* in 1577; Harrison revised his discussion of the social hierarchy in the next edition (1587), but he left this particular passage unchanged.

[7] *Ibid.*, I, 274.

[8] *De Republica Anglorum: A Discourse on the Commonwealth of England*, ed. Leonard Alston (Cambridge, 1906), p. 31. For a discussion of the relationship of Harrison and Smith's passages on the social hierarchy, see Mary Dewar, 'A Question of Plagiarism: The "Harrison Chapters" in Sir Thomas Smith's De Republica Anglorum', *Historical Journal*, 22 (1979), 921–9. Dewar argues that Smith took the passages from Harrison's manuscript before the first edition of Holinshed's *Chronicles* was published; when *De Republica Anglorum* was published in 1583, Harrison liked Smith's changes, and adopted them.

[9] *Ibid.*, pp. 41–2, 46.

'citizens' were 'those who hold offices in their respective cities, and are elected to sit in parliaments'.[10]

Harrison's use of the term 'citizen', while acceptable to Smith and Camden, was more restrictive than that of many of his contemporaries; the word was frequently used to describe any freeman of a city.[11] Traditionally, therefore, 'citizen' was accompanied by an adjective when it referred to the civic elite. In the thirteenth-century records of London, for example, leaders in ward politics were called 'the more sufficient' or 'the more powerful' citizens, while the mayor and aldermen were styled 'sovereign lords'.[12] In Elizabeth's reign the members of the city elite were variously described as 'the best citizens', 'principal citizens', 'rich citizens', or 'substantial citizens' while the rest of the city population was termed 'the commonalty'.[13] I shall adopt this terminology and refer to Harrison's group as 'principal citizens'.

Principal citizens were in fact the same men Mulcaster described as 'merchants' and the apologist termed 'merchants and chief retailers'. In order to rise to the rank of principal citizen, a man had to attain stature in his gild as well as in city politics, all the while increasing his fortune. Thus, a young merchant would start doing committee work in his company at about the same time he was appointed to committees in his parish; he could become a warden of his company at about the time he became a vestryman of his parish; and finally, after holding numerous offices in his company and serving on the Common Council of the city, he might become

[10] William Camden, *Britannia: or, a Chorographical Description of the Flourishing Kingdoms of England, Scotland and Ireland, and the Islands Adjacent; from the Earliest Antiquity*, translated from the edition of 1607 by Richard Gough (London, 1789), pp. cxxiv, cxliii.

[11] In Thomas Heywood's *1 Edward IV*, the lord mayor says he was found as a baby by a poor citizen, a shoemaker (Heywood, I, 57); in Robert Wilson's *Three Lords and Three Ladies of London*, the clown Simplicity expresses pride in his London citizenship, though he is only a ballad-monger (Dodsley, VI, 404).

[12] Sylvia Thrupp, *The Merchant Class of Medieval London* (Chicago, 1948), pp. 15–17.

[13] John Stow, *Annals, or, a General Chronicle of England . . . to 1631* (London, 1631), pp. 274–5. Stow contrasts the behaviour of the 'common people' with that of the 'Chief Citizens' and 'worshipful and best sort of the Citizens' in a riot against John of Gaunt. Later, he says that the mayor, sheriffs and 'other of the best Citizens' were arrested in 1392 when London refused to loan Richard II £1000 (p. 306); when Richard again looked on London with favour, according to Stow, 'the principal Citizens all in one livery' rode to meet him (p. 307). For a reference to 'substantial citizens', see the play *Sir Thomas More*, II, iv, line 229, in the *Shakespeare Apocrypha*.

master of his company at about the same time he became an alder-man.[14] Very few men reached the top ranks of city government. In London, there were only 212 men on the Common Council and twenty-six on the Court of Aldermen in any given year of Elizabeth's reign.[15] To rise to these heights a merchant had to be very wealthy; to be of 'some likely substance' to be an alderman of London, a merchant had to own property worth £10,000 and the expenses of being an alderman were so immense that half the 140 men elected to that office between 1600 and 1625 paid fines of between £100 and £800 in order to avoid serving. At the lower ranks of city office, however, the financial burden of serving the city was lighter; in London, the thousand men who served as vestrymen of parishes, executive officials in ward inquests and assistants of companies seldom declined an office because of the expense it entailed.[16]

Principal citizens formed a small civic elite bound closely by ties of business, political responsibility and marriage. This was especially true in the highest city ranks. In Elizabethan London, for example, 70% of the aldermen, sheriffs and leading common coun-cillors were grocers, haberdashers, merchant taylors, mercers, clothworkers or drapers. Many of them were involved in foreign trade as well as domestic; in James' reign, half the men elected to the Court of Aldermen invested in overseas trade, three quarters of them through the merchant adventurers.[17] The men who thus knew each other in mercantile and political capacities were also related to each other, for marriage alliances between wealthy merchant families were common, and promising sons were frequently apprenticed into one of the great companies. During Elizabeth's reign, for example, one-third of the men elected to the Court of Aldermen in London were related to other aldermanic families or had aldermanic descendants in the next generation, and two-thirds

---

[14] Frank F. Foster, 'Merchants and Bureaucrats in Elizabethan London', *The Guild-hall Miscellany*, 4 (1971–3), 158–9.

[15] Frank F. Foster, *The Politics of Stability: A Portrait of the Rulers in Elizabethan London* (London, 1977), pp. 180–3.

[16] Pearl, *London and the Puritan Revolution*, p. 60; R.G.Lang, 'Social Origins and Social Aspirations of Jacobean London Merchants', *EcHR*, series 2, 27 (1974), 42–5. On the number of local officers in Elizabethan London, see Foster, 'London Government', p. 277.

[17] Foster, 'Merchants and Bureaucrats', 158; Robert Brenner, 'The Civil War Politics of London's Merchant Community', *PP*, 58 (1973), 64.

of the lord mayors were related to the families of aldermen. Roughly one-third of the men elected to the Court of Aldermen in the reign of James I were the sons of the preceding generation of wealthy London merchants and retailers; and the most prosperous and powerful members of the Levant Company in the 1630s (men who were also prominent in city government) were related by birth or marriage to the men who had entered the company between 1581 and 1605.[18]

Harrison, Smith and Camden were apparently aware of the ties which made principal citizens a recognizable civic social group. But according to their definition, principal citizens were not just members of a civic group, but members of one of the four principal divisions of Elizabethan society. Unlike modern historians, they did not think of principal citizens as members of an 'occupational hierarchy' which was not clearly integrated with the rural status hierarchy; they did not think of principal citizens as 'urban gentry', men who had no sense they were different from country gentlemen; they did not even think the quick 'conversion' of merchants into gentlemen interfered with the cohesion of principal citizens.[19] A principal citizen, according to the Elizabethans who defined his status, was a member of the second highest of four social groups; there was no question about his status in society so long as he was a wealthy civic officer.

In fact, Smith and Harrison found it much simpler to define a principal citizen than to define a gentleman; for while a principal citizen could be distinguished from men in other social groups by his wealth and civic stature, a gentleman had to be defined less clearly. Harrison and Smith agreed that gentlemen were supposed to have some visible characteristics which made them worthy of their status, but they admitted that in practice, any student, lawyer, military officer or academic who could maintain the 'port, charge and countenance' of a gentleman without stooping to manual labour was considered a gentleman.[20] A civic leader could be defined by what he did; a gentleman could be defined only by what he was.

Outside social theory, the distinction between a merchant and a

[18] Lang, 'Social Origins', 31–4; Brenner, 'Civil War Politics', 61–2.
[19] In the order mentioned: Stone, 'Social Mobility', p. 18; Carl Bridenbaugh, *Vexed and Troubled Englishmen 1590–1642* (New York, 1968), p. 176 ('urban gentry'); Laslett, *World We Have Lost*, p. 49; Hexter, *Reappraisals*, p. 97.
[20] Holinshed, I, 273.

gentleman was not so clear as Harrison and Smith made it. At the highest ranks, principal citizens were in fact gentlemen; in London, the lord mayor was knighted after 1519, and the office of sheriff automatically bestowed gentility upon its holder.[21] In popular literature, even merchants of lower rank were called 'gentlemen' and addressed as 'master'. But a close examination of these examples shows that it was possible to *call* a merchant a gentleman without actually considering him to be one because of the ambiguity that surrounded the term 'gentleman'.

To begin with, while many authors agreed with Philip Stubbes that the title 'master' was proper to 'the Godly wise, for some special virtue inherent, either else in respect of their birth or calling, due to them', the exact relationship of the term to a man's status was unclear.[22] Harrison's implication that it referred only to gentlemen with coat-armour is certainly misleading; Shakespeare's father was called 'master' in town records as much as twenty-eight years before he received a coat of arms. The term was commonly used to give respect to men of stature in a given community, even if they were not gentle: Thomas Westcote noted that yeomen in Devonshire were called 'master' because they 'were gentlemen's equals by estate'.[23] But being a gentleman's equal by estate was not the same as being a gentleman. In one case that came before the Court of Chivalry concerning 'scandalous words provocative of a duel' (a case in which the plaintiff had to prove he was a gentleman in order to claim the court's protection) one plaintiff successfully defended his gentility by proving he was always called 'Master Rigby', never 'Goodman Rigby'. In another case, however, it was admitted that the defendant was called 'master' by his neighbours, but was *not* reputed to be a gentleman.[24] 'Master', then, while certainly implying respect due to men of wealth and status in a given community, was not a title used exclusively for gentry.

The term 'gentleman', as it was used in popular literature, was also one which could be used merely to imply respect without designating social status exactly. In Thomas Deloney's novel *The Gentle Craft, Part I*, a poor shoemaker named Simon Eyre tells his wife that

[21] Stow, *Survey*, II, 181.
[22] *Anatomy of the Abuses in England*, ed. F.J. Furnival, The New Shakespeare Society Publications, series 6 (London, 1877–9) Part I, 122.
[23] Holinshed, I, 273; Campbell, *English Yeoman*, p. 40.
[24] G.D. Squibb, *The High Court of Chivalry: A Study of Civil Law in England* (Oxford, 1959), pp. 174–5.

he has heard of an investment which, if he could make it, would make him 'a Gentleman forever'. He defines gentlemen in a standard way: they are men 'whose lands are answerable to their virtues, and whose rents can maintain the greatness of their mind'. But Eyre is called a gentleman long before he buys land and moves to the country. When he makes the investment, the lord mayor of London is so impressed with what seems to be the extent of his wealth that he invites Eyre and his wife to dinner. On this occasion, the shoemaker is called a gentleman for the first time in his life. Mistress Eyre's breathless recollection of the scene that night leaves no doubt of the importance she attaches to the appellation:

> Nay, and do you not remember, when the rich Citizen drank to you (which craved pardon because he knew not your name) what my Lord Mayor said? Sir (quoth he) his name is Master Eyre, did you mark that? and presently thereupon he added these words: this is the Gentleman that bought, and so forth. The Gentleman understood you, did you hear him speak that word?

In fact, however, Mistress Eyre is excited simply because the lord mayor and the 'rich citizen' have treated her husband as an equal. So far as Deloney tells the reader, Eyre's investment does not earn him land and rents; it earns him a place in the civic hierarchy. Eyre does become a gentleman some years after making the investment, but his gentility is bestowed upon him by the office of sheriff, later lord mayor. The promotions, far from taking him out of the ranks of principal citizens, are the honours due to the most rich and able of citizens. When he becomes lord mayor, Eyre does not look for a country estate – he gives a feast for all the apprentices in London and builds Leaden Hall at his own expense.[25]

Not all the merchants in Elizabethan popular literature rise to the gentility of civic office, but several are called gentlemen, just as Eyre is, because they are wealthy citizens. Occasionally, this appellation even conflicts with the thrust of the plot. In the play *The Fair Maid of the Exchange*, for example, the subplot concerns a feckless young gentleman who marries the daughter of a merchant to whom he is in debt. When she tells her father of the marriage, he is outraged; but the new son-in-law reminds him that 'the difference of our blood' makes the match a good one in spite of the poverty of

---

[25] Deloney, *Works*, pp. 112, 117, 124. When the servant who brings tidings of Eyre's appointment as sheriff finds Mistress Eyre, he tells her, 'Mistress, God give you joy, for you are now a Gentlewoman.'

the gentleman in question. Apparently it does, for the father for-gives them both. In a play which thus depends upon an acceptance of the distinction between a merchant and a gentleman, one would not expect merchants to be called gentlemen. But though the Fair Maid of the Exchange is a merchant's daughter, she is called a gentlewoman, her father is called a gentleman, and the three mer-chants who court her are also called gentlemen.[26]

A similar contradiction appears in the domestic tragedy, *A Warning for Fair Women*. The heroine, a merchant's wife, is per-suaded to reject her husband when a false fortune-teller informs her that when her husband dies she will marry a gentleman: ' 'Tis plainly figured here, and this is called, the Ladder of Promotion.' But while the thought of promotion into the gentry is enough to incite a weak woman to consent to the murder of her husband, the merchant she betrays is called a gentleman at the moment his murder is dis-covered. The old man who discovers his corpse cries, 'Ah weladay! see where another lies, a handsome, comely ancient gentleman: what an age live we in!'[27] The playwright, here as in *The Fair Maid*, is well aware of the importance of the difference between merchants and gentlemen, but he sees no incongruity in calling a merchant a gentleman.

The semantic ambiguity of the term 'gentleman', then, does not blur the distinction between merchants and gentlemen in Elizabethan literature. Principal citizens have 'next place to gentry', and so like the wealthiest yeomen in the country, they are called 'master', perhaps considered 'gentlemen's equals by estate'. But while Master Rigby in the country is reputed a gentleman among his neighbours because of his local prestige, in the city the most respected men have a different avenue of promotion: the principal citizenry. They may indeed rise to the gentility of high civic office, but their status is defined by their civic sphere of influence.

The civic prestige of a principal citizen may have entitled him to the respectful form of address due to a gentleman; but his occu-

---

[26] Scene of forgiveness, Heywood, II, 81. But the Fair Maid's servant tells another character, 'I serve a Gentleman, that Gentleman is father to this Gentlewoman, this Gentlewoman is a maid, this maid is fair' (Heywood, II, 48). In other places (II, 60, 67) the dialogue firmly establishes the two elder suitors as merchants; their younger brother, whose suit is successful, is unlikely to be any more gentle than they, but all three brothers are labelled 'gent' in the cast of characters.

[27] *A Warning for Fair Women*, Act I, lines 635–8, Act II, lines 585–6, in Simpson, *School of Shakespere*, Vol. II.

pation as a merchant was generally held to keep him from true gentility. In Elizabeth's reign (and long after) trade was considered ignoble; the author of *The Blazon of Gentry* even considered merchants to be further from gentle status than husbandmen because merchants were tarnished by trade and greed.[28] Snobbism aside, however, there were few Elizabethans who wished to sharpen the distinction between merchants and gentlemen by insisting that merchants should be prevented from investing in the gentry's most precious commodity – land. In 1559, for example, an article was included in the proposal for what later became the Statute of Artificers which limited the amount of land a merchant might buy; but when the Statute became law, the clause was omitted.[29] The pamphleteer George Whetstone made a similar proposal twenty-five years later in his *Mirror for Magistrates of Cities* (1584): to the end of furthering trade (and controlling vice), merchants should be required to put all their money into commerce and forbidden to purchase more land than 'a garden for recreation'. But the pamphlet was apparently no mirror of Elizabethan views on magistrates; it had only one edition.[30]

There was, however, considerable resistance to the idea that a man could be a gentleman while engaging in trade. The arguments on this point multiplied after James I's sale of knighthoods enabled any rich merchant to buy one, whether or not he was a gentleman by virtue of his civic office. If a merchant could be a knight, why could he not be a gentleman (at considerably less expense)? Some men actually proved they were gentle in the Court of Chivalry, though they were drapers, goldsmiths, or even soap-boilers.[31] One work written in 1629 agreed with these decisions, insisting that a man's trade did not erase his claim to gentility, if he were of gentle stock. But the idea that a man's trade could *make* him a gentleman even though he remained in business was shocking; when Baptist Hicks

---

[28] Sir John Ferne, *The Blazon of Gentry* (London, 1586), p. 72. This book was not a best-seller; in fact, it took two impressions to get rid of the copies of the one edition there was.

[29] R.H. Tawney and Eileen Power, *Tudor Economic Documents* (3 vols., 1924; rpt. London, 1951), I, 326.

[30] *A Mirror for Magistrates of Cities*, quoted in Wright, *Middle-Class Culture*, p. 21n.

[31] Squibb, *Court of Chivalry*, pp. 176–7. Some trades were considered more inimical to gentility than others. If a man occupied himself with 'base and mechanical arts' his gentility was impaired; but as Squibb points out, 'the line between "base and mechanical arts" and occupations consistent with the rank of gentleman must have been a difficult one to draw precisely'.

obtained a knighthood and continued to keep his shop he was flying in the face of society.[32] It was not until the very end of the seventeenth century that merchants moved into the most fashionable districts of London and tried to consider themselves gentlemen's equals; it was not until 1722 that a literary merchant could say with some dignity:

> give me leave to say that we merchants are a species of gentry that have grown into the world this last century and are as honourable and almost as useful as you landed folks that have always thought yourselves so much above us.[33]

Nor did the emergence of merchants as 'a species of gentry' occur without opposition; the social myth of the inimical values of the 'landed interest' and the 'moneyed interest' dominated many political decisions in the late seventeenth and early eighteenth centuries and resulted in the passage of the Property Qualifications Act of 1710.

Trade, then, was considered an impediment to gentility in the Elizabethan era and over a century after it. It was viewed as an occupation which, while it might be necessary to the commonwealth as a whole, lessened the dignity and lowered the social status of the men who participated in it. The implications of this familiar idea must be taken into account if one wishes to understand the kind of cohesion Elizabethan authors expected to find among principal citizens. They assumed that merchants were bound into a respectable social group by the simple fact that they were the most powerful inhabitants of cities and towns. Though a merchant's wealth made him a principal citizen, the way in which he obtained that wealth was only of negative importance to his status. Far from perceiving the economic activity of merchants as a force which would unite them in a recognition of their common interests, the authors considered it relevant to their place in the social hierarchy only because it separated them from gentlemen. This is a social consciousness

---

[32] Edmund Bolton, *The City's Advocate, In this Case a Question of Honour or Arms; Whether Apprenticeship Extinguisheth Gentry?* (London, 1629). The passion with which Bolton argues that apprenticeship does not extinguish gentility suggests that he was writing against considerable opposition. For Hicks's knighthood, see *DNB*, *sub* Baptist Hicks.

[33] Richard Steele, *The Conscious Lovers*, in *Six Eighteenth-Century Plays*, ed. John H. Wilson (Boston, 1963), p. 105. For a brief description of the movements of late seventeenth- and early eighteenth-century merchants into more-fashionable districts of London and the effect this movement had on the theatres, see John Loftis, *Comedy and Society from Congreve to Fielding* (Stanford, 1959), pp. 9–19.

untouched by the idea that class solidarity is closely related to economic interests and values.

The Elizabethan definition of social status in terms of social and political ties left the provincial businessman in a peculiar no-man's-land in the middle of the social hierarchy. Harrison and Smith did not include clothiers among principal citizens, for they lived in the country and were clearly *not* linked to the rulers of towns and cities. This negative perception was fundamentally accurate: a few clothiers apprenticed their sons to London merchants, but as a rule, clothier families intermarried with other clothier families in their counties, or (in some cases) with the local gentry, but not with the families of principal citizens. And since clothiers, whatever their wealth, did not have a specific sphere of influence in the political life of the county, there was nothing to distinguish them as a separate social unit. William Stumpe, the Wiltshire clothier whose genius for making money eventually brought him into the select ranks of county rulers, was an exceptional figure – and an Henrician one. By Elizabeth's reign, the Wiltshire gentry had become jealous of clothier families with large estates and seats in parliament and reasserted their innate superiority over men of trade. Consequently, after 1562 there were few clothiers in parliament, and the gentry did their best to keep clothiers in their places in other ways. In 1576, for example, the gentry inserted a chapter (c. 16) into the Statute 18 Elizabeth that limited clothier landownership in Wiltshire, Somerset and Gloucester to twenty acres. The statute was never enforced, but it was obviously made in an effort to clarify an ambiguous situation. Clothiers were not gentle; they were to remain men of second rank in the counties with holdings roughly the same as those of yeomen. Industrial wealth did not allow a man the political and social privileges of the gentry.[34]

This situation is clearly revealed in Deloney's novel *Jack of Newbury* (1597), a book written specifically to show that a wealthy clothier can be as honourable and just as a gentleman. The point needs to be made because Jack is *not* a gentleman, even in Deloney's eyes. He is as rich as Simon Eyre, he obtains a seat in parliament (at which time he is called 'master' for the first time), he is in fact a prince in his own domain – but for all this, he remains Jack of Newbury, a 'brave Yeoman' to the end of the book. When he tells

[34] G.D. Ramsay, *The Wiltshire Woollen Industry in the Sixteenth and Seventeenth Centuries* (2nd edn, London, 1965), Chapter III, especially pp. 46–69.

a knight who has seduced one of his maids 'I account the poorest wench in my house too good to be your whore, were you ten knights', he is not speaking gentleman-to-gentleman; he is informing a social superior that he will not be dishonoured even though he is not gentle.[35]

Jack deals with merchants, of course, and even helps a London merchant out of debt, but he has little in common with principal citizens. When Jack is married, it is not the children of London's principal citizens who accompany his bride to the altar, but the sons of Sir Thomas Parry and Sir Francis Hungerford, for the marriage is a county affair.[36] Even when economic crisis threatens the prosperity of all men of trade, the merchants and clothiers do not unite to defend their common interests. When war halts trade with the Netherlands, causing a severe depression in the clothing industry, Jack recognizes the hardships of poor workers who have been laid off and urges all clothiers to petition the king for a resumption of commerce. He insists on the need for unity in the matter, reminding the clothiers 'this sore of necessity can no way be cured but by concord', and concluding 'our trade will maintain us, if we will uphold it; and there is nothing base, but that which is basely used'. The brotherhood Jack encourages is rewarded: Henry VIII, remarking that clothiers are 'the chief Yeomen of our land', arranges a way for the merchants to 'freely traffic' with each other, and the clothiers go back to work.[37] But where were the merchants when the petition was presented? Deloney does not say, and the omission is interesting, for Holinshed's account of the affair specifically says that Henry renewed trade with the Netherlands at the advice of the Imperial ambassadors and the entreaties of England's 'merchants and clothiers'.[38] While Deloney is the only author in the Elizabethan era who portrays businessmen acting as a political and economic unit, he does not see that the economic interests uniting clothiers might extend *beyond* Jack's followers and unite businessmen in the city with businessmen in the country. Even for Deloney, a man's status is defined by the social circles in which he moves (or fails to move), and his status in these circles is much more important to his general status than is his economic interest.

It should not be surprising to students of Elizabethan history that

---

[35] Deloney, *Works*, p. 58 ('master'); p. 64 ('brave Yeoman'); p. 67 (knight and serving-maid).
[36] *Ibid.*, p. 22.   [37] *Ibid.*, pp. 43–4.   [38] Holinshed, III, 735.

a man's status in the social hierarchy should be determined to a large extent by his rank in his own city or county.[39] If, however, a man's social and political status is defined exclusively by his local stature, authors may praise men of his rank in terms which have nothing to do with his economic interest – especially if his occupation is generally considered to be demeaning. This is what happened as the portrait of the merchant changed in Elizabethan popular literature. The authors who praised merchants ignored their financial dealings entirely and celebrated the valuable political services of principal citizens. Thus, the changing cultural image of merchants did not initially force new values upon non-commercial society; it restated old values by applying the virtues of rulers to the men who ruled cities.

The literary merchant of the 1590s was, therefore, a product of a peculiar mixture of new social consciousness and traditional values; but as such, he reflected an aspect of merchants' careers that many merchants valued highly – civic rule, the 'chief glory' of the city elite.[40] And so, though the literary merchant was not an exemplum of diligence, thrift or business instinct (or perhaps, *because* he was not), he was a very popular figure. Merchants could be described and glorified in the language of the gentry in order to prove that the second-highest class in the realm had a tradition worth recording. That very praise, however, depended upon the assumption that merchants' values were exactly the same as aristocratic values. Was this a paradox in the sixteenth century? Were the authors aware of the peculiar hybrids they were creating? A few of them were, at least at some level, for when they described merchants in the language of the elite, their words lost standard meanings, their plots disintegrated, and they stopped in confusion. When they described the heroism of merchants, the popular authors – men who made their livings by manipulating words and ideas – found there was no language and no plot that permitted them to develop the ideas they were exploring in their works. Praise led to paradox, and finally, to silence.

[39] Neale, *The Elizabethan House of Commons* (1949; rpt. Harmondsworth, Middlesex, 1963), p. 20; Christianson, 'The Causes of the English Revolution: a Reappraisal', *JBS*, 15, 2 (1976), 58–9.
[40] Foster, 'Merchants and Bureaucrats', p. 150.

5. The merchant as usurer: a stock image in decline

If one were to take seriously the portraits of mercantile activity which appeared in Elizabethan sermons and moral pamphlets, one would be forced to believe that the merchant's primary concern was lending money at an extortionate rate of interest. The moralists did not, of course, single out the financier as the only member of society who had chosen Mammon over God; they pointed out that the usurer kept evil company with the rack-renting landlord, the corrupt magistrate, the greedy lawyer, and the pluralist clergyman.[1] One may doubt that Elizabethan readers seriously thought that all merchants were usurers, any more than they thought all gentlemen were greedy landlords. But in literary terms, the gentleman had an advantage over the merchant because he had alternate images as knight, courtier and governor, whereas the merchant's image, until quite late in Elizabeth's reign, was determined almost exclusively by the moralists. A few chroniclers might insert the good deeds of merchants in their works, but until these good deeds started to be portrayed on the stage, the merchant was most familiar to Elizabethans as a man who beggared the poor in order to enrich himself, a godless man who went to church only to arrest debtors, and a miser who thought only of his money on his deathbed.[2]

In the middle of Elizabeth's reign, however, a statute was passed which complicated the moral context in which the stock merchant-usurer appeared. This was the statute of 1571 which, while insisting that usury was 'forbidden by the Law of God' as 'sin and detestable'

---

[1] See, for example, Stubbes, *Anatomy of Abuses*, I, 116–17 on covetousness; Bullein, *Dialogue*, pp. 21–5 for covetous lawyers. For a 'specialized' treatment of greedy gentlemen, see Robert Cleaver, *A Godly Form of Household Government* (London, 1598), pp. 146–8, 285–6.

[2] The usurer who goes to church only to arrest debtors appears in Robert Wapull, *The Tide Tarrieth No Man*, lines 1078–90 (in *English Morality Plays*), and in Bullein, *Dialogue*, p. 12. In both these works, the usurer cannot think of God when he dies (*Tide Tarrieth*, lines 1653–60; Bullein, *Dialogue*, p. 11).

and permitting debtors to take creditors to court for taking interest, legalized interest rates of 10% or less.[3] The language of the statute reflected the strength of the moral condemnation of usury; that condemnation had had such force in the past that (except for the brief period between 1545 and 1552) interest-taking had been illegal in England for centuries. But the permission to take interest also reflected the necessity of making credit cheaply available. Before interest was legalized, it had been illegally available at the rates of 12–15%.[4] This had not accommodated the business community nor the gentry; nor had it accommodated the crown, which after the revolt of the Netherlands had had to turn to London instead of Antwerp for loans.[5] Largely because the crown saw the necessity of making credit available at a lower cost, parliament reluctantly legalized the sins of the usurer; if the moralists were horrified, debtors rejoiced to get money on such easy terms, and creditors, while at first trying to circumvent the statute, gradually settled upon taking the maximum rate.[6]

The legalization of interest-taking began an era in which credit transactions increased dramatically. The crown was only the most prestigious of the financiers' customers; credit also became necessary to gentlemen whose incomes lay in their land. That income, which was determined largely by rents which were paid only every six months and fixed for long periods of time by leases, was prone to dramatic fluctuations. Even if a gentleman's tenants paid punctually, he was master of the whole of his estate only in the interval between the death of his mother and the marriage of his daughters. If a gentleman's daughter married in a year when no leases fell due and his mother was mistress of one-third of his estate, he was likely to turn to a financier; he could then either take advantage of the complex legal network of bills, bonds, statutes and mortgages which enabled him to use his land as security for a loan, or he could buy goods on credit and pray for happier days to come. All the means of obtaining credit were cumbersome because the standard period for a loan was six months and so contracts had to be renewed frequently. Credit was also expensive: financiers generally demanded security of double the amount of the loan as well as interest. The

---

[3] *Tudor Economic Documents*, II, 162. [4] Stone, *Crisis*, p. 530.
[5] Robert Ashton, 'Usury and High Finance in the Age of Shakespeare and Jonson', *Renaissance and Modern Studies*, 4 (1960), 24.
[6] Stone, *Crisis*, p. 530.

elite grumbled, the moralists condemned – but gentlemen and aristocrats continued to borrow money. London, fast becoming the social centre of the nation, came to be a centre for money-lending; as more and more gentlemen borrowed, more and more merchants found it profitable to capitalize upon their needs. As a result, between 1580 and 1620, almost all of the principal citizens of London began to lend money at interest.[7]

Thus, the merchant-financier became a prominent figure in fact as well as in image. But he was no calculating, greedy man who broke the law of God and man to make money; he was one of the most respected men in the city who lent at a legal rate of interest to the most respected men in the country. The moralists, however, did not let changing times alter their image of the usurer. Twelve years after interest-taking had been legalized, Philip Stubbes compared a usurer to a murderer, a thief, a Jew and a Judas, only to conclude that the usurer was more sinful than any of the others. In the same year, Gervase Babington argued that usury was one form of theft and thus prohibited by the commandment 'thou shalt not steal'. A decade later, Henry Smith could still portray usury as 'a kind of cruelty, a kind of extortion, and a kind of persecution' which showed a man to be incapable of love. He also argued, in a rare personal attack on the business habits of London's principal citizens, that the sons of London aldermen who lent at interest were turning out badly because of the unjust lending practices of their fathers.[8] And all the prominent preachers of the last decade of Elizabeth's reign agreed that the usurer who wished to atone for his sins should give a fraction of his estate to the poor, thus charitably restoring what he had uncharitably taken.[9]

In formulating their arguments against usury, the preachers and satirists drew from a long medieval tradition, but they were influenced primarily by John Calvin, who had said that usury was a sin against the Christian's duty to love his neighbour. Calvin, however, had also argued that usury could be distinguished from interest-taking because it did not adhere to the Golden Rule. Lending at extortionate rates, lending at interest to poor men obviously dis-

[7] *Ibid.*, pp. 505–8 (fluctuations of gentry income), pp. 515–28 (methods and costs of borrowing), pp. 541–3 (attitudes towards debt), p. 533 (principal citizens).

[8] Stubbes, *Anatomy of Abuses*, I, 125–7; Babington, *A Very Fruitful Exposition of the Commandments by Way of Questions and Answers for Greater Plainness* (London, 1583), p. 354; Smith, *Sermons*, pp. 95, 108.

[9] Smith, *Sermons*, p. 116; Perkins, *Works*, II, 197–8; Greenham, *Works*, p. 72.

obeyed the Rule and therefore was sinful; but lending at moderate rates to wealthy men hurt nobody and was therefore permissible.[10] Only one Elizabethan preacher followed Calvin's example on this issue. William Perkins, the Puritan most given to making theological distinctions, explicitly approved of the statute of 1571 because it limited the interest charged by covetous men; he also argued that it was licit for rich men to charge interest between themselves, as they would charge hire for a horse.[11]

Most of the Elizabethan moralists, however, did not distinguish interest from usury and condemned all interest-taking. As a result, when they touched upon the fact that interest-taking was legal and credit was necessary, they reached a philosophical impasse. Philip Stubbes, for example, having argued that the legalization of interest did not discharge the sin of usury in the eyes of God, lamely admitted that the legalization of this particular sin limited usurers 'within certain meers and banks (to bridle the insatiable desires of covetous men)'.[12] But this admission weakened his argument that a usurer was a worse sinner than a murderer or a traitor – if interest-taking had really been a sin on the order of murder, legalizing it would hardly have been salutary.

Henry Smith ran into similar trouble at the end of a pair of eloquent sermons which proved that usury was a sin against God and man. As he began to sum up his arguments, Smith found himself concluding uneasily that *borrowing* from a usurer was probably not prohibited by the Bible, for 'he which lendeth for usury, lendeth for covetousness, but he which borroweth upon usury, borroweth for necessity'. There were, he added with an atypical lack of conviction, many reasons why borrowing at interest was licit 'which I cannot refute, and therefore I will not contract them: yet I mean not to decide the question, because I will not be mistaken'.[13] He concluded that he could not discourage a man who asked him if he might borrow from a usurer to save his life, credit or living; he would leave it to the man's conscience. Smith then shifted to more-comfortable moral territory and condemned men who borrowed not for necessity but to make themselves rich. But the damage was done. To sanc-

---

[10] John T. Noonan, Jr, *The Scholastic Analysis of Usury* (Cambridge, Mass., 1957), pp. 365–7. Noonan discusses the medieval attitude towards usury in Chapters I–IX.
[11] Perkins, *Works*, II, 116 (laws on usury); II, 19, III, 94–5 (lending between rich men). Perkins condemned usury, as distinct from interest, and insisted that free lending to the poor was a form of alms required of all rich men (II, 19; III, 94–5).
[12] *Anatomy of Abuses*, I, 123.   [13] Smith, *Sermons*, pp. 111–12.

tion borrowing and not lending at interest was clearly illogical; and to imply that one could borrow money without being covetous was to raise the possibility that one could lend money without being covetous, too. Furthermore, to leave the matter up to the individual conscience because the preacher could not make up his mind about the matter was to admit that, in the face of financial necessity, that preacher had lost his moral nerve.

And so, in the 1590s, the condemnation of usury continued to be attractive to audiences (judging from the popularity of Smith's sermons against it), but it had lost its way. It is possible that the stock portraits of the usurer as a godless, grasping man appealed to men who were in debt; one might note in passing that banks and 'loan-sharks' still fail to inspire the sympathy of the holders of mortgages and short-term loans. But the arguments which equated all profit with greed and then shamefacedly admitted that some forms of profit were legal and perhaps necessary were so weak that one suspects their appeal was primarily rhetorical. The usurer in these tracts had little in common with the respectable London citizens who lent money to gentlemen at the legal rate; as a result, the literary stereotype of the merchant-as-usurer in sermons and satires lost its credibility.

The decline of the stock usurer of the complaints is particularly visible in the drama of the latter half of Elizabeth's reign. The stage merchant, traditionally, was a villainous usurer who lent money to a prodigal gentleman; the paradigm was drawn from medieval satires and from everyday experience in every century since the twelfth.[14] Literary critics and historians have customarily seen a conflict between the 'moneyed interest' and the 'landed interest' in Elizabethan usurer plays; they have suggested that the dramatists were 'holding a mirror to reality' and reflecting the general disapproval of merchants' lending to gentlemen.[15] Some doubt should be cast on this judgment. The increase in borrowing by the elite may well have made the usurer–prodigal paradigm attractive to playwrights who wished to insert a note of contemporaneity into their plays, but there is little in the plays which suggests that the increase

[14] Hexter, *Reappraisals*, p. 79. For a discussion of the paradigm in medieval satires and complaints, see G.R. Owst, *Literature and Pulpit*, pp. 352–3.

[15] See, for example, Ashton, 'Usury and High Finance', p. 30; and Thomas Wilson, *A Discourse upon Usury*, ed. R.H. Tawney (1925; rpt., London, 1962), Introduction, pp. 33–4.

of money-lending was matched by increasing dramatic disapproval of credit transactions before Elizabeth's death. In fact, there is no evidence that the later usurer plays of the period stemmed from moral concern with either interest-taking or aristocratic debt.

The early Elizabethan plays in which the usurer–prodigal paradigm appeared took the tone of the sermons and satires. In George Wapulls' morality play *The Tide Tarrieth No Man* (1576), for example, a courtier named Willing-to-Win-Worship borrows money from the merchant Greediness. Greediness is the personification of the uncharitable man condemned by the moralists; he is completely caught up in the pursuit of gain and thinks only of his money, even when he is dying. He makes short work of the courtier, charging him £40 for a loan of £30. Willing-to-Win-Worship, ruined, goes back to the country, stating Wapull's views about usury:

> But what villainy is there in such,
> Who, knowing a man of their help to have need,
> Will encroach upon him so unreasonably much,
> Their own greedy desires to feed?

> The vicious man only seeketh his own gain.
> Yea, twice vicious may they be named
> Who do avarice so much embrace.[16]

Wapull's condemnation of Greediness's usury is whole-hearted, and the young gentleman is treated with sympathy.

A similar presentation of the usurer's greed appeared some fourteen years later in Lodge and Greene's *A Looking Glass for London and England* (c. 1590), a late morality play which condemned the sins of Londoners. One of the sinners is the Usurer, who lends money to Thrasybulus, a young man who has given his lands as security. When the hour of payment approaches, Thrasybulus produces the money, calling the Usurer a 'covetous caterpillar' and telling him that he has 'made extreme shift' to get the money rather than fall into the hands of 'such a ravening panther'. And the Usurer earns the abuse thus heaped upon him. As Thrasybulus counts out the money, a clock strikes four; noting that the bond specifies payment *between* three and four, the Usurer demands the security. Thrasybulus takes him to court, but the Usurer bribes the judge and

---

[16] *The Tide Tarrieth No Man*, lines 886–93, 1010–18.

wins his case. Thrasybulus, utterly ruined, laments the 'miserable time, wherein gold is above God', and is forced to pawn stolen goods to the Usurer in order to pay off the debt.[17]

A Looking Glass revived old morality-play figures as it adopted the form of the moralities; but by 1590, the stereotype of the usurer was already beginning to change. During the last fourteen years of Elizabeth's reign there were five other plays written in which the usurer–prodigal motif appeared, but the condemnation of usury in these plays became decreasingly important to their plots and themes. Only one of the plays, *The Merchant of Venice* (c. 1596), treated usury as a practice which required moral consideration; two of the others ignored the usurer's business practices entirely, and the last two used the usurer–prodigal confrontation as the basis for comedy. The unfortunate debtor of the moralities became a scapegrace hero in love with the usurer's daughter; the usurer ceased to be important as a money-lender and appeared in the role of an unjust father. Moral concern with the sin of usury shifted to romantic concern with the plight of the lovers and a comic resolution of their problems. Apparently, in the atmosphere of increasing money-lending, the situation of a young man in debt to a greedy usurer could no longer arouse interest unless the play were primarily concerned with something else.

In the two usurer plays written at about the same time as *A Looking Glass*, the emphasis remained on the sins of the usurer, but these sins had little to do with lending at interest. Usury, for example, was only the mildest of the sins of Barabas in Marlowe's *Jew of Malta* (c. 1589); he was a villain because he arranged a duel in which his daughter's lover was killed, he poisoned the entire population of a nunnery, and murdered two priests. Similarly, though on a less heroic scale of villainy, the usurer Servio in *A Knack to Know an Honest Man* (1594) was not condemned for his usury *per se*; his downfall was brought about by his treachery and his imprisonment of two innocent young men. Usury in these plays was not equated with villainy. Although the playwrights may have tacitly assumed that a usurer was capable of any crime, the villainy the audience *saw* had nothing to do with lending at interest.

As the usurer play developed in the late 1590s, the usurer's money-lending received minimal attention, but his other sins

[17]Greene, *Works*, XIV, 22 ('covetous caterpillar'), pp. 35–41.

became increasingly trivial. Pisaro, the usurer in William Haughton's farce *Englishman for My Money, or A Woman Will Have Her Will* (1598) is not a murderer or a traitor but merely a tyrannical father. He has three impudent daughters who want to marry three English gentlemen, all of whom are in debt to him. Pisaro wants the girls to marry three grotesque but solvent foreign merchants, but the girls plan to elope with their English lovers. Pisaro, overhearing their plans, arranges to have them met by the merchants instead. In the dark night, all the plans miscarry, but the gentlemen, with true English ingenuity, manage either to marry or to deflower their loves before daybreak, and Pisaro is forced to accept the *fait accompli*.

While the emphasis of the play is obviously on courtship, not usury, Pisaro's money-lending does receive some attention. The three gentlemen, however, are perfectly capable of defending themselves against Pisaro's greed. When he chides them for their prodigality and threatens to imprison them for debt, they do not lament the time wherein gold is above God. Instead, they threaten him with prison in return:

> Have you our land in mortgage for your money?
> Nay, since 'tis so, we owe you not a penny.
> Fret not, fume not, never bend the brow:
> You take ten in the hundred more than law.
> We can complain – extortion – simony –
> Newgate hath room, there's law enough in England.

Pisaro's daughters consider his greed a vice to be exploited, not lamented. They have offered to marry the gentlemen so they can get their cash without having to go through the painful process of repaying their loans. As one of them tells her love, 'i' God's name, spend at large: / What, man, our marriage-day will all discharge.' And her sister adds:

> Go to th' Exchange, crave gold as you intend,
> Pisaro scrapes for us; for us you spend . . .

> We here, you there; ask gold, and gold you shall:
> We'll pay the interest and the principal.[18]

---

[18] Dodsley, X, 540, 485.

Pisaro's greed is the object of ridicule, and it is he, not the gentle-men, who is finally exploited. In the terms of this play, usury is merely used to make the plot move and supply the characters with a few jokes. Once the lovers have married the girls, the usury theme disappears entirely. One might expect Pisaro to atone for his greed by giving the lands back to the gentlemen as a wedding-gift – one critic of the play, in fact, says he does.[19] But Pisaro does not mention the lands in his final speech of reconciliation; he merely accepts his daughters' independence, wishes the couples happiness and promises to give them a wedding feast.

In *Englishmen for My Money*, introducing a man as a usurer indi-cates that he is the play's villain, even though his villainy is far from convincing. In the last Elizabethan play in which the usurer–prodigal paradigm appears, the usurer is not a villain but a kindly old man. Berry, the 'usurer' in *The Fair Maid of the Exchange* (c. 1602), has lent money to Barnard, a young man notably short of both funds and brains. Barnard is unable to pay Berry back; faced with the possibility of debtor's prison, he goes to a party instead of thinking of a way to repay the loan. The 'brain' of the play, the Cripple of Fenchurch, is the man who thinks of Barnard's solution – he must marry Berry's daughter Moll so the debt will be forgiven. Fortunately, Moll is fickle enough to be talked into the arrangement and all ends happily. But in the midst of the intrigue, the Cripple chastises Berry for usury with some violence:

> thou wretch, thou miser, thou vile slave
> And drudge to money, bondman to thy wealth,
> Apprentice to a penny, thou that hoards up
> The fry of silver pence and half-pennies,
> With show of charity to give the poor,
> But put'st them to increase . . .
>
> The forfeit of his bond, O I could spit
> My heart into his face; thou blood-hound that dost hunt
> The dear, dear life of noble gentry.[20]

This sounds like the invective of the morality plays, but in context, it is merely a rhetorical flourish. The Cripple is not angry at Berry for lending money; he is annoyed because Berry has associated him

---

[19] A.B. Stonex, 'The Usurer in Elizabethan Drama', *PMLA*, 31 (1919), 200.
[20] Heywood, II, 29.

with Barnard and the other feckless hero of the subplot. Irritated at being accused of being as stupid as the gentleman he seems to defend, the Cripple proves his mettle by showing the eloquence he has at his fingertips. In *The Fair Maid*, the condemnation of usury has become a stock speech; the paradigm of the usurer and the prodigal has ceased to have a moral message and is simply a gimmick used to organize a subplot.

As one moves from *The Tide Tarrieth No Man* to *The Fair Maid of the Exchange*, one can see that what was once a subject for moralization has become a subject for comedy. The playwrights borrow motifs from each other, but in so doing they shift the emphasis further and further away from the sin of lending at interest. There is one play of this period, however, that does give serious consideration to the practice of usury. Shakespeare's *The Merchant of Venice*, following the morality plays, *The Jew of Malta* and *A Knack to Know an Honest Man*, draws the precedents set by the earlier plays together, with ambiguous results. While retaining the morality framework by implicitly comparing Antonio and Shylock as figures of charity and greed, Shakespeare complicates the moral issue by showing the limitations of Antonio's charity. Shylock hates Antonio because

> in low simplicity
> He lends out money gratis and brings down
> The rate of usance here with us in Venice.

But Antonio's charity does not extend to Shylock; he humiliates Shylock in public in a manner which makes one wonder if such a man can indeed be charitable. When he then comes to Shylock in private to borrow money, offering to pay the very interest he has so often railed at the Jew for taking, Shylock is quick to point out his hypocrisy:

> You call me misbeliever, cut-throat dog,
> And spet upon my Jewish gaberdine,
> And all for use of that which is mine own.
> Well then, it now appears you need my help.
> Go to, then, you come to me, and you say
> 'Shylock, we would have moneys', you say so –
> You, that did void your rheum upon my beard
> And foot me as you spurn a stranger cur
> Over your threshold; moneys is your suit.

Antonio's reply confirms Shylock's point, for he does not try to defend himself, but simply repeats that he needs money:

> I am as like to call thee so again,
> To spet on thee again, to spurn thee too.
> If thou wilt lend this money, lend it not
> As to thy friends, for when did friendship take
> A breed for barren metal of his friend?[21]

Antonio may lend money freely, but he is not necessarily charitable to the men with whom he does business. For his love of Bassanio, Antonio will 'break a custom', financing the quest of a 'lady richly left' with the ducats of a man he hates. This is the dark side of Venetian society; money is absolutely necessary to the way men live (to life itself, as Antonio and Shylock both say later), and since this is so, a man must take money where he can get it by whatever means are available.[22] Both the law of Shylock and the law of Venice recognize this kind of necessity; Shylock 'cites scriptures for his purpose' in his defence of usury, and Antonio, to seal his bond with Shylock, goes to a notary. Shylock's daughter Jessica exhibits the immorality to which the necessity of money can lead when she finances her marriage to a prodigal by stealing from her father, thus breaking both the law of Shylock and the law of Venice. The dark side of the commercial world puts the play's 'sympathetic' characters in an ambiguous moral position. They profit richly from the very thing they despise in Shylock – heartless and (in Jessica's case) immoral acquisition of money.[23]

But the harsh treatment Shylock receives makes him a sympathetic figure only so long as the play deals with money. In the trial scene, Shakespeare moves to higher considerations. Antonio prepares to give up his life for his friend in what approaches an imitation of Christ-like charity; Shylock, on the other hand, denies even his own law and refuses to admit there is any power but

---

[21] *The Merchant of Venice*, I, iii, lines 43–7, 111–19, 130–4, in *The Riverside Shakespeare*, ed. G. Blakemore Evans (Boston, 1974). All references to Shakespeare's plays are to this edition.

[22] When Shylock's goods are confiscated, he says, 'you take my life / When you do take the means whereby I live' (IV, i, lines 376–7). When Portia tells Antonio some of his ships are safe, he says, 'Sweet lady, you have given me life and living' (V, i, line 286). And the failure of these ships to come in earlier almost cost Antonio his life.

[23] Siguard Burckhardt discusses the importance of money in the world of Venice in *Shakespearean Meanings* (Princeton, 1968), pp. 212–14.

Venetian law. Sharpening his knife, he asks, 'What judgment shall I dread, doing no wrong?'[24] It is not money that is at stake now (Shylock refuses Bassanio's offer of triple payment), but life itself. Shylock loses the sympathy of the audience when he invokes legal sanction for murder.

Shylock does not murder Antonio, for Portia foils him on a legal point; he may take only a pound of flesh, no blood. But the judgment does more than save Antonio; it shows that Venetian law, Judaic law and Christian charity are woven together in the complex fabric of Venetian society and that any attempt to deny this fact leads to unkind and immoral actions. Portia's adherence to Venetian law makes Shylock obey Judaic law by not committing murder; the Duke's pardon makes Shylock see the necessity of charity. Antonio, for the first time in the play, does not rail at Shylock; he insists only that Shylock be charitable to Jessica and become a Christian. Antonio's charity is not hypocritical, as Shylock said it was. But Shylock's usury is not the only heartless and uncharitable way of acquiring money. Portia's emphasis on the inter-dependence of law and charity proves that the negative judgments of Shylock and Antonio are far too simple to be made in commercial society. The old stereotypes of usurer and prodigal must be related to the complexities which the necessity of money thrusts upon society.

The Merchant of Venice does not judge harshly, and in this it is like the other usurer–prodigal plays of the 1590s. While it does give serious consideration to the social sin of usury, it is also a romantic comedy. The prodigals, Bassanio, Lorenzo, and even Antonio (according to Shylock), profit richly by the downfall of the usurer: Bassanio marries a wealthy woman, Lorenzo and Jessica inherit Shylock's money, and Antonio does not have to repay his loan.[25] The usurer, who seemed to be such a threatening figure, is in fact outwitted by an intelligent woman. In spite of the dark side of *The Merchant of Venice*, the usurer–prodigal motif is turned to purposes other than moralization.

All the usurer–prodigal plays of the 1590s, then, suggest that the morality plays' stereotypes of greedy usurer and needy prodigal are no longer morally relevant figures. They are familiar figures, to be sure, but their familiarity invites comedy, not condemnation. This

---

[24] *Merchant of Venice*, IV, i, line 89.   [25] *Ibid.*, III, i, line 47.

suggests that the moral complexities which Shakespeare portrayed in *The Merchant of Venice* also thrust themselves upon the lesser playwrights of the 1590s. In an atmosphere in which interest-taking was legal, borrowing was necessary, and even the preachers' condemnations of usury were beginning to ring a little false, the greedy, heartless usurer was a stock figure left over from an earlier age.

Students of Jacobean drama, however, will argue that within a year of Elizabeth's death, the morality-play usurer was revived on the stage, and that he was again given a prodigal gentleman to exploit. There were indeed several usurer–prodigal plays performed in the first decade of James' reign, and the theme of all of them is summed up by Quomodo, the usurer in Thomas Middleton's *Michaelmas Term* (c. 1605):

> There are means and way enow to hook in gentry,
> Besides our deadly enmity, which thus stands,
> They're busy 'bout our wives, we 'bout their lands.[26]

Though these plays were by no means uniformly ill tempered, they gave new teeth to the old condemnations of merchants. The new vogue of these plays has been said to stem from the gentry's hatred of capitalism and the men who practised it. Tawney, for example, has argued that they reflect a 'dislike of a debtor class for its creditors', and L.C. Knights has suggested they reflect a dislike of merchants, 'who stood outside the current traditions' of the social hierarchy.[27] While these interpretations have some validity, it seems curious that hatred of capitalism should spring up overnight in drama and odd that serious dislike of lending money should reappear within months of the first production of *The Fair Maid of the Exchange*. And one may ask further why financiers should suddenly be the victims of 'bad press' at the very time interest rates were going down and borrowing by the aristocracy was beginning to diminish.[28]

The problem can be solved by observing what Middleton and his contemporaries considered to be the principal sin of the usurers in their plays. Surprisingly enough, the sin they objected to was not

[26] *Michaelmas Term*, I, ii, lines 110–12, in *The Works of Thomas Middleton*, ed. A.H. Bullen (8 vols.; London, 1885), I.

[27] Wilson, *Discourse*, p. 42; Knights, *Drama and Society in the Age of Jonson* (Harmondsworth, Middlesex, 1962), p. 148.

[28] Stone, *Crisis*, pp. 530–1, 542–3.

greed, but social ambition. Quomodo wants land, not money; he waxes eloquent over the (anticipated) pleasure of riding to his country estate, dressed in elegant clothes. He has also taken care to bring up his son as a gentleman; that son has gone to a university and learned prodigality.[29] Quomodo's counterpart Hoard in Middleton's *Trick to Catch the Old One* (1606) has similar desires to become a gentleman. So does Sir Giles Overreach in Massinger's *New Way to Pay Old Debts*. The Jacobean usurer, then, has acquired a new vice; he has lost his morality-play role as a figure of greed only to gain a new stereotype of the social climber.[30]

The new emphasis of the Jacobean usurer plays appeared within a year of the time in which James began the 'inflation of honours' by making 1161 knights in the first nine months of his reign. The overly generous creation of knighthoods was far more dignified than the wholesale commerce in higher titles which began with Buckingham's period of influence. But it was shocking enough to a generation accustomed to Elizabeth's parsimony with honour – and it was the first dignity that the crown allowed to be sold. Gentility had long been a reward for and a sign of ancient riches; now it was a reward for the possession of ready cash. And a knighthood could be purchased not just from the king, but from such financiers as Lionel Cranfield, who bought the making of six knights for £375 in 1606.[31]

In this atmosphere, the usurer could be reshaped into a socially relevant figure – a man who wished to purchase status with his money. In some plays he was given a social-climbing wife who indulged her social ambitions by becoming a gentleman's mistress. And this stereotype of the merchant, unlike the older one, did not decline. The dramatic portrait of the citizen as usurer, parvenu or cuckold retained its popularity until the very end of the seventeenth century.[32]

In Elizabeth's reign, however, the inflation of honours was yet to

[29] *Michaelmas Term*, II, iii, lines 91–100; III, iv, lines 13–19 (country estate), and IV, iv, lines 20–52; V, i, lines 1–19 (prodigal son).
[30] The exception here is Ben Jonson, whose plays condemn social climbing with less fervour than they condemn greed. But Jonson does not limit himself to condemning the greed of the 'capitalist class'. Volpone is not just a usurer; the other characters in the play (only one of whom is a merchant) are fully as much in love with money as he. Penyboy Senior's love of Pecunia is condemned, but so is Sir Epicure Mammon's worship of money and the greed of the characters in *The Devil is an Ass*.
[31] Stone, *Crisis*, p. 74 (knighthoods); p. 81 (selling of titles); pp. 76–7 (Cranfield).
[32] For a discussion of the theme of social ambition in merchants as portrayed by seventeenth-century dramatists, see Loftis, *Comedy and Society*, Chapter III.

come. The practice of lending at interest had received general acceptance by the 1590s, though it was still attacked on theoretical grounds by the moralists. And the portrait of the merchant as a figure of greed had ceased to be believable. As the merchant shed his old literary caricature, he was given a new one to try – the image of the valiant principal citizen. This image eventually failed, for it was never even suggested that the spotless character of a principal citizen should be tarnished by a business deal. The same social forces that permitted the revival of the usurer contributed to the demise of the principal citizen, for the satirists who deplored social climbing were quick to prove that the pretensions the new literary merchants had encouraged could easily lead to social ambition in men unworthy of gentility. But at the time the literary merchant-hero first appeared as an alternative to the greedy usurer, he was very popular, and his weaknesses, if they were noticed at all, were ignored.

6. *The merchant as knight, courtier and prince*

It was no accident that the valiant principal citizen appeared in Elizabethan literature at the same time as the stereotype of the usurer was in decline; the authors who celebrated the virtues of merchants created the new image in a conscious effort to replace the old. Turning to the past for source material, Deloney, Heywood, Dekker and a handful of lesser writers brought the exploits of famous and semi-legendary men of trade to the attention of the Elizabethan audience; together, their works formed a popular history of merchants which showed that businessmen had a long tradition of service to the commonwealth and, more particularly, to the crown.

In portraying the close ties of merchants and their sovereigns, these authors depicted a continuing political and economic reality. Elizabeth was increasingly dependent on the loans of London merchants as her reign progressed, and the court, like the country, profited from England's trade. London's principal citizens also gave Elizabeth military assistance; they raised nearly one-tenth of all the troops levied during her reign. In return for this kind of support, Elizabeth's privy council honoured the autonomy of London's government and helped the City Fathers act effectively in times of need, obtaining such things as extra food for the city in times of scarcity.[1] These are the kinds of ties one might expect to see reflected in the new works on merchants, those of political and economic understanding.

In fact, however, none of the Elizabethan authors portrayed mercantile service in the terms which political reality would lead one to anticipate. While their praise of merchants reflected an appreciation of principal citizens' service to the crown, they chose to present merchants and monarchs together in situations in which

[1] Foster, 'London Government', pp. 12–13, 18–19.

trade was irrelevant. They showed how the wealth of merchants served the crown by describing sumptuous banquets which merchants gave for kings, not by suggesting that merchants were generous with their loans. And when they wanted to celebrate the political services of merchants, the authors described the few isolated incidents in which merchants had personally defended the king's person or the king's peace with their swords. The Elizabethan merchant, in his new guise, did not reflect a new awareness of the importance of business to the commonwealth; he reflected a mentality which saw service to the realm in traditional, chivalric, quasi-feudal terms.

The man primarily responsible for fostering the noble tradition of the principal citizen was John Stow; in his chronicles the pale figures from earlier London histories became the heroes of the 1590s. Stow apparently came upon his vocation as the champion of principal citizens gradually: there is no evidence in the 1565 version of his *Summary of English Chronicles* that he intended to portray eminent Londoners. As Stow became increasingly absorbed in his research, however, he discovered a great deal of material which recorded the deeds and charities of London's principal citizens. By the time the *Summary* had expanded into the *Chronicles of England* (1580), Stow had collected numerous anecdotes which praised city leaders; and in his *Survey of London* (1598) he even compiled what amounts to an index to great merchants in his chronicles, entitling it 'Honour of Citizens and Worthiness of Men'.[2] It is to Stow's

---

[2] Stow, *Survey*, I, 104. Many of the entries are clearly designed to send the reader to Stow's chronicles. For example, the passage on Sir Thomas White merely mentions that he founded St John's College, Oxford, and adds that he was generous to the poor, 'as in my Summary' (I, 113). The story of Henry Picard's feast breaks off in the middle with an '&c.'(I, 106), and the stories of Philpot and Walworth are mostly much shorter than their equivalents in the chronicles. The reader who turns to the 1565 edition of Stow's *Summary of English Chronicles* for these references will find little: Picard's feast and Philpot's piracy expedition are not mentioned, and the Walworth story is brief (fo. 127). Sir Thomas White's charities appear, but in no detail (fo. 225). In the 1570 *Summary of the Chronicles of England*, the story of Philpot's expedition appears briefly, without Philpot's oration (fo. 230), the Walworth story appears as it did in 1565 (fo. 234), and the description of White's charities appears in a detail greatly out of proportion to the rest of the episodes in the *Summary* (fos. 373–4). In 1580, Stow published the ever-expanding *Summary* as *The Chronicles of England*; here the stories of Philpot and Picard appeared with the rhetoric discussed in the text, the Walworth story appeared with the praise of Walworth's 'incomparable boldness' (p. 483), and White's charities were again described in detail (pp. 1075–6). By 1580, Stow had discovered and celebrated the most famous merchants of London – ten years before the heroic merchant began to appear in other literature.

chronicles, then, that one must turn to see how the vogue of merchant heroes began.

The merchants in Stow's chronicles are all of a type – loyal to their king and country, true to themselves, and capable of acting worthily in any sort of situation. One of the earliest merchants whom Stow praises in detail is Henry Picard, a vintner who gave a banquet for Edward III, King John of France, King David of Scotland and the King of Cyprus in 1357. Holinshed recorded the feast without comment, but Stow added to the Londoner's glory by telling a tale which proved Picard's generosity. After the banquet, he says, the King of Cyprus began to gamble with Picard. At the beginning of the game, Picard lost 50 marks, but 'being very skillful at that art', he soon recouped his losses and won 50 marks besides. Noticing that the King was beginning to chafe at his misfortune, Picard said graciously, 'My Lord and King be not aggrieved, I covet not your gold but your play, for I have not bid you hither that I might grieve you, but amongst other things I might try your play.' There-upon, he gave back the King his money and bestowed 'rich gifts' upon the King's retinue and upon the other nobles at the feast, an action which brought 'great glory' to 'the Citizens of London in those days'.[3] Here was a man who could play his hand better than a king and lose 50 marks without batting an eye. He was a merchant, but Stow presented him as a princely man who could give lavish gifts to the entourages of four kings and play the courtier with grace and ease.

While Stow considered it a virtue for a merchant to lose money to a king when hospitality demanded it, he was careful to point out that merchants did not automatically defer to the men above them on the social scale; the respect of a merchant, he implied, had to be earned. For example, Stow tells the story of the Scottish pirate John the Mercer, who raided English ports in 1379 because of the negli-gence of the 'Duke of Lancaster and other lords that ought to have defended the realm'. This negligence angered one John Philpot, a goldsmith and an alderman of London, so he raised 'at his own cost' 1000 men and a navy to fight the pirate. The pirate was defeated, but the lords were offended ('although they knew themselves guilty'). They called the merchant before them to answer for his insubordi-nation, but he, unafraid of the consequences, gave them a lecture on political duty:

[3] *The Chronicles of England*, pp. 455–6. The story also appears in *The Annals of England* (1592), pp. 409–10.

I neither sent my money nor men to the dangers of the Seas, that I should take away from you or your fellows, the good renown of Chivalry, and win it to me, but being sorrowful to see the peoples' misery, in my country, which now through your sloth-fulness, of the most Lady of Nations, is brought to lie open to the spoiling of every vilest nation, when there is not one of you that doth put his hand to the defence thereof. I have therefore set forth myself and mine, for the saving of my nation and Country.

And Stow concludes triumphantly that the lords 'had naught to answer'.[4]

One may doubt that any merchant in the fourteenth century (or the sixteenth) could have accused the cream of the aristocracy of sloth and negligence without suffering dire consequences. Stow is merely dramatizing his point – that some merchants have been more concerned with England's welfare than men who seek the 'renown of Chivalry', and they have not been afraid to act as they saw fit. In passing, it is of note that Stow does *not* tell the story to show that Philpot's trade has made him wealthy enough to ignore the dis-pleasure of the peers, or to show that trade is superior to chivalry. The issue is public service; Picard's care for England may have been made possible by the wealth he gained by trade, but the story emphasizes his nobility of character.

There are many principal citizens in Stow's chronicles who are praised for serving their country or for their charitable actions. Some, like Picard or Philpot, are allowed to speak for themselves; others, like Sir Thomas White, are praised at length for their charities.[5] Many of them never became heroes on the stage or in stories, Philpot and Picard among them. But all the merchant-heroes had in common the grace and vision of Stow's heroes and spoke in the same rhetoric about their love for their country and king. It was Stow, not Holinshed, who set the tone for the writers who later celebrated the deeds of principal citizens.

For all the virtues of Stow's research, however, his chronicles

---

[4] *The Chronicles of England*, pp. 476–7. The story also appears in *The Annals* (1592), pp. 441–2. Holinshed recorded the expedition in both editions of his *Chronicles*, but he did not include Philpot's speech. See *The Last Volume of the Chronicles of England, Scotland and Ireland* (London, 1577), p. 1009; and Holinshed, II. 718–19.

[5] See n. 2 for White's charities. Stow did not include them in the *Annals*; apparently he considered them better fit for the *Summary* and *Chronicles*, which maintained the format of the city chronicle, dated by mayors' and sheriffs' tenures of office, than for his more general *Annals*.

could not in themselves have popularized the valiant principal citizen. The organizational principle of history as Stow wrote it was chronology; he gave Londoners a place in that chronology, but only as their deeds fit into his year-by-year accounts of the past. Thus, until the 'Honour of Citizens' provided a catalogue of merchants' great deeds, a reader had to plough through what Thomas Nash called accounts of 'Mayors and Sheriffs, and the dear year, and the great Frost' to find the heroes Stow had described.[6] It was the poets and playwrights who selected principal citizens out of their chronological slots and focussed attention on their traditions – but the traditions they celebrated, like those Stow discovered, touched upon merchants' trade only indirectly.

The most popular principal citizen drawn from the chronicles, for example, was William Walworth, fishmonger and mayor of London in 1381; his story appeared in two plays, a Lord Mayor's Show, and two long poems written in the 1590s. Walworth had been a contemporary of Philpot and a citizen similarly powerful and devoted to London; but his literary fame rested in his personal, chivalric defence of Richard II against the leader of the Jack Straw Rebellion. In Richard Johnson's *Nine Worthies of London*, Walworth appeared as an elderly warrior who, despite his anger at Wat Tyler's personal rudeness to Richard II, hesitated to silence him because the aristocrats in the king's company hung back, and 'It were no manners nobles to disgrace'. But as the rebels' presumption increased, Walworth strode alone through the crowd and stabbed their leader. Johnson described him as a man who would do anything to 'profit his country and purchase honour', and one who scorned 'death or grievous pain' when it came to protecting his king; he was 'an eagle' amidst the timid aristocrats who would not give their lives for their sovereign.[7] In the play *The Life and Death of Jack Straw*, Walworth was made to speak of his 'honour' again, and his 'magnanimity' was carefully compared to that of the ancient Romans. At the play's end, Walworth was knighted by the king and spoke at some length about his duty to his monarch:

> My gracious lord, this honourable grace,
> So far above desert (sith what I did,

---

[6] *Pierce Penniless his Supplication to the Devil* (1592), in *The Works of Thomas Nash*, ed. Ronald B. McKerrow (5 vols.; Oxford, 1958), I, 194.
[7] In *The Harleian Miscellany*, ed. William Oldys and Thomas Park (London, 1811), VIII, 440–4. This work had only one edition.

My duty and allegiance bad me do),
Binds me and my successors evermore
With sweet encouragement to th' like attempt.
Your majesty and all your royal peers
Shall find your London such a storehouse still,
As not alone you shall command our wealth,
But loyal hearts, the treasure of a prince,
Shall grow like grains sown in a fertile soil.
And God I praise, that with this holy hand,
Hath given me heart to free my prince and land.[8]

This rhetoric is far more chivalric than anything in Stow's chronicles. Richard is Walworth's 'gracious lord', Walworth's service is the result of his 'duty and allegiance' to an overlord, and its success has made his hand 'holy'. Walworth speaks of the wealth of London, but he expresses pride in his service and his city in the language of the court, not the counting-house. And his action has bought his city its most precious commodity – honour.

Walworth's service was, of course, exceptional. It is not every day that a fishmonger can prove he is the king's loyal vassal. But Walworth was not the only merchant hero who was praised for chivalric service. When Thomas Heywood wanted to glorify London businessmen in *1 Edward IV*, he too placed them in a heroic setting. One act of the play is taken up with the stout attempts of the London business community to defend the city against the Bastard Fauconbridge and his rebels. The audience is assured that

whole companies
Of Mercers, Grocers, Drapers, and the rest,
Are drawn together for their best defence,
Beside the tower,

ready to fight for Edward's right to rule England. The lord mayor reminds these warlike men of trade that they are acting in accordance with London's tradition of service to the king:

Think that in Richard's time even such a rebel
Was then by Walworth, the lord Mayor of London,
Stabbed dead in Smithfield.
Then show yourselves as it befits the time,

[8] Dodsley, V, 406, 413.

And let this find a hundred Walworths now
Dare stab a rebel, were he made of brass.

The apprentices chime in by telling the rebels about the 'memorable actions' apprentices have performed in past battles.[9] And the valour of the citizens is illustrated in a series of skirmishes in which the rebels are soundly defeated.

The heroes of the Walworth stories and Heywood's plays are obviously designed to appeal to London citizens' pride in the city's tradition of service to the realm. But the service which glorifies fishmongers, mercers, grocers, drapers and the rest is personal chivalry which is related very minimally to trade. These wealthy merchants do not bank-roll troops; they fight like knights in the colours of their companies. In order to praise the service of principal citizens, the authors turn London from a storehouse into a battlefield; they put merchants in armour and make them talk of 'duty', 'honour', and 'holy' loyalty to the king. Heywood and his contemporaries see no incongruity in using chivalric motifs, based in a pre-capitalist system of values, to appeal to the social consciousness of urban businessmen. Episodes which could show that merchants have a dignified tradition of *mercantile* service are ignored; the authors wish to show that merchants have the same kinds of traditions as the elite.

One of the authors in the 1590s did try to reconcile chivalric ideals to bourgeois service in the praise of his hero. Thomas Deloney, a silk-weaver and the most influential of the authors who praised men of trade, took up the problem Stow had touched upon in his presentation of Philpot and presented a businessman who could serve his monarch on the battlefield not because he was brave but because he was rich. But Deloney pressed beyond Stow's treatment of the theme, and his manipulation of old and new social values resulted in a work with implications perhaps more searching than he intended.

The hero of Deloney's *Jack of Newbury* was a famous and semi-legendary clothier who had lived in the reign of Henry VIII.[10] Deloney adopted Jack's legend and enhanced it by telling of his rise to fortune, portraying his mythical clothing establishment, and relating a series of tales which proved he was worthy of his wealth. One of the first episodes in the book concerns Jack's loyalty to his

[9]Heywood, I, 13–14, 17–18.   [10]*DNB*, *sub*. John Winchcombe.

king as it is expressed in military terms. When the Scots invade England in 1513, Jack (who is technically a yeoman) is required to bring six men to the field. Instead, he brings 150, all dressed in 'white coats, and red caps with yellow feathers'. He leads these liveried retainers personally, arrayed 'in complete armour on a goodly Barbed Horse'. It is a pretty sight and a walike one; Deloney assures the reader that each of Jack's soldiers is 'so expert in the handling of his weapon, as few better were found in the field'. Most of the county elite admire Jack's showy contribution, but others are envious and say that he is 'more prodigal than prudent, and more vain-glorious than well-advised, seeing that the best Nobleman in the Country would scarce have done so much'. A nobleman, they add sagely, would, of course, know that the king often asks for troops, so he 'would do at one time as [he] might be able to do at another'.

Jack, however, denies that he is being ostentatious. He observes to Queen Catherine that the gentlemen are merely jealous because he has surpassed them in 'hearty affection' to his 'Sovereign Lord'. And he is careful to let her know that he is not a nobleman who counts the cost of service, but a humble clothier who will give everything he has to serve her:

> Gentlemen I am none, nor the son of a Gentleman, but a poor Clothier, whose lands are his Looms, having no other Rents but what I get from the backs of little sheep: nor can I claim any cognizance but a wooden shuttle. Nevertheless, most gracious Queen, these my poor servants and myself, with life and goods, are ready at your Majesty's command, not only to spend our bloods, but also to lose our lives in defence of our King and Country.[11]

The scene is still that of the Walworth stories and *1 Edward IV*; a monarch in need meets a businessman in armour and is assured of the businessman's undying loyalty. But the businessman in this case is not a single knight but the mounted, armed leader of a larger host of liveried retainers than the 'best Nobleman in the Country' can muster. The value of businessmen is still measured by the standards of the elite, for Jack does what a loyal vassal is supposed to do in times of military need. But this episode puts greater pressure on those standards than the Walworth stories did. Valour is expected

---

[11] Deloney, *Works*, pp. 23–4.

of a knight, so Walworth's heroism does not disturb the concept of knighthood. But Jack's appearance as a lord does disturb the concept of lordship, for he is not a gentleman or even a gentleman's son. He has no land, only looms; no rents, only sheep; his retainers are humble men who turn wool into cloth. 'Nevertheless', his ignoble trade allows him to serve his country nobly. It also allows him to show the queen what he is: not just the most loyal, but the most powerful man in Berkshire.

Whatever the wider implications of the episode, it is used merely to prove that Jack is the king's loyal vassal. The language Deloney uses neither invites nor permits him to say that trade makes clothiers as a class more powerful than aristocrats as a class. He lets the matter rest when he has proved that a clothier's loyalty can be as useful as a lord's. But it is possible that Deloney was disturbed by the social implications of the scene. He did not portray any of his later heroes in similar positions of military power. The valorous shoemakers in *The Gentle Craft* are disguised princes or courtiers; the clothiers in *Thomas of Reading* leave war to their betters.

The stories that appealed to the social pride of merchants and clothiers were not all concerned with the military exploits of their heroes; there were many tales which praised principal citizens for their peace-time services. But these stories too were circumscribed by pre-capitalist assumptions, and their heroes, like Walworth and the citizens in *1 Edward IV*, were judged by the standards of the elite. Consequently, although trade was praised in these stories, it was never praised in quite the terms one might expect.

For example, when an author wishes to assert the dignity of trade, he does not argue that trade is good for the nation; he says that gentlemen think well enough of merchants to apprentice their sons to them. Thus, in Heywood's *Four Prentices of London*, one learns that the four 'prentices' are in fact the sons of the banished Earl of Boulogne who, despite their noble blood, 'have no scorn' of their civic trades because London citizens are such stout fellows. In *The Gentle Craft, Part I*, Deloney promises to tell the reader about 'worthy and renowned Kings, / And divers lords and Knights also', who took up shoemaking in hard times and found shoemakers fine companions; Dekker adopts this motif in *The Shoemakers' Holiday*. And in the opening paragraphs of *Thomas of Reading*, Deloney writes an encomium of the clothing trade in which he says it was held in such 'high reputation' that 'the younger sons of Knights and Gentlemen, to whom their Fathers would leave no lands, were most commonly preferred to learn this trade, to the end that thereby they might live in good estate, and drive forth their days in prosperity'.[12] Furthermore, the 'prosperity' of trade is not presented as its chief attraction to the superfluous sons of the elite; while the authors assume a great merchant or clothier will be wealthy, they are concerned to show that a gentleman who enters trade need give up none of his aristocratic ideals. The tales prove that merchants are not narrow misers who think of nothing but cloth and spices but men with a dignified tradition of aristocratic magnificence who (to all appearances) simply practise trade in their spare time. In spite of this, however, the authors are concerned to show that the gentlemanlike merchants in their stories are proud of being merchants and do not stand in awe of men who are technically their social superiors. Behind each story is a hint of the consciousness that, all rank aside, merchants are slightly better than the elite at the sort of thing which a lord is supposed to do.

One of the chief virtues of a member of the elite was his beneficence, and the authors who glorified merchants were careful to present their heroes as beneficent men.[13] The most popular means of expressing a merchant's beneficence was to show that a merchant could give a feast which was literally fit for a king. Henry Picard's feast, as described by Stow, may have served as a general model, for none of the heroes said to have given banquets for their monarchs actually did so. If this is so, the authors adopted the most obvious points from the Picard story and used the scene to show both that the merchant was capable of expressing his loyalty extravagantly and that the merchant's self-confidence allowed him to act with more grace than a courtier – or in some cases, with more grace than a king.

In Dekker's *Shoemakers' Holiday*, for example, Simon Eyre, a shoemaker who has become lord mayor of London, gives a feast to which he invites all the apprentices of London and the king. Dekker uses the scene to imply that the monarch, merchant and apprentices are all united by their wit and good fellowship. Eyre is not at all

---

[12] *Four Prentices*, in Heywood, II, 168; *Gentle Craft*, Deloney, *Works*, p. 71; *Thomas of Reading*, Deloney, *Works*, p. 213.

[13] Sir Thomas Elyot suggests that 'magnificence' is the virtue of monarchs, and 'beneficence and liberality' the equivalent virtues in subjects. *The Book Named the Governor* (1531), Facsimile (Menston, Yorkshire, 1970), Book II, Chapter X.

courtly, though he is courteous to the king. He calls attention to his lowly occupation even as he expresses his loyalty:

> I beseech your grace pardon by rude behaviour, I am a handi-crafts man, yet my heart is without craft, I would be sorry at my soul, that my boldness would offend my king.

This is humble, but it is not the speech of a man who is nervous about having risen from handicraftsman to lord mayor of London. Once he is assured that the king approves of his 'madness', Eyre continues to express his loyalty in the rhetoric he uses in addressing equals, subordinates and superiors alike:

> you see not a white hair on my head, not a grey in this beard, every hair I assure thy majesty that sticks in this beard, Sim Eyre values at the king of Babylon's ransom. Tamar Cham's beard was a rubbing brush to it: yet I'll shave it off, and stuff tennis balls with it to please my bully king.[14]

Eyre's familiarity does not limit the deference he feels for the king, but he is not self-deprecating. He thanks the king for coming to his 'poor' banquet, but clearly the fare he offers is 'poor' only because nothing is worthy of the king's grace. He uses his 'rough-ness' to imply that the relationship between kings and merchants is so friendly that the merchant does not need to adopt the rhetoric of the court in the king's presence. The scene has a double aspect. It shows that Eyre can live up to courtly standards of liberality, fidelity and personal charm. But it also shows that Eyre is his own man as well as the king's, and it suggests that a monarch must appreciate a merchant for what he is.

In Heywood's *1 Edward IV* there appears a banquet scene which is more challenging in its attitude toward genteel virtues than Dekker's feast. The banquet is given for Edward IV by John Crosby, and it is carefully presented as the high point of Crosby's life. Crosby was a foundling, raised at a hospital, apprenticed to the Grocers' Company, and finally risen to the mayoralty and knighted by Edward for his services against Fauconbridge. Although he preens himself before the mirror before the king arrives, reflecting upon his past life and looking forward to the banquet, Crosby is no fawning parvenu. When Edward arrives, the mayor greets him with all the grace of an experienced courtier; he dismisses his heroism as

---

[14] *The Shoemakers' Holiday*, V, v, lines 9–24, in *The Dramatic Works of Thomas Dekker*, ed. Fredson Bowers (Cambridge, 1955) II.

the duty which should be expected of a loyal vassal and welcomes his overlord to his home:

> My gracious lord, what then we did,
> We did account no more than was our duty,
> Thereto obliged by true subjects' zeal;
> And may he never live that not defends
> The honour of his King and Country!
> Next thank I God, it likes your majesty
> To bless my poor roof with your royal presence.
> To me could come no greater happiness.

But the banquet which thus starts so ceremoniously ends in disaster; Edward meets Mistress Shore at Crosby's house and is so taken with her that he ignores the mayor completely. Finally, overcome by his feelings, he 'starts from the table', says brusquely, 'Thanks for my cheer, Lord Mayor! I am not well', and leaves abruptly. Crosby is crushed ('Oh, God! here to be ill! My house to cause my Sovereign's discontent!'), but he remains loyal. Standing alone upon the stage with the uneaten banquet heaped before him, he sighs:

> His highness did intend to be right merry;
> And God he knows how it would glad my soul,
> If I had seen his highness satisfied
> With the poor entertainment of his Mayor,
> His humble vassal, whose lands, whose life, and all,
> Are, and in duty must be always, his.

Here, the 'humble vassal' has displayed a far greater depth of fidelity than the king. The play does not judge Edward harshly, but this scene and the scenes in which Edward seduces Mistress Shore suggest that Edward's courtly behaviour, unlike the London citizens' loyal conduct, is merely a cover for what in Heywood's plays are consistently the greatest of faults – callousness and ingratitude.[15]

[15] Heywood, I, 58–63. The scene calls to mind a passage in the Second Prayerbook of Edward VI, in which 'people negligent to come to the holy Communion' were chastised in the following way:

> You know how grievous and unkind a thing it is, when a man hath prepared a rich feast, decked his table with all kind of provision, so that there lacketh nothing but the guests to sit down; and yet they which be called, without any cause most unthankfully refuse to come. Which of you, in such a case, would not be moved? Who would not think a great injury and wrong done to him?
> (*The First and Second Prayer Books of Edward VI* (Everyman's Library, no. 448; London, 1949) pp. 283–3.)

It is in the hands of Deloney, however, that the social commentary in the banquet scene takes on a truly challenging aspect. Like the other authors, Deloney uses the banquet to demonstrate the wealth and personal merit of his hero. But he makes his point by comparing Jack of Newbury to the greatest of Henry VIII's courtiers; and this changes the issue from fellowship and good manners to the problem of the proper use of wealth, status and power. Again, by using the language of the elite to glorify his clothier, Deloney has turned that language inside out.

The merchants in other bourgeois tales began their feasts by showing their monarchs what loyal vassals they were. Jack takes a different approach; he does not entertain Henry VIII until the king has recognized him as a prince in his own domain. When he hears that Henry is in Berkshire, Jack dresses thirty of his men in livery and gives them swords; he dresses himself in a russet coat and slops, attire fitting his yeoman status. He and his men go to an anthill near the road along which Henry and his train are to pass and pretend to defend it. The king sees them and sends a herald to ask who they are. Jack informs the herald that he is 'poor Jack of Newbury, who being scant Marquis of Molehill, is chosen Prince of Ants'; he adds that he is defending the ants against the 'furious wrath of the Prince of Butterflies'. The king is amused, but he does not fully grasp the implications of Jack's pose. He sends for Jack to come speak to him. But Jack replies to the shocked herald: 'his Grace hath a horse and I am on foot; therefore will him to come to me'. Surprisingly enough, Henry comes, saying he is content to ride to this 'Emperor of Ants, that is so careful in his government'.

Once Henry has accepted Jack as an emperor, Jack becomes a loyal vassal. Claiming the arrival of the king has dispersed his foes, he explains the war of the Ants and Butterflies. The Butterfly, he says, was oppressing the industrious commonwealth of Ants, but the Ants dared not complain because of the Butterfly's 'golden apparel'. Since nobody stopped the Butterfly, he became 'so ambitious and malapert, that the poor Ant could no sooner get an egg into her nest, but he would have it away'. Then the Butterfly 'assembled a great many other of his own coat, by windy wars to root this painful people out of the land, that he himself might be seated above them all'. At this point, Jack assembled his men to withstand the Butterfly; but the arrival of the king put all the Butterflies to flight. The Butterfly is of course Cardinal Wolsey, whose wars caused heavy taxation and a depression in the clothing industry. Wolsey understands the allegory only too well, but Henry is delighted with the tale. When Jack adds that he means to 'humbly yield' all his 'Sovereign rule and dignity, both of life and goods' to the king now that he has saved the ants, Henry is so pleased that he decides to see Jack's house.[16]

When Henry arrives at Jack's establishment, he is given a costly gift; but although its cost is not ignored, its importance lies in its political lesson. It is a golden beehive, out of which springs a 'flourishing green tree, which bore golden Apples'. Tree and beehive are beset by 'diverse Serpents', but the serpents are trodden down by two virtues. The virtues hold an inscription which explains that the icon is 'The figure of a flourishing Commonwealth: / Where virtuous subjects labour with delight.' Ambition, Envy and Treason, their 'power prepared with bad intent', try to destroy the commonwealth, but they are 'dispersed' by Prudence and Fortitude. And thus, concludes the inscription, 'are they foiled that mount with means unmeet, / And so like slaves are trodden under feet'. Jack's present points out iconographically that the tree of commonwealth is supported by the busy community of clothiers. Both the clothiers and the commonwealth are threatened by the powerful and ambitious Wolsey, who has risen by improper means; Wolsey can be controlled only with the help of the monarch's prudence and fortitude.[17]

There follows a magnificent feast, 'served all in glass' and washed down with claret wine and sack, which are 'as plentiful as small Ale'. Cardinal Wolsey, still 'galled by the Allegory of the Ants', does not enjoy himself. He remarks to the king that he should note the 'vainglory of these Artificers' and especially of Jack, 'the fellow of this house'. He adds that Jack has 'stuck not to undo himself' in order to attain fame for giving a banquet for the king, but that in time of war or subsidy, Jack will 'grudge and repine'. Catherine points out that Jack in fact brought 150 men to the field in times of war, so Wolsey is silenced.

After the banquet, Jack takes Henry on a tour of his establish-

---

[16] Deloney, *Works*, pp. 27–9.

[17] *Ibid.*, p. 29. Max Dorsinville has suggested that this icon compares Henry's commonwealth, which is beset by idle courtiers, to Jack's, 'where pride in hard work is celebrated as the ideal life style' ('Design in *Jack of Newbury*', *PMLA*, 88 (1973), 235). But surely the point is simply that Jack's miniature commonwealth supports the realm, while Wolsey's pride threatens its destruction.

ment. The reader, who has been on an identical tour ten pages earlier as Jack showed his household to his prospective father-in-law, may wonder why he is being shown the workers twice. But Deloney is not quite so clumsy as he seems. The first tour simply demonstrated Jack's wealth; the second is designed to show the king why the Commonwealth of Ants deserves protection from the Prince of Butterflies. It is difficult for a modern reader to see the tour as anything but a comparison of Jack's diligent labour and Wolsey's conspicuous expenditure. The contrast is indeed implicit in the scene; an Elizabethan reader familiar with Cavendish's *Life and Death of Cardinal Wolsey* through the chronicles of Stow or Holinshed could easily have compared Jack's fruitful establishment with Wolsey's household of gaudily dressed cooks, ushers, servants, yeomen, and chapel processions of forty priests in matching copes.[18] A close reading of the passage, however, reveals that Jack does not ask Henry to protect the realm from the idleness and display of the Butterflies, but from the social woes which are the result of the Prince of Butterfly's pride.

In the first room the king finds 200 men working at 100 looms, happily singing about the benefits of lowly estate; he remarks on their good cheer and gives them 100 angels to spend on a feast. In the next room, Henry finds a great number of pretty spinners and carders contentedly singing about the treachery of a Scot; he casts them 'a great reward'. By the time the king has seen the fulling mills and the dye house, where more people are happily working, he has learned the lesson Jack hopes to teach. He remarks at 'what a great number of people were by this one man set on work', and he adds 'that no Trade in all the Land was so much to be cherished and maintained as this, which (quoth he) may well be called, The life of the poor'. The nation of Ants deserves protection because it supports men and women who would otherwise be poor and unemployed.

But Jack can employ the poor only under certain conditions, and the last pageant Henry sees drives home that point. The pageant is put on by ninety-six poor children who make their money by picking burrs out of wool. One of these children, dressed as Diana, presents the king with four prisoners: Bellona, goddess of war, and her three daughters, Famine, Sword and Fire. All four are terrifyingly dressed, and Famine is described in particular detail. This is a plea

[18] Holinshed, III, 760–1.

of the poor for an end to Wolsey's 'windy wars', which (as Deloney has carefully explained) caused a depression in the clothing industry and widespread unemployment among the families of the poor children. The children do not wish the king to end war at the expense of honour – they present him with two servants, Fame and Victory, and tell them to wait upon their prince forever. But they do suggest that the clothing industry cannot be 'the life of the poor' unless the king realizes the welfare of the Commonwealth of Ants is more important to England's well-being than the ambitious wars of the Prince of Butterflies. The courtiers, however, have a short-term solution to the problem of the poor children. The queen remarks that 'God gives as fair children to the poor as to the rich, and fairer many times.' She, Henry and the noblemen in their train acknowledge this fact by adopting all ninety-six children, giving them places at court, an education at the universities, or gentlemen's livings. Each of the children is so worthy of promotion that all of them become 'men of great account' in the realm.[19]

And so, Jack has instructed his monarch in the duties of governance. He has proved that a clothier who is not a gentleman or a gentleman's son can give as lavish a feast as any courtier in the realm, Wolsey included. He has taught the king that clothiers are important to the commonwealth because they set the poor on work. And he has taught the king that he should be a prince like Jack, who cares for his people and sees his position as a social obligation, not a prince like Wolsey who uses his power only to heap further glories upon himself at the expense of the poor. What Henry is *not* expected to learn from Jack, however, is that he should change his value system. Deloney does not compare Jack to the aristocracy of birth, nor does he condemn courtiers *per se*. It is not suggested for an instant that the king's court is extravagant and wasteful while Jack and his Ants are diligent and thrifty. Jack's banquet, after all, is conspicuous expenditure at its height, and ninety-six of his workers are promoted to a life of leisure which Deloney unhesitatingly presents as being far better than any employment Jack can give them. Deloney is careful to compare Jack only to a man who has risen from origins as humble as his own and forgotten that the *existing* value system thrusts social responsibility upon men of

[19]Deloney, *Works*, pp. 36–8.

wealth and position.[20] It is Wolsey's pride, not his idleness and extravagance, which makes him beggar the poor by conjuring up wars to win. And it is Jack's sense of justice and charity, not his belief in the intrinsic value of hard work, that makes him look out for the welfare of his weavers, spinners and carders.

As Henry VIII leaves Jack's house, he wishes to thank Jack by knighting him. But Jack, unlike Mayor Crosby, William Walworth and other heroes of Elizabethan tales about merchants, declines the offer. He asks to remain a 'poor clothier' among his people, whose welfare he values more than 'all the vain titles of Gentility: for these are the labouring Ants whom I seek to defend, and these be the Bees which I keep: who labour in this life, not for ourselves, but for the glory of God, and to do service to our dread Sovereign'. Henry presses the honour on Jack, but Jack is firm. Honour, he says, makes men forget their origins, 'and to the end I may still keep in mind from whence I came, and what I am, I beseech your Grace let me rest in my russet coat, a poor Clothier to my dying day'.[21] Accepting the honour would put Jack in Wolsey's category – that of proud men who seek their own advancement, forget their origins, and also forget that the ants in the commonwealth need protection.

But there is more in Jack's refusal of a knighthood than his mere desire to avoid the sin of pride. The phrases in which he denies himself honour recall all the incidents in which he has shown himself to be a prince. He asks to remain a 'poor Clothier' in his 'russet coat'; but it was 'poor Jack of Newbury' who identified himself to the herald as King of Ants, and it was the man in the russet coat who refused to come when the king commanded. Jack asks to live among his people, but he describes them as his subjects: they are the ants he *defends*, the bees which he *keeps*. To a man who is a prince in his own commonwealth, a knighthood is indeed a 'vain title of gentility'.

In describing Jack as a prince, however, Deloney raises problems which he cannot solve. It is all very well to show that Jack is a model to his monarch and a governor whose social commitment puts

---

[20] Dorsinville argues that Jack is 'the epitome of the rising Elizabethan mercantile class that wishes to counterbalance the power of the courtiers', but has to 'be careful if he wants to replace the power of those of noble birth' ('Design in *Jack Newbury*', p. 236). But if Jack wants to replace anybody in Henry's esteem, it is not the courtiers of *noble* birth; Deloney compares him to Wolsey and *only* to Wolsey. No other courtier in Henry's train is mentioned by name.

[21] Deloney, *Works*, p. 38.

ambitious Wolsey to shame. But one cannot ignore the fact that Wolsey has become a prince by conventional courtly channels, while Jack has become a prince by running a clothing empire. Jack's method of attaining princely dignity puts pressure on the concept of princeliness, even though all his values are those of the elite. For if he is really a prince, then princeliness must depend not on high birth and royal favour, but on the great wealth that comes from industrial service.

This brings up the fundamental question of what Jack is – and the question is never answered in the book. Deloney's most perceptive critic argues that Deloney is more interested in Jack's roles than in his status, and this is certainly true to an extent, for Jack is, among other things, an actor.[22] His monarchy is part of a pose which (like his pageants) is put on for allegorical purposes; and clearly, his anthill is a *model* commonwealth, not a commonwealth in fact. But though Jack's princeliness is allegorical fiction, his power is not; he is able to bring 150 men with him to the battlefield, advise the king on the proper use of power, and (in a later chapter) reverse the trend of foreign policy which hurts the clothing industry. If Jack is not a prince or a lord in fact, he is not a yeoman either. He says he is a poor clothier, but this too is simply a pose: 'poor' in this context loses its standard meaning, and 'clothier' comes very close to meaning 'lord'. If Deloney consciously described Jack's roles rather than Jack's status, he was making a virtue of necessity, for there was no word in Elizabethan vocabulary to describe what Jack really is. Jack remains, perforce, a man of undetermined place in the social hierarchy. He performs the actions of a model governor – gives a great banquet, relieves many poor men at his wedding, takes good care of his servants, becomes an MP. A clothier can prove the merit of the values of the elite, while Cardinal Wolsey and 'the best Noblemen in the Country' shirk their responsibilities; but that clothier has no place in society.

Deloney does not say (and quite possibly had no way of saying) that Jack does not fit into the social hierarchy because his sort of power must be defined in terms of economic and political interest, not good blood, preferment, and a tradition of noble action. However searching the implied questions in *Jack of Newbury* may be, they are only implied, not asked or answered. Finally, Jack is a

---

[22] Walter R. Davis, *Idea and Act in Elizabethan Fiction* (Princeton, 1969), p. 250.

figure like Picard, Philpot, Walworth, Eyre and Crosby: he is a businessman described in terms of the elite. He perfectly exemplifies the difficulties of using the values of one class to appeal to the pride of another; sooner or later the hybrid figure which is created will raise questions that threaten established social ideology.

Interestingly enough, Deloney turned away from most of the questions *Jack of Newbury* pressed upon him. He began his last novel, *Thomas of Reading*, with an encomium of the clothing trade as it existed (anachronistically) in the reign of Henry I. Clothing provided a living for the sons of the elite, he said, but it also supported half of England's humbler population, 'and in such good sort, that in the Commonwealth there were few or no beggars at all . . . Idleness was then banished our coast, so that it was a rare thing to hear of a thief in those days. Therefore it was not without cause that Clothiers were then both honoured and loved.'[23] Again, Deloney insists that one of the chief values of the clothing trade is its support of the poor; the Golden Age he describes here contrasts sharply with the Elizabethan age, in which beggars abounded and the mid-century slump in the clothing trade had left clothiers less powerful and wealthy than they had been earlier. But in *Thomas of Reading*, the clothiers who employ the poor are not heroes of Jack's dimensions. In fact, Deloney seems consciously to have made them provincial so that they do not threaten the values of the elite. When these clothiers meet the king, one remarks sagely that he 'had rather speak to his King's Majesty, than to many Justices of peace'. When they give a banquet for the princes of England, one of them asks the cook to make a 'good store of pottage', and another fails to attend because he has been strung up like a sausage on the rafters of an inn as punishment for trying to seduce the innkeeper's wife.[24] These clothiers are wealthy, but they are by their own admission 'country folk' who talk country language, not princes who can speak the language of chivalry. They are valuable subjects; their trade supports England's poor and the valour of England's aristocracy, as Henry I notices appreciatively.[25] But the trade which supports them does not make them princely. In *Thomas of Reading*, Deloney adheres to the social ideal of Harrison, in which men of second rank

[23] Deloney, *Works*, p. 213.   [24] *Ibid.*, pp. 228, 229, 232.   [25] *Ibid.*, pp. 241, 215.

in the county are yeomen who accept the intrinsic superiority of the elite.

Ironically, *Thomas of Reading* had more influence on other writers of tales about merchants and craftsmen than any of Deloney's other works. It was the source for four plays (all of which are lost) and a novel, while *The Gentle Craft* was used as a model for only two plays. But the playwrights never touched *Jack of Newbury*. It may have lent itself to dramatic treatment for the same reasons Deloney's other works did; but its social implications, it seems, were unstageable. The ideas in Deloney's most searching work remained unrevived and unexamined throughout the remaining years of the life of the businessman in armour, though the book itself sold better than almost all other works of fiction in the seventeenth century.

The businessman in armour did not in fact survive Deloney by many years: the silk-weaver died in 1600 and the vogue of the merchant hero came to an end in 1605.[26] During these years there arose a new vogue of witty, polished 'citizen comedy', created by Jonson, Middleton, Marston and Massinger. This comedy was about London society and was certainly concerned with problems of social status, but, as I have shown in the last chapter, it revived the merchant's stereotype as a usurer and frequently suggested he was an ineffectual governor even in his own household.

The creators of citizen comedy were not above poking fun at the playwrights who pandered to the popular, unsophisticated taste for bombast and civic heroism. In *Westward Ho!* (1605), Jonson, Marston and Chapman pointed out that the old comedy appealed to citizens who could not possibly live up to aristocratic ideals. They created Touchstone, a diligent goldsmith whose morality is formed entirely by time-worn aphorisms, but whose imagination is fired by civic heroes like Gresham or Whittington (both heroes of plays produced in 1605). When Touchstone's 'thrifty' apprentice becomes an alderman's deputy, Touchstone dreams happily of the time when his deeds will be played 'by the best companies of actors, and be called their get-penny'. But the youth who is thus supposed to get actors a long run is such a miser that he flinches at the thought of having a feast at his own wedding, insisting that the left-overs from

[26] In that year Heywood's *2 If You Know Not Me, You Know Nobody* appeared; its hero was Sir Thomas Gresham. That play mentions another merchant-hero play, *Richard Whittington*, which had just been produced (it is now lost). Only one more 'citizen' play appeared thereafter: William Rowley's *A Shoemaker, A Gentleman* (c. 1608).

the wedding of Touchstone's social-climbing daughter will furnish his own table 'with bounty'.[27] The virtue of magnificence is utterly beyond his imagination.

Two years later, Beaumont and Fletcher again satirized citizen taste in *The Knight of the Burning Pestle*. The central figures of the play are a grocer and his wife, who have a great deal of imagination, but make up for it by having terrible taste and no grasp of the slightest complication of dramatic plot and theme. Sitting on the stage of the play they wish to see, they force the actors to make their apprentice play the lead; then they insist that he kill a lion, court a princess, rescue prisoners from a giant, and die nobly at the end of the comedy. The 'old comedy' over which they and citizens like them tyrannize, according to Beaumont and Fletcher, is romance-fed, childish fantasy.

This kind of satire did not kill the taste for merchant heroes, as the continued popularity of Deloney's novels – and the stage failure of *The Knight of the Burning Pestle* – prove. The satirists simply hastened the death of the old comedy by showing it to be a second-rate literary fad. The fad was particularly subject to satire because the Jacobean inflation of honours exposed the implications of the fantasies in the older works. The possibility that stories about heroic merchants could encourage a financier like Baptist Hicks to pose as a William Walworth or a Simon Eyre may well have added barbs to the pens already sharpened to attack cheapened titles that any wealthy man of trade could buy from a courtier – or worse still, from Lionel Cranfield.[28] And the implication that such men, like John Philpot or Jack of Newbury, might be as powerful as lords because of their wealth was hardly reassuring.

But while the inflation of honours and the satire which it inspired worked together to halt the creation of valiant principal citizens, it is quite possible that the businessman in armour was moribund in any case. He was a fragile figure, despite his justly earned pride in his achievements and his confident dealings with kings and peers. His fragility did not lie in what he was, for his historical achievements gave merchants a tradition of which they could be proud. The fragility of the merchant-hero lay rather in the impossibility of developing him into a figure relevant to the increase in Elizabethan money-lending, the growth of London's commercial activity, or the beginning of the expansion of English trade. The Elizabethan authors could repeat stories of merchant heroism and lavish merchant banquets *ad nauseam* (and surely it was this repetition, as much as anything else, which provoked satire) – but they failed to show that trade had *intrinsic merit*. They could develop the merchant into a man who could live up to the standards of the gentry, but they could not develop him further into a man of trade whose pride was founded in the belief that he was different from the gentry.

One can see what is absent from Elizabethan literature on merchants more clearly if one looks ahead to the works that praised merchants in the eighteenth century. In 1712, for example, Richard Steele wrote:

> there is no Man whom I so highly honour as the Merchant. This is he who turns all the Disadvantages of our Situation into our Profit and Honour. His Care and Industry ties his Country to the Continent, and the Whole Globe pays his Nation a voluntary Tribute due to her from his Merit. His Handwriting has the Weight of Coin, and his good Character is Riches to the rest of his Countrymen.

Merchants gain honour for themselves and for England – but they gain it by the 'care' and 'industry' by which they practise trade, not by the valour with which they defend their kings. Nine years later, Steele compared merchants to gentlemen in his play *The Conscious Lovers*; but he compared them in merchants' terms. Mr Sealand, a merchant, remarks that men like him

> are as honourable and almost as useful as you landed folk that have always thought yourselves so much above us; for your trading, forsooth, is extended no farther than a load of hay or a fat ox. You are pleasant people, indeed, because you are bred up to be lazy; therefore, I warrant you, industry is dishonourable.[29]

'Honour', as it is defined by the gentry, is laziness. True honour, as defined by merchants, is the honour of 'trading' and 'industry', the attributes of a useful class of men.

[29] The first passage is from *The Englishman*, October 12, 1713, as outlined in Loftis, *Comedy and Society*, pp. 94–5. The second is from *The Conscious Lovers*, in *Six Eighteenth Century Plays*, p. 105.

This kind of consciousness was based on the idea that there were two sets of values in society – that of the gentry and that of the men of trade. Defoe, like Steele, considered the two value systems opposed to each other. When he praised the tradition of men of trade, he praised the tradition of trade:

the rising greatness of the British nation is not owing to war and conquests, to enlarging its dominion by the sword, or subjecting the people of other countries to our power; but it is all owing to trade, to the increase of our commerce at home, and the extending it abroad.

Conquest – the outcome of aristocratic chivalry – is far inferior to trade as a means to greatness. And the gentry, in not recognizing this fact, are simply clinging to bygone values:

it is a Scandal upon the Understanding of the Gentry, to think contemptibly of the trading part of the Nation; seeing however the Gentlemen may value themselves upon their Birth and Blood, the Case begins to turn against them so evidently, as to Fortune and Estate, that though they say, the Tradesmen cannot be made Gentlemen; yet the Tradesmen are, at this time, able to buy the Gentlemen almost in every part of the Kingdom.[30]

Gentlemen are no longer governors whom merchants should imitate; they are men of so little understanding that they believe in the antiquated notion that status and innate superiority follow 'birth and blood'. In fact, however, superiority is a product of utility and the 'fortune and estate' which comes from it. The works of Defoe and Steele reveal the development of a language and a habit of mind which enable merchants to take pride in themselves as men of trade, not as social miniatures of the elite.

The consciousness of the Elizabethan tales about heroic merchants is less straightforward than the consciousness of Defoe and Steele. It is the peculiar mixture of social values that preceded the idea that men of trade were 'conscious of themselves as something like a separate order, with an outlook on religion and politics peculiarly their own'.[31] For the brief vogue of the heroic merchant is a double phenomenon. It affirms, on the one hand, Lawrence

---

[30] *The Complete English Tradesman, in Familiar Letters* (1727) (2 vols., New York, 1969), I, 315; and *A Plan of the English Commerce* (1729). The Shakespeare Head Edition of the Novels and Selected Writings of Daniel Defoe, Vol. X (Oxford, 1927), pp. 60–1.
[31] R.H. Tawney, *Religion and the Rise of Capitalism* (1926; rpt. New York, 1954), p. 173.

Stone's observation that in Elizabethan England 'the dominant value system remained that of the landed gentleman', in spite of the emerging ' "middle class culture" of educated artisans, small shopkeepers, and merchants.'[32] But on the other hand, it suggests that the consciousness that men of trade had a dignified position in the social hierarchy was pressing against the confines of that dominant value system. In order to appeal to the social pride of merchants, the popular Elizabethan authors had to experiment with the flexibility of the accepted value system, stretching it this way and that in their efforts to create a basis for what a century later had clearly emerged as a middle-class pride.

Stow, Deloney, Heywood and Dekker were not philosophers; they were not even well-educated men. They were perceptive enough professionally to realize that there was a market for works that glorified principal citizens, but they did not have the social vision to see why the glorifications were by and large unsatisfactory. Faced with the incongruities of making merchants act like knights and the dangers of showing that wealthy clothiers were more powerful than lords, they simply stopped writing about men whose power lay in their wealth. Quite possibly, theirs was the only solution available at the beginning of the seventeenth century. In trying to describe the social consciousness of merchants, they had reached the limits of Elizabethan social theory, and no new social theory appeared to solve their dilemma. In *Jack of Newbury*, Deloney hovered on the threshold of a new theory which suggested that status could be defined in terms of money and power and that trade served the commonwealth better than the wars and displays of the elite. But it was a threshold which he did not, and possibly could not, cross.

[32] Stone, *Crisis*, p. 39.

7. Lessons in diligence and thrift

The contrast between the Elizabethan businessman in armour and the merchant of the 'moneyed interest' described by Defoe and Steele raises a fundamental problem about the Elizabethan adherence to the Protestant work ethic. Half a century has elapsed since R.H. Tawney published *Religion and the Rise of Capitalism*; and in spite of the debate over the nature of the connection between Calvinism and capitalism, there is still generally scholarly agreement that the Puritans' doctrine of the calling engendered a new appreciation of diligent labour and a gradually developing certainty that the wealth which resulted from diligence should be considered a measure of godly activity.[1] In its original form, Tawney's thesis dealt mainly with the 'later phases' of Puritanism – the post-Restoration theology of Richard Baxter and his contemporaries. At this time, according to Tawney, Puritanism discarded the suspicion of economic motives which had been a characteristic of earlier reform movements:

> and offered a moral creed, in which the duties of religion and the calls of business ended their long estrangement in an unanticipated reconciliation . . . It insisted, in short, that money-making, if not free from spritual dangers, was not a danger and nothing else, but that it could be, and ought to be, carried on for the greater glory of God.[2]

Scholars of pre-revolutionary England, however, have been quick to suggest that the gospel of work was preached to a bourgeois

---

[1] H.R. Trevor-Roper has disputed this idea in 'Religion, the Reformation and Social Change', in *Religion, The Reformation and Social Change and other Essays* (London, 1967), pp. 1–45. Christopher Hill has suggested that the doctrine of individuality of conscience may have had more to do with the reconciliation of Calvinism and capitalism than the work ethic. See 'Protestantism and the Rise of Capitalism', in F.J. Fisher, ed., *Essays in the Economic and Social History of Tudor and Stuart England, in Honour of R.H. Tawney* (Cambridge, 1961), pp. 15–39.
[2] *Religion and the Rise of Capitalism*, p. 199.

congregation nearly a century before 1660. Wright, for example, has argued that the 'glorification of diligence and thrift' in the sermons of the Elizabethan puritan William Perkins gives that preacher 'unusual significance in the history of bourgeois ideas and ideals'. Hill follows Wright's lead; Perkins, he says, preached what amounted to 'justification by success', and his contemporaries Dod and Cleaver preached that 'labour was a duty to one's neighbour'. David Little, while disputing Hill's interpretations of Perkins' sermons, admits that there is in the preacher's works 'a tendency to equate prosperity with the sign of God's blessing'. Even the Georges, who argue that ' "the spirit of capitalism" in its Protestant guise . . . simply does not exist in England before 1640', suggest that pre-revolutionary Protestants thought 'the most obviously godly calling [was] the most obviously economic or productive one'.[3] The gospel of work, Wright argues, obviously appealed to men like John Browne, whose *Merchant's Avizo* contains maxims which 'epitomize the bourgeois philosophy that virtue pays in things of this world', and Thomas Tusser, whose *Five Hundred Points of Good Husbandry* advises the reader to 'count no travail slavery / that brings in penny saverly'. And, according to critics of Elizabethan literature, the bourgeois doctrine of the calling was adopted by Dekker, Heywood and Deloney, whose works praised diligent, thrifty apprentices in stories which came close to equating financial success with election.[4]

These interpretations of the work ethic in Elizabethan England are obviously opposed to the suggestion, made in the previous chapter, that the sixteenth-century works which glorified merchants did so before the 'development of the bourgeois point of view'.[5] For what could be more bourgeois than praise of diligence and thrift? And who can better exemplify God's blessing of bourgeois entrepreneurs than the diligent apprentice who becomes lord mayor of

[3] Wright, 'William Perkins: Elizabethan Apostle of "Practical Divinity" ', *HLQ*, 3 (1940), 182; Hill, *Society and Puritanism*, pp. 129–30, and *Puritanism and Revolution: Studies in Interpretation of the English Revolution of the Seventeenth Century* (1958; rpt. New York, 1967), p. 229; Little, *Religion, Order and Law: A Study in Pre-Revolutionary England* (New York, 1969), p. 119; Charles and Katherine George, *The Protestant Mind of the English Reformation, 1570–1640* (Princeton, 1961), pp. 172, 143.

[4] Wright, *Middle-Class Culture*, p. 161 (Browne), p. 198n. (Tusser), pp. 637–8 (Dekker, Heywood), pp. 190–1 (Deloney); Davis, *Idea and Act*, p. 252 (financial success and election).

[5] Wright, *Middle-Class Culture*, p. 657.

London? All of the opinions above, however, are based on the unexamined assumption that diligence and thrift are virtues which appeal only to the bourgeoisie – and this assumption is incorrect. Discussion of the connection between working hard in a calling and becoming an entrepreneur may bring to mind such historical figures as Benjamin Franklin, Samuel Smiles and other apostles of the self-made man; but does a man *necessarily* have to be a middle-class capitalist to realize that extravagance leads quickly to poverty, while 'money in thy purse is always in fashion'?[6] Does a man have to be bourgeois to realize that 'the way to get wealth' is to pay attention to his assets and make good investments in whatever commodity he deals in?[7] The Elizabethan gentlemen responsible for the two preceding quotations certainly did not think so. Similarly, one may ask if the belief that prosperity is God's gift necessarily leads to the belief that God smiles upon men who work hard to get rich. Why could not the belief encourage its adherents to ignore the acquisition of wealth (since the source of all wealth is divine) and concentrate upon the obligations a wealthy man has to his fellow man? Potentially, at least, the doctrines of providence and the calling can be of interest to all but the very poorest members of society.[8] And because this is true, one cannot simply examine Elizabethan literature for lessons in diligence and thrift and (having found them) conclude that bourgeois values flourished in the late sixteenth century. One must instead examine the *context* of Elizabethan discussions of diligence, thrift, and prosperity to see if one can detect a development of a 'way of life, a code of ethics' which bourgeois men could adopt to distinguish their values from those of the elite.[9]

Elizabethan preachers, both Anglican and Puritan, did not condemn wealth as trenchantly as did fourteenth-century English divines or even the more conservative of the mid-sixteenth-century

[6]'Sir Walter Raleigh's Instructions to His Son and to Posterity', (1632), in *Advice to a Son: precepts of Lord Burghley, Sir Walter Raleigh, and Francis Osborne*, ed. Louis R. Wright, Folger Documents of Tudor and Stuart Civilization (Ithaca, New York, 1962), p. 29.
[7]Gervase Markham, *A Way To Get Wealth* (London, 1623). This is an *omnium gatherum* of re-issues from Markham's earlier pamphlets on husbandry. Its first section is primarily concerned with the proper buying and keeping of horses and hounds.
[8]Thomas, *Religion and the Decline of Magic*, p. 111. Thomas suggests that 'those at the bottom end of the social scale' are more likely to believe in 'luck' than in providence.
[9]Wright, *Middle-Class Culture*, p. 3.

commonwealth philosophers.[10] Despite their repeated assurances that riches were 'veils set betwixt God and us', and 'no argument that he loveth us', they exhibited an increasing interest in defining the kinds of gain which could be legitimately acquired by diligent labour.[11] Gain which provided for one's family was certainly legitimate; Robert Cleaver, for example, encouraged every 'household governor' to work at his calling, 'that it may bring in honest gain, whereby the necessaries for the family may be prepared'. The 'necessary riches' which should be acquired as 'honest gain' received careful definition from William Perkins. They were, he said, of two kinds: goods necessary to sustain life and goods necessary to support social status.

> Goods necessary to nature, are those, without which nature and life cannot be well preserved; and these are most needful. Necessary in respect of a man's person, are those goods, without which a man's state, condition, and dignity wherein he is, cannot be preserved.

Money beyond necessary wealth, thus defined, Perkins called 'abundant riches'. This kind of wealth might also be legitimate, and it was certainly not a necessary evil. A man who used his money well could enjoy it in good conscience:

> If God give abundance, when we neither desire it, nor seek it, we may take it, hold it and use it, as God's stewards. Abraham and Joseph of Arimathea, are commended for their riches, and yet they obtained them not by their own seeking and moiling; but [as they walked] in their callings, God in his providence blessed and multiplied their wealth . . . [I]f we have possessions and abundance, we may with good conscience enjoy them as blessings and gifts of God.[12]

The Puritans' definition of legitimate wealth sanctioned both necessary and abundant riches.

It is essential to notice, however, that the abundant wealth which Perkins described was a free gift from God, given to men who neither desired nor sought to become rich. This was not merely cautionary rhetoric; prohibitions against seeking abundance lay at

[10] On the subject of Anglican and Puritan attitudes towards wealth, see T.H. Breen, 'The Non-existent Controversy: Puritan and Anglican Attitudes on Work and Wealth, 1600–1640', *CH*, 25 (1966), 273–87; Richard L. Greaves, *Society and Religion in Elizabethan England* (Minneapolis, 1981), pp. 548–54.

[11] Greenham, *Works*, pp. 19, 104.

[12] Cleaver, *Household Government*, p. 62; Perkins, *Works*, II, 125–6.

the heart of the Elizabethan doctrine of the calling. Readers were encouraged to pray and labour in the confident hope that God would 'so prosper [their] endeavours' that 'nothing [should] be wanting unto them'; but the divines told them repeatedly that they were not permitted to work for – or even hope and pray for – abundant wealth. Christ, insisted Alexander Gee, taught men to pray for their daily bread – that is, he allowed prayer *only* for 'all things necessary for this poor and miserable life'.[13] The injunction to pray for daily bread, according to Perkins, was given to teach that we can 'ask no more' of God than what we need, even in our prayers, and to teach us 'moderation in our diet, apparel, houses'. Furthermore, since no man is permitted to work for something he cannot legitimately pray for, it follows that he may not seek abundance in his calling either. Once he has made enough money to maintain himself and his family, 'a pause must be made, and he may not proceed further, to enlarge his estate'. The man who desires and works for wealth disobeys God's commandment to pray only for what is necessary. Moreover, in 'seeking and moiling' after wealth, he proves that he does not trust that 'special Providence' of God which provides for the welfare of all men. And finally, he risks damnation, for 'it is a hard thing to become rich without injustice', and 'what know we, whether God will keep and preserve us from sin, when we seek and labour for abundance?'[14] The man who works diligently to become rich is in effect asking the God he disobeys and distrusts to preserve him from the damnable sin of covetousness.

Once a man allows his heart to be snared by 'distrustfulness, and inward greediness of the world', Arthur Dent assures his readers, he is 'set on fire, and utterly undone'. The evil of covetousness infects not just the greedy man, but the whole of society, for a covetous man does not hesitate to rob rich and poor men alike for the sake of his own gain. Such a man may try to disguise covetousness as the kind of diligence, thrift and social duty the preachers encourage in the pursuit of necessary wealth, but his attempts to make sin respectable can easily be detected. The man who raises his prices in times of dearth obviously puts his own gain before the welfare of the poor, says Greenham, even though he does nothing technically

---

[13] John Norden, *A Pensive Man's Practice* (London, 1589), p. 10; Alexander Gee, *The Ground of Christianity* (London, 1584), p. 25. Norden was a topographer, not a divine.
[14] Perkins, *Works*, I, 339, 769; II, 125–6.

illegal. The man who justifies labour for wealth by saying he will be good to the poor when he is rich, according to Perkins, is trying to justify evil deeds by saying 'that good may come thereof'. The man who justifies the oppression of widows and orphans by saying he has a duty to support his own children is certain to suffer the fate of 'the wicked, in the lake that burneth with fire and brimstone', thunders Cleaver. And furthermore, he adds elsewhere, the man who half-starves his servants in order to save money is certainly not thrifty, for 'this is no more to be counted frugality, or good husbandry, than to rob a poor man, to give to the rich, is true liberality'.[15]

In the face of statements such as these, it is difficult to believe that Perkins, Greenham, Cleaver, Dent and the other leaders of Puritanism in what Tawney might call 'its earlier phases' had discarded their suspicion of economic motives. There is nothing in their works which has the ambivalence of Richard Baxter's Direction (1673) that riches may be sought 'in subordination to higher things . . . That is, you may labour in that manner as tendeth most to your success and lawful gain.' Baxter, while insisting that one should labour to be 'Rich for God, not for flesh and sin', came close to suggesting that entrepreneurial inspirations were not covetous, but gifts of God: 'If God show you a way in which you may lawfully get more than in another way, (without wrong to your soul, or to any other) if you refuse this, and choose the less gainful way, you cross one of the ends of your Calling, and you refuse to be God's Steward, and to accept his gifts.'[16] God did not intervene with the process of money-making so directly in the sixteenth century.

The fact remains, however, that sixteenth-century Puritans did not frown on wealth if it were God's gift, not man's goal. And the distinction between wealth which is the result of God's multiplication of a blessed man's income and wealth which is the secular reward of diligence and business sense is far easier to make in theory than in practice. Could not a hard-working man say that his wealth was proof that God blessed entrepreneurial inspiration? And if so, how could Puritanism help but be a religion which appealed primarily to middle-class men whose self-definition depended upon their approval of the pursuit of abundant riches? Christopher Hill

[15] Dent, *Plain Man's Pathway*, p. 68; Greenham, *Works*, p. 194; Perkins, *Works*, II, 126; Cleaver, *Household Government*, pp. 285–6 (misnumbered 186); pp. 77–8.
[16] Baxter, *A Christian Directory: or, A Sum of Practical Theology* (London, 1673), p. 450.

claims that Perkins' sermons did appeal to such men: any 'good bourgeois' in the preacher's congregation could easily ignore his injunctions against covetousness as 'traditional qualifications' of his approval of wealth and listen only to his 'new concessions' to the wealthy.[17] But this interpretation is open to question, even if one assumes that the 'good bourgeois' in Cambridge could ignore the centrality of Perkins' condemnations of money-making as completely as Hill does. For Hill does not ask who 'the wealthy' are or what kind of diligent labour they are supposed to do. And more importantly, he fails to see that once a man reached a certain point of affluence, the Puritans insisted that he be diligent in a calling which involved not making money, but spending it.

The essential fact to remember when dealing with the calling is that it is considerably more than that by which 'temporal life is preserved and maintained'. The calling is also, in Perkins' words, 'a certain kind of life', the goal of which is service of God and society: 'the end of a man's calling, is not to gather riches for himself, for his family, for the poor, but to serve God in the serving of men, and in seeking the good of all men; and to this end men must apply their lives and labours'. The way a man serves the commonwealth depends on his social status, for God made a calling to go with each rank.[18] Poor men, then, serve society by doing manual labour diligently, and it is their duty to be virtuous in their modest capacities, 'that is, humble lowly, dutiful, painful, ready to help and ready to please'. Men of moderate means are to support their families by working diligently and honestly in some trade, taking care not to envy the wealth and status of their betters.[19]

In this scheme of things, rich men are also expected to have a calling, but their duties extend beyond supporting themselves. They must, of course, maintain their own estates; but they must also educate their children carefully so that they can, in their turn, fulfil their social obligations when they reach the age of responsibility. They must be just and charitable with their servants, taking care not to work them too hard in order to increase their productivity. And outside the household, rich men must be devoted to relieving the

[17] *Puritanism and Revolution*, p. 230. David Little has pointed out that the quotations Hill uses to support his idea are misleadingly abbreviated (*Religion, Law and Order*, p. 119). Hill in fact neglects to quote *all* Perkins' qualifying words on wealth, and so considers his views out of their Elizabethan context.

[18] Perkins, *Works*, I, 480; I, 750–1; II, 126 (end of calling).

[19] Dent, *Plain Man's Pathway*, pp. 177–8; Perkins, *Works*, I, 771; II, 136.

plight of the poor: 'The right rich man, that duly deserveth that name, is not known by his possessions, by his costly fare, and costly building, by his sumptuous palace, by his plate, jewels, and substance, but by considering the poor and needy.'[20]

If they have any intellectual, spiritual or political talents in addition to their money, rich men are required to devote these to the church and commonwealth. Not even lords, ladies and 'other great ones', says Dent, are allowed to live without such service, for to this end 'our wits, our learning, our reading, our skill, our policy, our wealth, our health, our wisdom, and authority, are to be referred'. Rich men labour with their minds, not their hands, says Babington: 'the magistrate must govern, cherish, and defend, the judges determine the causes of the people, the ministers deliver their gifts to the Church, and every one in some sort of sweat, that is in some Godly endeavour of body and mind derive unto himself the use of their outward things'. And idleness among men in these callings is especially lamentable. Dent, for example, deplores the viciousness of magistrates who neglect their duties and preachers who give themselves over to pride, covetousness and even husbandry, among 'other worldly affairs': he entreats them to 'cast off idleness and sloth: and with diligence, faithfulness, care and conscience, perform the duties of their places'.[21]

Elizabethan Puritan preachers condemned idle rich men for refusing to act as philanthropists, magistrates, judges, or ministers, not for refusing to labour in a fixed, bourgeois calling. They insisted that the children of rich men be educated so that they could learn some 'lawful calling' instead of being totally dependent on their estates – for wealth, they agreed, was transitory.[22] But the calling of the rich man was the calling of the public servant, the 'good housekeeper' who relieved the poor, the preacher or teacher. And these callings demanded a considerable outlay of capital. Philanthropy included such expensive tasks as founding poor-houses, hospitals and schools. Ministers were notoriously poorly paid. And while some court positions could yield great 'fruits of office', there were

[20] Cleaver, *Household Government*, pp. 331–2 (education); Babington, *Commandments*, pp. 178–9 (care of servants – Babington insists that servants not be made to work on Sundays); Smith, *Sermons*, p. 511 (charity).

[21] Dent, *Plain Man's Pathway*, pp. 172–3 (lords and ladies), p. 176 (idle magistrates and preachers); Babington, *Commandments*, p. 380. See also Perkins, *Works*, I, 754–5.

[22] Cleaver, *Household Government*, pp. 146–7.

many men who were broken by the expenses expected of a courtier. At the lower levels of office, the financial burden was still considerable; to be an alderman of London, one should remember, a principal citizen had to be worth £10,000 in goods so he could bear the expense.[23]

As it concerned the rich man, then, the doctrine of the calling was used to impress upon men of wealth and status the importance of their serving the commonwealth with all their ability. The appeal did not go unheeded; the Puritan gentry under Elizabeth and her successors were indeed committed to serving the realm with all their obstinate political talents, and London merchants of the same period, according to W.K. Jordan, contributed to charitable causes with unprecedented generosity.[24] For our purposes, however, what is important about the Puritan portrait of the rich man's calling is that it had nothing to do with trade or other means of becoming rich. The godly rich man was not engaged in the pursuit of wealth; he was *already* wealthy. The source of his income, whether inheritance or business, was irrelevant. Cleaver seems to have assumed that wealthy men were rentiers; but Smith, Perkins and Dent included merchants in their ranks of ideal rich men.[25] The calling of the rich man, so far as they were concerned, applied to all kinds of men with money, for the rich man's duty to the commonwealth was fulfilled not by what he got but by what he spent and how he spent it. Diligence was not necessarily lucrative work in a given job, but a vigorous social energy turned to the good of the commonwealth. Its concomitants were not thrift and business sense, but justice, temperance, liberality, charity – the virtues of Elyot's governor.

It is one thing to say that the doctrine of the calling was linked to the values of the elite in theory; it is quite another, of course, to say that the newly emphasized virtues of diligence and moderation were not used to appeal to the self-consciousness of the bourgeoisie in some other popularized form. What about the maxims in Tusser's *Five Hundred Points of Good Husbandry* or the moral instructions

---

[23] Stone, *Crisis*, pp. 449–63; Pearl, *London and Revolution*, p. 60.

[24] Jordan, *The Charities of London*, pp. 63–78.

[25] In *Household Government*, pp. 185–6, 269–70, 331–3, Cleaver's condemnations of rich worldlings imply that they do nothing but hawk, eat, play dice and build. But Dent condemns the idleness of rich citizens (*Plain Man's Pathway*, pp. 170–1), Smith insists that merchants should give alms (*Sermons*, p. 509), and Perkins' passage about just gain never implies that wealthy men live only on their rents (*Works*, II, 125–9).

in Browne's *Merchant's Avizo*? What about the diligent apprentices in Heywood's plays and Deloney's fiction? Do they not show that the Puritan ethic appealed to bourgeois men even in the sixteenth century?

Let us begin with Tusser's *Five Hundred Points of Good Husbandry*. It does indeed commend diligence and thrift enthusiastically in such introductory poems as 'The Ladder to Thrift'; and its agricultural instructions are mixed with advice to work hard the year 'round and run an efficient household so that one's coffers will stay full. But the *Five Hundred Points* antedates the great age of Elizabethan Puritan sermons by over a decade, and it is in fact merely one of many expanded editions of Tusser's original *One Hundred Points of Good Husbandry*, first published in 1557. Tusser's 'source' for the commendations of diligence and thrift is not sixteenth-century theology, but the georgic tradition of Hesiod, the Elder Cato, Varro and Virgil. Both the Greek and Roman georgics advocated diligence and austerity. Hesiod, writing a century or so after the death of Homer, had insisted: 'Work is no reproach: the reproach is idleness. But if thou wilt work, soon shall the idle man envy thee thy wealth: on wealth attend good and glory. And whatever be thy lot, work is best, if thou wilt turn thy foolish mind from the goods of other men to work and study livelihood as I bid thee.' It is certain that Tusser, a gentleman educated at Eton and Trinity College, Cambridge, a courtier who retired after ten years from the court to become a farmer, was well acquainted with the georgic tradition.[26] And in writing in this tradition he was doing nothing new. In 1523, one Master Fitzherbert first published a prose agricultural treatise called *The Book of Husbandry* which remained popular throughout Elizabeth's reign.[27] Fitzherbert's manual, like Tusser's, mixed advice about crop-planting and diseases in animals with paragraphs on 'Riches', 'Diligence', and the sins of prodigality, and ended with a series of moral and religious essays.

Neither Fitzherbert's prose treatise nor Tusser's poetic one was aimed at small farmers. For both writers adopted the pose of the

---

[26] 'Works and Days', in *Hesiod: The Poems and Fragments*, ed. and trans. A.W. Mair (Oxford, 1908), p. 12. On the possible influence of Hesiod upon Tusser, see James Davies, *Hesiod and Theognis* (Philadelphia, 1880), pp. 118–25.

[27] *The Book of Husbandry, by Master Fitzherbert*, ed. Walter W. Skeat (London, 1882), attributes the authorship to Sir Anthony Fitzherbert, Justice of Common Pleas. This attribution has been corrected by F.L. Boersma in *Law Library Journal*, 71 (1978), 387–400.

classical georgic authors, who had written works which appeared to be everyday agricultural books in order to teach the duties of farming and the value of simple, industrious living to aristocratic men who had retired from the army or politics and wished to become gentleman farmers. Thus, Fitzherbert began his book with a discussion of ploughs which was of interest primarily to a man who had never used one, incorporated a good deal of Latin into his 'simple text', and included a section entitled 'A Short Information for a Young Gentleman that Intendeth to Thrive', which told the gentleman to spend a good deal of time making sure his steward and tenants were farming his land correctly.[28] And although Tusser's doggerel verse and the relative scarcity of his Latin maxims give the impression that he is appealing to simple men, this is in large part a pose. For the book is dedicated to Lord William Paget in a poem whose initial letters spell 'Thomas Tusser Made Me'; one of its concluding poems is another attempt at university wit in which every word begins with a 'T'. And the advice between the two poems, while it is practical (in the best tradition of Cato and Varro), is for the most part far too elementary to appeal to a working husbandman – even if he could read it. Similarly, the portion of the work which treats 'Good Housewivery' is dedicated to Lady Paget and teaches the 'thrifty housewife' to manage a large household of servants and be sure that her son gets a proper musical education when he grows up.[29] Tusser's belief in the value of simple country life is not a pose; his dedication to farming rings true and may very well have led to his interest in georgic poetry. The popularity of his book (and its twenty editions made it one of the fifteen most popular books in Elizabethan England) is probably attributable to his sincerity as well as to his classical imitation or his agricultural advice. But while the book may have appealed to yeomen and town dwellers nostalgic for the rhythms of rural life, it was written primarily for gentlemen who had been introduced to the classical virtues of diligence, simplicity, and frugality in grammar school and found the application of these virtues to English agriculture amusing and instructive.

John Browne's *Merchant's Avizo* (1589), like Tusser's georgic,

---

[28] *Ibid.*, pp. 9–13, 90–3.
[29] Tusser, *Five Hundred Pointes of Good Husbandry*, ed. W. Payne and S.J. Herrtage (London, 1878), pp. 5, 137, 168–79, 185–6. 'Thrift' in Tusser's poem usually means 'thriving', not 'frugality'.

antedates the published sermons of Greenham, Perkins and Smith. But it was printed after the appearance of Babington's popular treatises and Dent's *Sermon of Repentance*, and so it could easily have been affected by the early works in the Puritan tradition. The book is mainly a practical treatise for factors on their first trips abroad; it teaches these 'young beginners' how to make out bills, bonds, receipts and other forms properly and instructs them in writing informative letters to their masters and other merchants. It also, however, tells the young merchant how to conduct himself; here, if anywhere, one can expect to see how the doctrine of the calling could be used to mould a diligent capitalist. And the work ethic is readily apparent: Browne tells the young merchant to work diligently, bargain carefully, keep his dealings to himself while watching the transactions of more-experienced merchants intently, be scrupulously honest in his trading, and exercise his discretion in the 'small adventures' he is enabled to make in his own behalf. He is also to pray, mindful that if he remembers his 'duty and service to God, all things shall go well' for him.[30]

Out of context, this sounds very bourgeois. But what *is* the context? The moral passages in *The Merchant's Avizo* are not influenced so much by the Puritan sermon as they are by the aristocratic tradition of 'advice to a son'. And Browne consciously adopted this tradition; he ended his manual with a short fable about a young lion who comes to grief because he has not taken his experienced father's advice, not with a little treatise on the value of merchants to the commonwealth.[31] And thus – without questioning Browne's assumption that the young factor is not being sent abroad to *lose* his master's money – Browne's moral instruction is not so much concerned with the profit of the merchant as with the proper deportment of the man. The opening letter reminds the young factor repeatedly that he is an inexperienced subordinate who is shouldering important responsibilities for the first time. As an impression-

---

[30] *The Merchants Avizo*, pp. 9–12.

[31] *Ibid.*, pp. 57–9. It seems that Browne originally composed the *Avizo* for his son, so the tradition he used is entirely appropriate to the work (p. xiv). The *Avizo* begins with a poem which says that merchants are of great use to the commonwealth (p. 5). But the poem was written shortly after Bristol and the rest of the west country had been hard hit by the commercial crisis of 1586–7; it makes a plea for peaceable trade by showing that great unemployment will result from the interruption of merchants' business. In later editions, Browne added an explanatory note to the poem; he did not, apparently, feel that he could say trade was so important without explaining why he had originally done so (see pp. x–xii, and p. 60, n. 6).

able youth in Papist Spain, he is to worship God frequently with familiar Protestant prayers. He is to remember that he is on his master's business, not his own; and therefore he must take care to report his dealings to his master as quickly as possible and not exercise too much initiative in buying commodities other than those he was sent for. He must rely on the advice of senior merchants and show them great respect. He must be 'lowly and courteous' to the Spaniards; he must be particularly careful not to take offence if he is insulted by 'the rude and common sort of people'. He is not, in short, to be a swaggering, chauvinistic sea-dog, but a tactful, courteous youth who learns and respects the 'civil laws and customs' of the country in which he is a visitor. His good manners, discretion, diligence and respect for his elders may make him a good merchant; but Browne does not encourage him to be virtuous by telling him his good conduct will gain him customers and make him rich. Unlike Lord Burleigh, who in 1584 told his son Robert to be 'humble yet generous' to his superiors because such action 'prepares a way to advancement', Browne tells his young man to be courteous and thoughtful mainly because rude, thoughtless young men are objectionable.[32]

In fact, much of the advice in Browne's 'Godly Sentences Necessary for a Youth to Meditate Upon' is very like the advice in Burleigh's more famous 'Certain Precepts for the Well Ordering of a Man's Life', although one is obviously written for a merchant and the other for a courtier. Browne tells his young merchant to keep close tally on his expenses and shun the company of high-living, hard-drinking men and loose women; Burleigh gives Robert the same advice.[33] Browne tells his merchant to pay attention to the prices of the commodities he buys; Burleigh informs that 'there may be a penny in four saved betwixt buying at thy need or when the market and seasons serve fittest for it'.[34] And both Browne and Burleigh instruct their young men never to stand as surety for a friend in debt.[35] Neither Browne nor Burleigh is uninterested in the success of the youth he advises – the whole purpose of advising a son, after all, is to give him some moral ballast in the early voyages of his career so that his later voyages may bring him great rewards.

---

[32]*Merchants Avizo*, pp. 9–12; 'Certain Precepts for the Well Ordering of A Man's Life' (c. 1584), by William Cecil, Lord Burghley, in *Advice to a Son*, p. 12.
[33]*Merchants Avizo*, pp. 10–11, 56; *Advice*, pp. 10–11.
[34]*Merchants Avizo*, p. 10; *Advice*, p. 11.   [35]*Merchants Avizo*, p. 55; *Advice*, p. 12.

But both the experienced courtier and the experienced merchant know that a man who does not diligently attend to his responsibilities, a man who wastes his money and ruins his health in lewd living, and a man who does not pattern his behaviour on the example of the wise and experienced men in his profession will not succeed in that profession. Diligence and thrift, in the context of advices to sons, are not virtues which distinguish capitalistic merchants from feudal courtiers; they are two of the many virtues which are shared by all competent, responsible men of dignity.

Let us look further at the popularizations of Puritan morality as they appeared in the works of two secular Elizabethan authors who wrote in the late 1590s and were probably influenced (if only informally) by the late Elizabethan Puritan tradition. If Hill is right, 'good bourgeois' writers like Thomas Heywood and Thomas Deloney should see through the Puritans' 'traditional' injunctions against the pursuit of abundant wealth and present us with heroes whose diligent, thrifty accumulation of money is a great virtue. Now, we do find 'bourgeois' heroes in Heywood's plays and Deloney's fiction. We find poor boys who become dazzlingly wealthy overnight; we find merchants who are rich enough to buy jewels that princes cannot afford. But are these men examples of virtuous industry?

A glance at Heywood's plays reveals that his bourgeois heroes are not praised for virtues which earn them money. Look, for example, at John Crosby, the lord mayor in *1 Edward IV*. He has all the earmarks of a poor boy who has made good. He was a foundling, raised in a London hospital, apprenticed to the Grocers' Company; during the course of his business career, he rose to become lord mayor of London. This kind of spectacular success might inspire praise of the diligence with which Crosby climbed the London ladder to prosperity and status. But we hear no such praise. Crosby's whole business career is summarized in one line, spoken by himself: 'God pleased to bless my poor endeavours.' And Crosby is actually proud of his diligence as a rich man, not his industrious rise to wealth:

> The man that found me I have well requited,
> And to the Hospital, my fostering place,
> An hundred pound a year I give for ever.

> Likewise, in memory of me, John Crosby,
> In Bishopgate Street, a poor House have I built,
> And as my name have called it Crosby House.[36]

The diligence and thrift which have earned Crosby his fortune are ignored; Heywood chooses to portray his generosity in making us aware that the mayor is a virtuous merchant.

The hero of a later Heywood play, *2 If You Know Not Me, You Know Nobody* (1605) is the merchant prince Thomas Gresham. In the opening lines of the play, Gresham's factor and another merchant remark that Gresham's 'Care how to get, and forecast to increase' are 'especial virtues, being clear / From base extortion'. But this is the last the audience hears of diligence and thrift; Heywood in fact asks us to admire Gresham's ability to spend, even to lose, money. In the course of the play, Gresham loses £60,000 in a risky business venture; Heywood asks that we admire the casual lack of concern with which the merchant receives the news. Heywood also insists that Gresham can make extravagant gestures in the best tradition of aristocratic conspicuous expenditure: when the merchant gives a banquet for the Russian Ambassador, he buys a pearl for £1500, smashes it, mixes it with his wine, and drinks it as a toast to Queen Elizabeth.[37] Nothing further from thrift could be imagined. In parading Gresham's virtues, Heywood's chief concern is to let his audience know that the merchant is not greedy or miserly; he has money, and he knows how to spend it with cultured display.[38]

Heywood does not suggest that Gresham spends all his money in expensive gestures. A great deal of the play is concerned to praise Gresham's role in founding that most capitalistic of institutions, the Royal Exchange. But while we might expect to hear that the Exchange will enhance English trade, Heywood does not present it in these terms. Gresham first vows to build some sort of Exchange because he gets caught in the rain on Lombard Street, where merchants usually discuss their transactions; he finds it annoying that 'a famous city as this is' should have no place where merchants can

[36]Heywood, I, 57.   [37]*Ibid.*, I, 251, 300, 301.

[38]Gresham is not the only merchant in Elizabethan literature who is praised for spending money extravagantly. In Henry Robarts' *Haigh for Devonshire* (London, 1600), the factor of William, one of the 'six gallant Merchants of Devonshire', is praised for losing all his master's money by gambling with a Spanish duke who wants to test the courage of Englishmen (Chapter XVII).

meet when it rains. The idea takes firmer shape in his mind when he sees pictures of London dignitaries in the gallery at the Dean of St Paul's house. These men have given hospitals, schools, poor-houses and water conduits to the city; as he looks at their portraits, Gresham regrets his lack of generosity:

> We that are citizens, are rich as they were,
> Behold their charity in every street,
> Churches for prayer, alms-houses for the poor,
> Conduits which bring us water; all which good
> We do see, and are relieved withall,
> And yet we live like beasts, spend time and die,
> Leaving no good to be remembered by.[39]

The alternative to 'living like a beast' is participating in the tradition of loyal London citizens. But this is a tradition of charitable expenditure, not diligent acquisition. The Exchange is not presented as a mercantile investment which will enrich the city; it is presented as a contribution to the comfort of Londoners and their guests. Like water-conduits, gates and libraries, the Royal Exchange exhibits the diligent expenditure of wealthy philanthropists.

Heywood, then, presents his audience with self-made men and rich merchants, but he ignores the means by which they have become wealthy. The ability to work hard, to make a shrewd investment, is not a virtue in Heywood's eyes. It is in using money well, not in making it industriously, that the playwright's heroes prove themselves virtuous, and using money well involves engaging in charitable activities and gestures of loyalty which are far from thrifty. The 'spirit of capitalism' is simply not present in Heywood's plays.

We may turn to the fiction of Thomas Deloney with more hope of finding the industrious hero we are looking for. Among modern scholars, Deloney is known as an 'apologist for the middle class'. His heroes are clothiers and shoemakers, and many of them become rich before our very eyes, for Deloney does not ignore the process of becoming wealthy. Deloney's presentation of his most familiar poor-boy-made-good hero, Jack of Newbury, has led Herbert Donow to say that the author has 'unquestioning respect for the successful efforts of men to become wealthy'. It has led Max Dorsin-

[39] Heywood, I, 268, 277.

ville to argue that Jack is 'the epitome of the rising Elizabethan mercantile class that wishes to counter-balance the power of the courtiers'.[40] But a careful reading of Deloney's works reveals many episodes which cast doubt upon the belief that Deloney praises entrepreneurs on the make. He recognizes the spirit of capitalism to be sure, but he presents it with a wry humour, not with approval.

The man for whom Deloney expresses the most unqualified admiration is Jack of Newbury, the hero of his first book. As a youth, Jack is 'of merry disposition, and honest conversation'; although he never drinks to excess, he is such a pleasant fellow that he receives the 'good estimation' of all and becomes 'every Gentleman's companion'. But even as a drinking companion, Jack is thrifty; he limits his beer expenditure to a shilling a week, and when it is spent, he leaves, reminding his companions 'twelve pence a Sunday being spent in good cheer / To fifty-two shillings amounts in the year'. Jack is also diligent. His mistress, noting how careful a man he is, commits to him the 'guiding of all her work-folks' when her husband dies, and he handles his obligations with such scrupulous care that her business prospers.

Jack's diligence and thrift serve him well – but not because they make him rich. His virtues bring him to the attention of people in a position to better his condition; Deloney thinks in terms of preferment, not self-made men: 'Thus was Jack's good government and discretion noted of the best and substantialest men of the Town: so that it wrought his great commendations, and his Dame thought herself not a little blessed to have such a servant, that was so obedient to her, and so careful of her profit.' Jack's mistress, seeing that he is attentive to her 'profit' and obedient to her as a good servant should be, decides that a man with such virtues might be a good investment as a husband. The decision is hers, and so is the courtship. Jack is completely passive in the matter, even though he is well aware (being a good businessman) of the convenience of being provided with 'a house ready furnished, servants ready taught, and all other things for his trade necessary'.[41] His mistress is his superior both in rank and in age; Jack decides that a marriage

[40] Meritt Lawlis, *Apology for the Middle Class: the Dramatic Novels of Thomas Deloney* (Bloomington, 1960); Herbert Donow, 'Thomas Deloney and Thomas Heywood: Two Views of the Elizabethan Merchant', Unpublished Ph.D. thesis, University of Iowa, 1966, p. 36; Dorsinville, 'Design in *Jack of Newbury*', p. 236.
[41] Deloney, *Works*, pp. 3–4, 8.

between them might not be a happy one. The mistress, however, plays the role of entrepreneur as she prepares to invest permanently in Jack's virtues. She wastes no time in striking the bargain: on a frosty night she crawls into his bed to warm her feet, and the next day she leads him to the altar and marries him.

The gentle bawdiness of the tale of courtship should not distract us from seeing how its humour enables Deloney to present Jack's rise to wealth. It puts Jack in the position of a man who is not at all aggressive when a clear chance for financial gain presents itself to him. He, like Perkins' ideal man, does not labour diligently to get rich; he is merely a 'kind young man', who, when he has wealth thrust upon him, will 'not say her nay'. Jack works hard, but he is not an entrepreneur; his virtue, by bringing him to the attention of his mistress, allows him to become rich, but it does not make him rich. In the opening chapters of *Jack of Newbury*, Deloney has portrayed Jack as a virtuous man who has become wealthy demonstrably through no effort of his own; he can then spend the rest of the book showing how justly Jack employs his virtuously acquired riches.[42]

In his next novel, *The Gentle Craft, Part I*, Deloney tries to treat Simon Eyre's rise to wealth and power in the same way he treated Jack's. Eyre is a diligent shoemaker; other heroes of his ilk in *The Gentle Craft* become wealthy because the king notices their good work and makes them his private shoemakers. Eyre, however, does not have to wait for this kind of recognition, for he hears from his journeyman that a great ship full of rare merchandise has been driven to shore and its merchant owner is willing to sell the cargo for whatever he can get. Eyre, well aware of the benefits to be had from buying the cargo of a ship at a low price, discusses his wish to buy it with his wife. In the discussion, the differences between Eyre and his wife emerge. When she hears that the ship could yield at least double profit on the investment, she 'was inflamed with the desire thereof, as women are (for the most part) very covetous: that matter running still in her mind, she could scant find in her heart to spare

---

[42] *Ibid.*, p. 15. Kurt-Michael Pätzold has pointed out that none of the characters who rise to social prominence in *Jack of Newbury* do so because of their diligence and thrift: Randoll Pert, the children in Jack's 'factory', and the maid Joan all 'make good' because of the generosity of their social superiors. *Historischer Roman und Realismus Das Erzählwerk Thomas Deloney*, Sprach und Literatur: Regensburger Arbeiten zur Anglistik und Amerikanistik (Regensberg, 1972), pp. 62–3.

him time to go to supper, for very eagerness to animate him on, to take that bargain upon him'. When they have eaten ('and given God thanks'), she encourages him to bargain for the whole community. He, it seems, thinks he cannot do it because he cannot raise a proper down-payment. But she sees the possibilities of the situation with the practised eye of an entrepreneur and outlines a plan to her husband which is shrewd and likely to work, albeit of questionable morality. Eyre, dressed as a shoemaker, will meet the merchant and bargain for the cargo, pretending to act on behalf of a rich alderman. He will leave his small down-payment with the merchant, promising the alderman will give him a bill for the rest. Then Eyre will dress as an alderman, meet the merchant, give him the bill, and take possession of the commodity. He will then sell the goods for enough to repay the merchant at the appointed time. The scheme will be so artfully contrived, adds Mistress Eyre, that not even their journeyman will know that Eyre is acting on his own behalf and not that of the alderman – but Eyre must be careful not to leave his name in writing.[43] The plan is executed as she outlines it, and Eyre, like Jack of Newbury, starts on the pathway to virtuous wealth.

By attributing all the ingenuity to Mistress Eyre, Deloney can celebrate Eyre's later achievements as a wise, just and charitable rich man without having had to portray him at first as an entrepreneur who has sullied himself by conjuring up a questionably honest business deal. The plan is laid at the feet of Mistress Eyre; its naked capitalistic shrewdness is decently covered by attributing it to a failing in womankind: covetousness. Eyre conveniently remains unaware of the business aspects of his fortune; to him, the ship has come because of God's grace. Mistress Eyre is not so humble. After she and Eyre have been entertained by the lord mayor and that dignitary has said jestingly that a man as rich as Eyre should be mayor, Mistress Eyre comments to her husband:

> Yea (thought I) he may thank his wife for that,
>   if it comes so to pass.
> Nay (said Simon) I thank God for it.
> Yea, and next him you may thank me (quoth she).

She is quite right, of course. But her lack of piety and her inability to sit back and let God shed his blessings upon her are, in Deloney's

---

[43] Deloney, *Works*, pp. 113–15.

eyes, faults, not virtues; they make her the weaker member of the partnership. Eyre's attitude toward his 'gift' is the proper one: he is concerned to give God 'eternal praise' for his success, and he humbly hopes that he may dispose of his money 'as may be to [God's] honour, and the comfort of his poor members on earth'.[44] And Eyre is diligent in his calling as a rich man: he is a good master to his servants, he gives a feast for all the apprentices in London, he founds Leaden Hall, and he serves the city first as sheriff, then as lord mayor.

And yet, there is considerable tension in Deloney's portrait of Eyre and his wife. The Puritans' ideal of the godly rich man is clearly visible, but so is the beginning of the spirit of capitalism. Mistress Eyre, in her covetousness, may design the scheme by which her husband becomes rich, but it is Eyre who carries it out. And while Deloney does not approve of Mistress Eyre's feminine greed, it is quite clear that her business sense is necessary to Eyre's success. It is possible that the entrepreneurial aspect of Eyre's rise disturbed Deloney. Between the chapter in which Mistress Eyre outlines her plan and the ensuing chapter, there is a strange break: the chapter which should present Eyre's dealing with the merchant and his invitation to the lord mayor's banquet is left out. This leaves the story oddly unfinished; and the omission suggests that Deloney did not know how to deal with the problem he had raised.[45]

Having approached a recognition of the spirit of capitalism, Deloney investigates the possibilities of gaining wealth still further in his next work. The hero of the first story in *The Gentle Craft, Part II* is Richard Casteler, the only one of Deloney's characters whose wealth cannot be attributed to God's mercy or his wife's aggression. Unlike Jack of Newbury, Casteler is the epitome of ambitious industry: 'The lovely Maidens of the City of Westminster, noting what a good husband Richard Casteler was and seeing how

---

[44] *Ibid.*, pp. 117, 121.

[45] Pätzold maintains that Eyre's story, like Jack's, indicates that Deloney does not think diligence is enough to make a man wealthy (*Historischer Roman*, pp, 64–5). But he does not say that Eyre is very nearly an entrepreneur, while Jack is not. When Dekker adopted Eyre's story in *The Shoemakers' Holiday*, he followed Deloney in making the transaction by which Eyre rises very vague. The audience knows Eyre will get a good deal on the ship and it sees Eyre put on fine clothes before talking to the merchant, but there is nothing in the play which suggests Eyre's transaction will be questionably honest. Dekker treats the whole episode without considering its entrepreneurial aspects. See *The Shoemakers' Holiday*, II, iii.

diligently he followed his business, judged in the end he would prove a rich man: for which cause may bore unto him a very good affection, and few there was that wished not themselves to be his wife.'[46] It is not altogether clear, however, that Deloney approves of Casteler's diligence; we must remember Deloney's attitude toward women who see a sure gain in sight. Deloney does not himself indulge in praising Casteler; he merely points out that the man's ambition wins him the admiration of Mistress Eyre's spiritual sisters in Westminster. The emphasis in the opening paragraphs of the story is not on Casteler but on the 'lovely Maidens' who wink at him in church, curtsey to him in his shop, give him flowers, and stand in their doorways watching him pass while they decide he is bound to be very wealthy since he is so 'wise and thrifty'. Here again, Deloney is laughing at the aggression and covetousness of womankind.

The smiles of the lovely maidens prepare us for another of Deloney's tales in which love and business are happily united. But in this story, Deloney treats fruitful marriage and devotion to business as being mutually exclusive. The plot concerns the industrious Richard's courtship by (not of) two Westminster maidens, Gillian of the George and Long Meg of Westminster. Gillian is an entrepreneur; she wants to marry Richard because he is a good businessman and is sure to be rich. She is, in fact, so sure that he is the best investment she can make that she has refused another man who is 'wealthy, and therewithall of very good conversation'. Meg, on the other hand, wants to share with Richard a life of good food, good wine, and abundant amorous delight. The ideal husband, as she describes him, is one who saves the best morsels of meat for his wife and spends the hours after supper 'fetching many stealing touches at her ruby lips', until, when he hears the clock strike eight, he calls her to bed for a sweet night of pleasure.[47]

Richard, the object of these affections, is known to be 'mightily addicted to the getting of money'. His diligence is proverbial: he is known as the 'cock of Westminster' because he rises at four in the morning to be at work. It is also known that he does not shut his shop until ten or eleven at night. This industrious man is courteous to Meg and Gillian when they visit him, but his heart is obviously not

---

[46] Deloney, *Works*, p. 141. Wright quotes this passage to show that Deloney's approval of diligence and thrift is unqualified (*Middle-Class Culture*, p. 190).
[47] Deloney, *Works*, pp. 143–5.

in the courtship. When they have left his shop, he expresses annoyance at the loss of his working time: 'here is a forenoon spent to no purpose, and all by means of a couple of giglets, that have greater desire to be playing with a man than to be mindful to follow their business: but if I live, I will suddenly avoid both their delights and their loves.'[48] Richard's coldness is in part a result of his distaste for the forwardness of Meg and Gillian. But Deloney repeatedly suggests that his rejection, especially of Meg, is expressive of the same nature that makes him so passionately devoted to his work: a nature in which something is missing.

In suggesting that Richard is a little imperfect in some way, Deloney takes advantage of the sexual undertones of Richard's nickname. Meg, for example, tells Gillian that she fears 'though he be a Cock by name, he will never prove a Cock of the game'. And later, after Richard has married a coy but industrious Dutch girl, Meg reflects again on the possible connections between his working habits and his lack of virility:

> by this good day I am glad I have 'scaped him, for I do now consider I should have never took rest after four o'clock in the morning, and alas, a young married wife would be loath to rise before eight or nine: beside that I should never have gone to bed before ten or eleven, or twelve o'clock by that means, what a deal of time should I have lost above other women: have him quoth you? now God bless me, I swear by Venus, the fair goddess of sweet love, in the mind I am in, I would not have him, if he had so much as would lie in Westminster Hall.[49]

This is certainly sour grapes; but Meg's suspicions are confirmed by Richard's matrimonial failings. Three years after Richard's wedding, his journeyman Robin teases him because he has no children. The ensuing dialogue, again playing on the implications of Richard's nickname, relates his childlessness to his diligence:

> Hold thy peace (quoth Richard) all this while I have but jested, but when I fall once in earnest, thou shalt see her belly will rise like a Tun of New Ale, thou knowst I am the Cock of Westminster.
>
> Aye (quoth Robin) you had that name,
> More for your rising, than your goodness in Venus' game.

Everybody laughs, but Deloney adds that the joke was remembered

---

[48] *Ibid.*, p. 152.   [49] *Ibid.*, pp. 145, 162.

for seven years after, for the Castelers remained childless:

> Therefore Robin would often say, that either his Master was no perfect Man, or else his Mistress was in her infancy nourished with the milk of a Mule, which bred such barrenness in her.[50]

The marriage of Richard and his pretty Dutch wife is sterile. We do not know who is at fault, and we certainly do not have to believe (as Meg implies) that Richard works so hard he has no time for amorous delights. Whatever connection there is between his childlessness and his working is much more subtle. Richard is never openly condemned for working hard; Deloney says at the end of the tale that Richard is generous to the poor throughout his life and at his death. This, however, is an afterthought, and Deloney never relates the increase of Richard's wealth to the increase of his responsibilities – he merely relates his diligence to his empty house. The implication is that there is something a little wrong with a man who is so 'mightily addicted to the getting of money' that he labours twenty hours out of twenty-four. Instead of using his Poor Richard's example to inculcate 'Industry and Frugality, as the Means of procuring Wealth, and thereby securing Virtue', Deloney relates Casteler's gain to his spiritual and sensual loss.[51]

Having thus turned away from the capitalistic implications of his presentation of Eyre, Deloney stops experimenting with ways of reconciling gain and accepted morality. In his last novel, *Thomas of Reading*, he retreats to the technique of Heywood, ignoring his heroes' acquisition of money entirely and talking only of the charitable ways they spend it. Far from using the preachers' approval of abundant wealth and diligent work as a doctrine which encourages poor boys to make good, Deloney uses Puritan morality as a retreat from the spirit of capitalism. The ideal of the diligent rich man allows him, as it allowed the Puritan preachers, to ignore the problem of money-making and praise the spirit of charity, liberality and social duty.

What is interesting about Deloney is that he comes very close to considering the spirit of diligent acquisition independently from the spirit of the diligent, godly rich man, but then turns away from the possibility. Finally, he admires poor boys *made* good, but not poor boys who *make themselves* good. The capitalistic spirit as he pre-

[50] *Ibid.*, p. 170.
[51] *The Autobiography of Benjamin Franklin*, ed. Leonard W. Labaree, *et al.* (New Haven and London, 1964), p. 164.

sents it in *Jack of Newbury* and the two parts of *The Gentle Craft* is not a virtue, but a flaw. The diligent pursuit of money is narrowing. It may be acceptable in a woman, but women are by nature narrow already; even the best of them think of nothing but financial security, social status and love (in that order), so a talented woman loses little of her attractiveness by being eager to accumulate material things. But devotion to making money is certainly not a good trait in a man, for men should be involved in the serious concerns of life: feeding the poor, caring for servants, filling public offices, defending the realm. The diligent man who has his priorities in order will keep his weaker half under control and leave covetousness, as he leaves courtship, to attractive, entrepreneurial women. Thus, while Deloney, like the Puritans, thinks that wealth is not necessarily evil, he does not think the good that can be done by wealthy men justifies 'seeking and moiling' after gain. In his reluctance to approve the spirit of capitalism, he assigns it, as he would certainly have assigned the first bite of the forbidden fruit, to the sex that caused the Fall.

It is clear, then, that while lessons in diligence and thrift did appear in many different types of Elizabethan popular literature, these virtues were not yet presented as the special attributes of businessmen. There was nothing in the doctrine the Puritans preached that came as a surprise to gentlemen schooled in the classical georgic tradition, with its appreciation of simplicity, hard work and frugality. Nor was there anything in the doctrine of the calling which made aristocrats think again about the values of *The Governor*. Diligence and thrift in the sixteenth century were simply two among many virtues in which the more responsible members of the elite believed; the others were charity, hospitality, courtesy, liberality, temperance, social duty and justice. The collective name for all these virtues was not 'the spirit of capitalism', but 'greatspiritedness' – magnanimity. And if Deloney, Heywood, Dekker and the lesser writers who celebrated businessmen applied the virtues of diligence and thrift to their heroes, they applied them along with the other virtues which were, as yet, inextricably linked with them. It was not until the late seventeenth century that the authors who wrote about men of trade selected out the virtues of diligence and thrift as the remnant of the aristocratic code which businessmen had retained and the elite had thrown away.

How different the sixteenth-century connotation of godly diligence is from the entrepreneurial ideal of the post-Restoration period can be seen if one compares Jack of Newbury, Simon Eyre, or even the young factor addressed in *The Merchant's Avizo* to the capitalists Defoe and Steele described in the early eighteenth century. When Defoe described the opportunities open to a merchant, magnanimity was far from his mind:

A Merchant, or perhaps a Man of a meaner Employ thrives by his honest Industry, Frugality, and a long series of diligent Application to Business, and being grown immensely rich, he marries his daughters to Gentlemen of the first Quality, perhaps a Coronet; then he leaves the Bulk of his Estate to his Heir, and he gets into the Rank of the Peerage; does the next Age make any scruple of their Blood, being thus mixed with the ancient Race?[52]

This is the spirit of capitalism. To Defoe, wealth is the goal of a man's diligence. Making a great deal of money by working hard is commendable (so long as the industry with which it is sought is 'honest'). And the attainment of wealth is not linked with social responsibility, but with comfort and prestige. The merchant who becomes wealthy enough to marry his daughters to gentlemen may leave a large estate to his heir; but he leaves to his class a legacy of diligence, frugality and ambition.

Steele, writing in 1711, suggested that the ideal of diligence and thrift separated merchants from gentlemen, even though 'the Trader is fed by the Product of the Land, and the landed Man cannot be clothed but by the Skill of the Trader'. In an amiable argument at Mr Spectator's Club, the Baronet Sir Roger De Coverly insists that nobility cannot be found in trading people, for they are interested only in gain. This interest makes them dishonest at worst, and small-minded at best:

what can there great and noble be expected from him whose Attention is for ever fixed upon ballancing his Books, and watching over his Expenses? And at best, let Frugality and Parsimony be the Virtues of the Merchant, how much is his punctual Dealing below a Gentleman's Charity to the Poor, or Hospitality among his neighbours?

Sir Andrew Freeport, a merchant, takes exception to Sir Roger's remarks. Even leaving aside the great charities which merchants

---

[52] *A Plan of the English Commerce*, p. 9.

have engaged in since the Reformation, he says, and allowing parsimony and frugality to be the only virtues of merchants, parsimony as merchants practise it is superior to hospitality as gentlemen engage in it:

> If to drink so many Hogsheads is to be hospitable, we do not contend for the Fame of that Virtue; but it would be worth while to consider, whether so many Artificers at work ten Days together by my Appointment, or so many Peasants made merry on Sir Roger's Charge, are the Men more obliged; I believe the Families of the Artificers will thank me, more than the Households of the Peasants shall Sir Roger. Sir Roger gives to his men, but I place mine above the Necessity or Obligation of my Bounty.[53]

And, he continues, as to keeping careful accounts, if gentlemen took care of the money they waste on horses and hounds and watched closely over the economy of their estates, they would never have to sully their blood by marrying into the families of merchants who got wealthy by working industriously and poring over their cashbooks.

To Steele and Defoe, the essential virtues of a good man are industry, frugality and attention to business. Men of the moneyed interest have these virtues, and hence they succeed in their endeavours. Gentlemen waste their money on 'charity' which does not help the poor in the long run, and 'hospitality' which consists of extravagant pursuit of pleasure with friends. Insofar as Steele and Defoe argue that diligence, thrift and attention to one's affairs are virtues which all men should adopt, they say nothing that Elizabethan authors would deny. But the context of their remarks is foreign to Elizabethan social sensibilities, for the virtues Defoe and Steele praise have been divorced from the 'aristocratic' virtues they used to accompany. Diligent, thrifty men of the moneyed interest oppose the idleness and extravagance of the elite; gentlemen look down on diligence and thrift because these virtues are associated with men of trade. The elite and the bourgeoisie have different value systems in the early eighteenth century; in the sixteenth century, they did not.

One cannot argue, then, that the 'spirit of capitalism' which

---

[53] *The Spectator*, ed. Donald F. Bond (5 vols.; Oxford, 1965), II, 186–7.

Tawney identified in post-Restoration literature was present in Elizabethan England. There were, of course, great fortunes made during Elizabeth's reign, and many of them were made by merchants. Harrison, in defining 'citizens', remarked upon the 'mutual conversion' of merchants and gentlemen in the sixteenth century as Defoe and Steele did in the eighteenth. But whatever the facts of capitalism, the *spirit* of capitalism – the sense that making oneself rich by working long hours at a profitable trade was something to be proud of, the idea that money-making could be carried on for the greater glory of God – was not even articulated, let alone familiar. The idea that a man of trade could make a fortune with the expressed ambition of joining the other men of his class who were wealthy enough to buy out most of the gentlemen in the kingdom was unheard of. The suggestion that attention to business accounts was a greater virtue than bravery, hospitality, magnificence and courtesy was unthinkable. And the idea that merchants could be superior to gentlemen in character because they made money while gentlemen simply lived on their rent-rolls was social heresy.

The social perceptions in the works of Elizabethan popular authors suggests, then, that the study of social developments of the seventeenth century should not begin with the premise that there was little self-consciousness among principal citizens until there were bourgeois values to bind this group together. It should instead begin with the realization that in the early seventeenth century, bourgeois pride was expressed in terms of the values of the elite, and by the end of the seventeenth century it was expressed in terms of the values of the middle class. The Elizabethan expression of merchant pride asserted that merchants participated in the traditions of the elite and argued that the gentry and aristocracy did not have a monopoly on political talent, wealth, historical service and social self-consciousness. But the very words in which the authors made their argument suggest that the elite still had an unchallenged monopoly on one precious commodity – a social ideology which even the most bourgeois authors believed to be the only one thinkable. The later consciousness, on the other hand, separated the values which could enable men to make money from the other values of the elite; it challenged the assumption that making money was less dignified than spending money, and it implicitly questioned the elite's monopoly on both power and values. Though the first consciousness developed into the second, they are fundamentally different if they are examined side by side.

It is beyond the scope of this work to say when the change in values occurred. Tentatively, however, it seems possible that the English Revolution was a precondition for, not a product of, this shift. The London oligarchy which remained loyal to Charles I almost to the eve of the Civil War, for example, was composed of men whose political consciousness was recognizably like that of the citizens in *1 Edward IV* or *The Nine Worthies of London*.[54] But the consciousness of the men of 'the moneyed interest' in the late seventeenth century was different from the one celebrated in Elizabethan England, for it was based on the idea that merchants were different from the aristocracy and the gentry. The social turmoil of the Civil War and the years that followed it may very well have precipitated the shift in values to which Deloney looked forward but which he could not clearly articulate.

Be that as it may, the Elizabethan expression of social consciousness in merchants is interesting in its own right, for it suggests that the values which we anachronistically assume to be bourgeois were once integral parts of the value system of the elite. It is difficult to grasp the sensibility of an Elizabethan author who cannot praise Jack of Newbury without making him act like a lord, or praise William Walworth without making him act like a knight. But that very difficulty should serve as a reminder that the context of Elizabethan social thought was different from that of later centuries. Even Elizabethan authors who engaged in trade, like Thomas Deloney or John Browne, could not praise a man for being diligent without considering him in the context of aristocratic virtues. And although Deloney could see (or perhaps merely sense) that the businessman did not fit into this context, he could not separate the values of his clothier from the other values of traditional society. If the historian can feel the distance between the groping consciousness of Deloney and the clearly articulated position of Steele, he can appreciate the anxieties and antagonisms which the change in social ideology thrust upon both gentlemen and merchants in the seventeenth century.

[54] Pearl, *London and Revolution*, Chapters III and IV.

Part III

The gentle craftsman

8. *Clown and rebel: the craftsman as one of 'the fourth sort of people'*

The popular authors who celebrated the achievements of merchants also wrote about lesser men of trade – craftsmen, journeymen, and apprentices. This is not surprising; there were many more craftsmen, journeymen and apprentices in Elizabethan England than there were merchants and rich clothiers, and the men who migrated to London and provincial towns in search of work, whatever their aspirations, were of this low commercial status (if in fact they were not merely unskilled rural labourers). The popular authors could attract an audience of these men by focussing their dreams of success – telling them how great merchants had once been poor men like themselves. Still, few apprentices and craftsmen could actually hope to rise to such economic heights, so the authors wisely balanced their stories of poor boys made good with others that asserted the innate worthiness of lesser men of trade who became neither rich nor famous.

When they approached craftsmen, the authors encountered a sociological problem rather different from the one they had faced in their stories about merchants. Merchants, as principal citizens, had a social position 'next place to gentry', formed one of the four major social groups of the hierarchy, and had a tradition of leadership which, along with the apocryphal tales of their wealth, could be used readily by authors who wished to replace the negative stereotype of the merchant as usurer. Craftsmen, however, had no such tradition; they were not the men by whom history was made. In society at large, in towns and in trading companies, they were inferior to merchants in status and power, and while they occasionally influenced political decisions, they did not make them. Apprentices and journeymen shared this dependent status with craftsmen, but they posed a problem easier to solve. Since their positions at the bottom of companies were (in theory) temporary, their consciousness could be raised by tales that appealed to the hopes and dreams of youth.

Most master craftsmen, however, had risen as far as they couldwhen they went into trade, and as members of the 'fourth sort of people', they had no positive historical or literary tradition except that of loyalty to a gild and participation in its pageants. In a society in which gild loyalty was breaking down and mystery plays had been outlawed, the craftsman was sorely in need of a new image.

The extent of the problem facing popular authors who wanted to create this new image is immediately visible when one turns to Harrison and Smith's discussions of Elizabethan social divisions. Both authors divided the realm, in Harrison's phrase, into four 'sorts' – 'gentlemen, citizens or burgesses, yeomen, and artificers or labourers'.[1] In their detailed considerations of the four social groups, Smith and Harrison called the lowest group 'the fourth sort of people which do not rule', and they said it was composed of 'day labourers, poor husbandmen, and some retailers (which have no free land), copy holders, and all artificers, as tailors, shoemakers, carpenters, brickmakers, masons &c.'[2] The term 'artificer', then, served only to distinguish craftsmen from the other men in the lowest social group; it was not a word which, like 'gentleman', 'citizen', and 'yeoman', designated a separate social class.

The fundamental distinction in the hierarchy, as Harrison and Smith made it, lay between the three highest classes who had 'voice and authority in the commonwealth', and men in the much larger fourth group who were fit only to be ruled. This all-important line was drawn roughly at the franchise, which, as it was defined by statute (8 Henry VI, c. 7), expressly limited the right to vote to

---

[1] Holinshed, I, 263. As F.J. Furnivall points out in *Harrison's Description of England in Shakspere's Youth* (London, 1877), the 1586 version of this quotation wrongly reads 'gentlemen, citizens or burgesses, yeomen, which are artificers, or labourers' (p. 105). I have quoted the version of 1577, as Furnivall does. Smith's version of this much-quoted passage is a textual puzzle. Alston, following the 1584 version of *De Republica Anglorum*, quotes Smith's assertion that the four groups are 'gentlemen, citizens, yeomen artificers, and labourers' (p. 31). But there is no such thing as a yeoman artificer, and if one checks other editions of *De Republica Anglorum* one can see that the commas in the phrase change places from edition to edition, apparently with more interest in justifying the lines at the right side of the page than in clarifying Smith's meaning. Since all the printed versions were published after Smith's death, and the first edition states that the manuscript was full of the 'contrariety and corruption of copies' which result from 'the errors and rashness of scribes', the most sensible assumption is probably that Smith, like Harrison, divided the groups into 'gentlemen, citizens, yeomen, artificers and labourers', since these are the basic divisions he considers in detail.

[2] Holinshed, I, 274; Smith, *De Republica Anglorum*, p. 46.

freeholders of substance and excluded men of the 'fourth sort', who were prone to be disorderly at elections.[3] Since the days of Henry VI, as Harrison and Smith were well aware, inflation had blurred the line between voters and non-voters – a trend that was to have important consequences in the early seventeenth century.[4] In the late 1570s and early 1580s, however, this was still to come; Harrison and Smith simply admitted that forty-shilling freeholders were lesser men than they had been in the past, and added that despite inflation, yeomen had 'a certain pre-eminence, and more estimation than labourers and the common sort of artificers'.[5] The distinction between men who ruled and men who obeyed was, in other words, as important as the distinction between gentlemen and everybody else – the difficulties of making either distinction simply confirmed their confidence that there was one to be made.

One of the major differences between the rulers and the ruled was that among the latter exact status was unimportant. Harrison and Smith spent pages discussing the differences between dukes, earls, lords, knights and gentlemen; they spent several paragraphs on principal citizens and yeomen, carefully defining the status and political power of each group. They were unconcerned, however, with nuances in status below the rank of yeoman. While they admitted that there were some men in this group with more money and a few more responsibilities than others, they paid little attention to the consequences of this fact. An odd juxtaposition of phrases in Harrison's treatment of the 'fourth sort' typifies this attitude. Some men of this status, he says, are 'not altogether neglected' in (local) political matters:

[3] The statute opens by saying that recent elections have been attended by 'very great, outrageous, and excessive Number of People . . . of the which most part was of People of small Substance, and of no Value, whereof every one of them pretended a Voice equivalent . . . with the most worthy Knights and Esquires dwelling in the same Counties; whereby Manslaughters, Riots, Batteries, and Divisions among the Gentlemen and other People, shall very likely rise . . . ' To prevent disorders, Parliament limits the county voters to those who have free land or tenement 'to the Value of Forty Shillings by the Year at the least above all Charges' (8 Henry VI, c. 7). It is not clear that the riots can be attributed solely to the 'people of small Substance'; but it is clear that Parliament thought their removal from the scene of elections would keep the peace.

[4] On Elizabethan borough franchises, see Neale, *Elizabethan House of Commons*, Chapter XII, especially pp. 236–8. Derek Hirst discusses the widening of these franchises in *The Representative of the People?* (Cambridge, 1975), Chapters III and V.

[5] Holinshed, I, 275; Smith, *De Republica Anglorum*, p. 42.

for in cities and corporate towns, for default of yeomen they are fain to make up their inquests of such manner of people. And in villages they are commonly made church wardens, sidemen, aleconners, now and then constables, and many times enjoy the name of headboroughs. Unto this sort also may our great swarms of idle serving men be referred, of whom there runneth a proverb; Young serving men old beggars, because service is none heritage.

Harrison slips without transition from a consideration of the respectable men who become constables to a discussion of the men constables are to arrest, apparently because he sees no fundamental distinctions between men of this 'sort'. In a subsequent passage, he fails to distinguish between farmers and skilled craftsmen; he remarks that both husbandmen and artificers are good in their trades. To him, men of the fourth sort are by definition very like each other despite their differences in occupation and wealth, for they share the common political and social fate of being ruled.[6]

Many craftsmen were aptly consigned to the 'fourth sort of people', along with husbandmen, copyholders and labourers. At their lowest level, craftsmen merged with the poor, for many of them did not pay taxes and some even received poor relief. But as a social group, craftsmen actually covered a wide range of the hierarchy. At their most prosperous, they approached yeomen in wealth, and at this level they had political voice, particularly in smaller towns where the wealthiest men in the corporations were of very modest means by the standards of London, Norwich, Bristol or Exeter.[7] In London, there was a wide gap between the wealthiest craftsmen and poor artisans and independent journeymen; the wealthier craftsmen could afford to give large charitable donations to schools and loan funds, whereas few artisans could afford to make even small charitable bequests. But even in provincial towns like Leicester, there was a great difference in wealth and 'estimation' between a well-to-do weaver who owned a six-room house and was worth £67 at his death and a weaver who rented a small cottage from the corporation and was so poor that the probate officials did not even bother to survey his estate.[8]

---

[6] Holinshed, I, 275–6.
[7] Hoskins, 'Leicester', pp. 54–5 discusses the comparatively modest scale of personal estates in Leicester; on the subject of poor craftsmen, see Hirst, *Representative of the People?*, pp. 93–4.
[8] Jordan, *Charities of London*, pp. 78–82; Hoskins, 'Leicester', pp. 56–7, 62–6.

Since craftsmen covered such a broad range of the social spectrum, one would suppose that there was some term which distinguished the 'common sort of artificers' from their more-fortunate counterparts. But there was no such term. At the local level, this lack of distinction probably caused no confusion; one knew who was a master craftsman and who was not, and in the larger companies there was an important difference between liverymen and yeomen. But unlike the distinction between a yeoman and a husbandman, the difference between types of craftsmen did not find its way into general social theory. Mulcaster, for example, distinguished only between merchants and manuaries; he did not add that there were gradations of wealth and power among manuaries. And the author of the 'Apology of the City of London' in Stow's *Survey* saw only three groups in that city: 'Merchants, Handicrafts men and Labourers'. Handicraftsmen formed a middle group between principal citizens ('merchants and chief retailers') and labourers (porters, carmen, watermen). They had 'not much to spare', and could thus be distinguished from merchants, but they were better off than labourers, who had 'need it were given unto them'.[9] The middle group, according to the apologist, was the largest of the three; this perception suggests either that he excluded the urban poor and unemployed from his group of 'labourers', or that he considered handicraftsmen to extend from the lowest ranks of merchants into the group of those who 'had need it were given unto them'. His description corresponds to the medieval term *mediocres* (the English equivalent of which is far from complimentary), used in London's records to designate the group below merchants; it included small artisans who took wares to market on their backs and wealthier members of lesser companies, some of whom had as many as eight men working in their shops. The wealthiest *mediocres*, from the fourteenth century to the sixteenth, were not seen as a separate entrepreneurial class – they were simply the most respectable members of the middling group.[10]

Insofar as Elizabethan social theorists thought about craftsmen at all, then, they perceived them as one of the social sub-divisions in the widely based ranks of the ruled – with the proviso that a few individual craftsmen might be worthy of a little political responsibility if no men of higher status could be found. Craftsmen were members of a social group collectively referred to as 'the commonalty', or 'the

[9] Mulcaster, *Positions*, p. 197; Stow, *Survey*, II, 207–9.
[10] Thrupp, *Merchant Class*, p. 32.

simple people', and 'simple' meant 'small in goods', with the connotation of being small in understanding.[11] There was, then, nothing in the definition of craftsman status the popular authors could select and accentuate when they wanted to appeal to craftsmen's social pride. Craftsmen had no social distinction; social theory made them members of a faceless, volatile mass of people.

The portrait of the craftsman as a member of 'the fourth sort of people' carried over from social theory into literature, particularly into drama. Until the late 1590s, the craftsman appeared on the Elizabethan stage as a stereotyped rustic clown. This stereotype had a long history; rustic clowns had appeared in classical drama as early as the fifth century BC and had quickly developed the 'stock' characteristics of stupidity, gluttony, provinciality and gullibility they retained in the coming ages. In early English drama, the rustic clown was either a shepherd whose jokes modified the solemnity of mystery plays, or a provincial peasant gulled by the Vices in morality plays.[12] After the founding of the theatres, however, the rustic clown, like the gentle craftsman who succeeded him, was generally an urban character: of the fifteen rustic clowns in Elizabethan drama, twelve were craftsmen.[13]

The craftsman clown was probably a victim of convenience rather than of a deliberate act of prejudice; in history plays, craftsmen fit more comfortably into civic episodes than shepherds or peasants would have. Nevertheless, the craftsman's eligibility for the rustic role was undoubtedly made possible by his close association with the lower orders of society.[14] Merchants never appeared

---

[11] *Ibid.*, pp. 14–16. See also Chapter 10.

[12] Allardyce Nicoll, *Masks, Mimes and Miracles: Studies in the Popular Theatre* (New York, 1931), pp. 40–1, 69–72, 181–2. On the development of mystery and morality play clowns, see Olive Busby, *Studies in the Development of the Fool in the Elizabethan Drama* (1923; rpt. Folcroft, Pennsylvania, 1969), p. 23.

[13] The three agricultural rustics were Turnop in Munday's *John à Kent and John à Cumber* (c. 1589), Bullithrumble in Greene's *Selimus* (c. 1592), and Much the Miller's Son in Munday and Chattle's *1* and *2 Robin Hood* (1598). One other rustic, who is neither a pastoral figure nor a craftsman clown, is Dogberry, the constable in Shakespeare's *Much Ado About Nothing* (c. 1598).

[14] The prejudice in the portraits of the craftsman clown was not necessarily a consciously held opinion – one need not believe that Elizabethan playwrights or their audiences thought all craftsmen were stupid and amoral, if they were closely questioned on the subject. But the later demise of the old stereotype suggests strongly that, by the end of Elizabeth's reign, playwrights no longer felt comfortable about creating stupid, thoughtless craftsmen because of the prejudice inherent in the role. To recognize this attitude, the modern movie goer has only to see a 1930s movie which presents Negroes as comic characters who dance, sing, and roll their eyes

as rustic clowns, for among the mandatory characteristics of the clown were low social status, inferior mental capacity, and lack of sophistication, none of which could be applied unthinkingly to the civic elite. Craftsmen, however, were historically associated with the 'commonalty' that had no political role in society except when led into rebellion by ambitious men. This simplicity and gullibility made them obvious candidates for the role of clown; making them gluttonous, absurd and stupid as well as a mere matter of literary tradition.

The implied criticism of craftsmen inherent in the early clowns is evident in all the plays in which they appear. They are typically concerned only with their appetites, and give most of their attention to drink and food (in that order). The earliest of the craftsman clowns, Simplicity the miller in Robert Wilson's *Three Ladies of London* (c. 1581), is unconcerned when Hospitality is killed by Usury because Hospitality served such humble fare to the men he invited to his house:

He had nothing but beef, bread, and cheese for me to eat.
Now I would have had some pies, or bag-puddings with great
    lumps of fat;
But, I warrant ye, he did keep my mouth well enough from that.
Faith, and he be dead, he is dead: let him go to the devil,
    and he will;
Or if he will not go thither, let him even lie there still.

Similarly, Derick, the clown in *The Famous Victories of Henry V* (1586), decides to give up being a carrier (thereby deserting his master) and become a cobbler so he can share the strong ale of his 'foil', John the Cobbler. Adam, a journeyman smith in Lodge and Greene's *Looking Glass for London and England* (c. 1590), is perpetually drunk, and at the end of the play when he is given a choice between fasting, as the rest of the population is doing, or hanging, he tells the city official:

I had rather be hanged than abide so long a fast. What, five days?
Come, I'll untruss. Is your halter, and the gallows, the ladder,
and all such furniture in readiness?

And finally, in the anonymous play *Locrine* (c. 1591) the cobbler

when they are frightened. He will feel uncomfortable now at what is clearly implied criticism of the capacities of Negroes, whereas forty years ago he could have laughed without question.

Strumbo's house is burned by the invading 'huns', and the king offers to rebuild it right next to the castle gates for protection, but Strumbo replies:

> Gate! I cry God mercy! Do you hear, master King? If you mean to gratify such poor men as we be, you must build our houses by the Tavern.[15]

With regard to women, craftsman clowns are usually inadequate in one way or another. Simplicity, for example, is very sensitive about the way 'the maidens' view him in *The Three Ladies of London*: he first resolves to give up being a miller because 'the maidens call me Dusty-poll', and he later declines to sell brooms because 'the maids would cosen me competually with their old shoon'. In *The Three Lords and Three Ladies of London* (c. 1588), Simplicity returns, a married man who lives in fear of his wife's sharp tongue. In *The Famous Victories*, John the Cobbler is married to an Amazon of a woman who beats him and throws stools at Derick; when Derick and John are drafted, Derick suggests that John's wife would serve the captain better in France than they will. Strumbo, too, has a shrewish wife who beats him; but after a couple of beatings he manages to silence her by throwing her down upon her bed and pleasing her so well she never scolds more – or so he says.[16]

Though the craftsman is thus concerned with food, drink and evading his shrewish wife, he tries to present himself as a sophisticated man of the world. His pretensions, however, merely make him abuse the English language, for he has a very weak intellect. When Simplicity reappears in *The Three Lords and Three Ladies of London*, for example, he tells the audience that his 'manners and misbehaviour is mended half and half', since he came to London – 'ye may see time doth much'. But time has only made him pompous. When the Three Lords have dispersed some Spanish lords who have tried to take over London and England (in an obvious reference to the Armada), Simplicity eagerly offers them a long 'supplantation' (supplication) that tells them how to rule the city. He also suggests

---

[15] Dodsley, VI, 318 (Simplicity); *The Famous Victories of Henry the Fifth*, lines 427–41, in Geoffrey Bullough, ed., *Narrative and Dramatic Sources of Shakespeare* (London, 1962), IV; *The Lamentable Tragedy of Locrine*, II, iii, 84–8, in *The Shakespeare Apocrypha*; *A Looking Glass for London and England*, p. 108, in Greene, *Works*, XIV.

[16] Dodsley, VI, 253, 326; *Famous Victories*, lines 897–934; *Locrine*, III, iii, and IV, lines 21–56.

he might be a good addition to the city council. In *Locrine*, Strumbo uses long words with little regard to their meaning; his love-letter, written to a simple country girl, is so incoherent that she cannot understand it. Seeing this, Strumbo laments that his 'great learning is an inconvenience' and sinks to courting her in plain English.[17]

The clowns' malapropisms and social aspirations are not without a certain charm. For all their faults, craftsmen clowns are at least men of flesh and blood – a welcome contrast to the paste-board aristocratic heroes in all these plays except *The Famous Victories*. The social possibilities of the contrast, in fact, are not lost upon the dramatists of the late 1590s; but in the 1580s, when playwrights are still looking for ways to present aristocratic virtue convincingly, it may be accidental. The early dramatists, in any case, take care to draw a sharp distinction between the virtuous, responsible members of the elite who are fit to rule, and the unreliable, questionably honest clown who is not. Simplicity, for example, is too simple minded to recognize virtue when he sees it in *The Three Ladies of London*: he asks Dissimulation to get a benefice for his cousin Sincerity, he tries to marry Dissimulation to Lady Love (so Simplicity, Love's servant, can eat better), and he deserts Conscience when she becomes poor, joining a group of beggars since their work is easier than selling brooms and the rewards are more immediate. In *The Famous Victories*, John the Cobbler manages to avoid fighting at Agincourt; after the battle, he and Derick rob corpses and desert the troops to go home. In *Locrine*, Strumbo runs away from the enemy soldiers, then plays dead on the battlefield instead of coming to the aid of Prince Albanact. And in *A Looking Glass*, Adam the Smith tries to seduce his master's wife, then beats his master when he objects.[18] For all the charm and vigour of the craftsman clown, he is presented as a child who requires a firm parental hand; he cannot be expected to act rationally, nobly or morally unless he is ruled.

The irresponsibility of the craftsman clown received its strongest treatment in the plays in which he appeared as a rebel, for here the dramatists drew not just upon dramatic tradition but upon the uncompromising Tudor attitude towards rebellion. The play-

[17] Dodsley, VI, 404, 487; *Locrine*, I, ii.
[18] Dodsley, VI, 292–3, 324, 326–7; *Famous Victories*, lines 1412–51; *Locrine*, II, iv and v; *Looking Glass*, pp. 65–7.

wrights, like every other Elizabethan subject who had learned the catechism, had learned in their earliest years that the Fifth Commandment required them to obey not just their parents, but 'the king and all that are put in authority under him', including 'governors, teachers, spiritual pastors and masters'. They had also heard, as had all other Elizabethans, the two homilies on obedience in the collection of *Certain Sermons or Homilies Appointed to be Read in Churches*, which taught that social order and social hierarchy had been ordained by God as part of the universal order of the sun, moon and stars; and that disobedience was the 'first and the greatest, and the very foot of all other sins' against God and the society he had created.[19] The doctrine of obedience and contentation was as familiar to the playwrights and their audiences as the air they breathed; and it was certainly a part of the books they read, for every author, divine or secular, who discussed the social order emphasized the importance of serving God and society in a calling, be it ever so lowly, and being content with one's status.[20] This repeated insistence on the doctrine by all in authority had a surprising power to enforce social order, even in difficult times. Disorder there was, but from the 1540s to the 1630s, all kinds of protest among the fourth sort of people, whether against enclosures or against the 'covetous caterpillars' thought to cause the rise of prices in times of dearth, were traditional and almost ritualistic. In years of

[19] Gorden J. Schochet, 'Patriarchalism, Politics, and Mass Attitudes in Stuart England', *HJ*, 12 (1969), 429–31. Schochet claims 'An analysis of over two hundred Tudor and Stuart glosses upon the official texts has revealed without exception that whenever the Decalogue was discussed, political duty was extracted from the Fifth Commandment.' *Certain Sermons*, Part II, pp. 275–6, Part I, p. 69.

[20] See, for example, Foxe, I, xxiv; Perkins; 'Treatise of the Vocations, or Callings of Men', in *Works*, I; Ling, *Politeuphia*, [fo. 120v); Edwards, *The Paradise of Dainty Devices* (London, 1576), pp. 79–80; Deloney, *Works*, pp. 31–2. Just how far the doctrine of obedience was to extend was, of course, a moot point; but the general assumption was that while subjects could not obey commandments against the dictates of charity or piety, they must limit their resistance to passive disobedience and do nothing which might cause 'insurrection, sedition, or tumults'. (See Babington, *Commandments*, p. 232; Perkins, *Works*, III, 136; *Certain Sermons*, I, 74–5.) Perhaps because of the power of the *Acts and Monuments*, it was tacitly assumed that martyrdom would be the only result of disobedience; at any rate, the doctrine of obedience was not discussed with as great intensity in Elizabeth's reign as it was in the next two reigns, when it became increasingly clear that the result of disobedience for conscience's sake might be civil war instead of martyrdom. For an analysis of the seventeenth-century discussions of the issue, see J. Sears McGee, *The Godly Man in Stuart England: Anglicans, Puritans and the Two Tables, 1620–1670* (New Haven, 1976), Chapter IV.

dearth, the poor did not riot to express their hunger; they took their complaints to men in authority, expecting these magistrates to curb the abuses of covetous middle-men and badgers. Only if the magistrates did nothing (or too little) to improve their lots would the poor take matters into their own hands; and when they did riot, they consistently attacked the goods of the offending middle-men, not the dwellings or the persons of the gentry.[21] In the absence of a police force and a standing army, the belief in God's social order and the sin of rebellion was in fact a strong deterrent to riot.

The doctrine of obedience and the set of reactions it encouraged had, however, a strikingly negative effect on the portrayals of craftsmen in the chronicles to which the playwrights turned for information on rebellions. For the only time the fourth set of people went beyond the ritualistic protests familiar throughout Elizabeth's reign, according to Stow and Holinshed, were the times their simplicity had been manipulated by ambitious men who misled them for their own purposes. And so, they portrayed rebels as brutish, irresponsible men who were easily led into sedition – thus confirming the idea that *all* men of low status were of low mental and moral capacity. For example, when Holinshed discussed the causes of Jack Straw's rebellion, he said plainly that the commons allowed themselves to be led by base men because they were prone to be 'set on by some devilish instinct and persuasion of their own beastly intentions, as men not content with the state whereunto they were called'. And when Stow discussed a London riot that had occurred in the reign of Richard I, he pointed out that the demagogue who had led it was a 'counterfeit friend to the poor' who persuaded them to rise against the rich; a 'man of evil life, a murderer, who slew a man with his hands', and one who had falsely accused his elder brother of treason. But the common people would not recognize the true nature of this man and considered him to be a martyr when he was hanged, even carrying away the gibbet for a holy relic.[22] Here the common people are not just simple; they have a basic moral flaw. They cannot tell true saviours from evil rabble-rousers.

The chroniclers' portraits of the moral failings of the fourth sort

---

[21] Roger B. Manning, 'Violence and Social Conflict in Mid-Tudor Rebellions', *Journal of British Studies*, 16 (1977), 18–40; John Walter and Keigh Wrightson, 'Dearth and the Social Order in Early Modern England', *PP*, 71 (1976), 22–42.
[22] Holinshed, II, 735; Stow, *Annals*, p. 162.

of people fit well into the dramatists' portrait of the craftsman clown, for the rebels could be made to be weak, self-seeking rustics whose aspirations, like those of Simplicity or Strumbo, were comic. The unreliability of the rebel clown, however, was presented as a danger rather than a comic flaw, and his aspirations resulted not in mistakes, but malicious actions. From a social point of view, the ease with which the rebel could be fit into the role of craftsman clown made the dramatic portrait of the craftsmen even more negative than the chroniclers' portrait. For 'the commonalty' in the chronicles were considered as a body; but in drama, all the rebels with speaking parts were specifically shown to be craftsmen. Almstakers, apprentices, labourers, or servants were conspicuously absent; and as a result, the disapproval which was meted out to all the fourth sort of people in the chronicles was centred upon craftsmen in drama. They became the representatives and leaders of the common people.

If the craftsman clown requires strong parental guidance, the craftsman rebel is a gullible child who is led astray in a world of politics by men who promise him great rewards. In the anonymous *Life and Death of Jack Straw* (c. 1591), for example, Jack is encouraged to lead a rebellion by Parson Ball, an ambitious priest who convinces him that England's problems lie in 'difference of degrees'. Ball persuades Jack that he will do a great service to his country if he can 'make division equally / Of each man's goods indifferently' – and Jack is so far from understanding equality that he promises to make Ball Archbishop of Canterbury and Chancellor of England once everybody is equal. Later, when his power has gone completely to his head, Jack promises Wat Tyler 'We will be lords every one.'[23] To simple men like Jack, there is no difference between 'equality' and 'greed'. In Shakespeare's *2 Henry VI* (c. 1591), Jack Cade is also manipulated by a man who appeals to his ambition; the Duke of York persuades him to call himself John Mortimer and gather a following by posing as a saviour prince. Cade does so, forming a rebel 'army' by appealing to the craftsman's proverbial interest in food and drink: 'There shall be in England seven halfpenny loaves sold for a penny; the three-hoop'd pot shall have ten hoops, and I will make it a felony to drink small beer. All the realm shall be in common, and in Cheapside shall my palfrey go to grass.'[24] This is

[23] Dodsley, V, 382, 394.   [24] *2 Henry VI*, IV, ii, lines 65–9.

so appealing that even Dick the Butcher and Smith the Weaver (who see through Cade's pretensions) decide to follow him to see what kind of a world they can make for themselves.

The social and political aspirations of the craftsman rebels are made to look absurd in these plays, but since the issue is human life, the simplicity of the rebels is horrible as well as funny. In *Jack Straw*, the Captain Tom Miller and the boy Nobs serve as clowns who amuse the audience with some crude buffoonery in the midst of the rebellion, as when Nobs steals a goose which Tom is about to pluck. But these buffoons also treat murder and destruction as a great joke; Nobs drags an innocent Fleming off to Smithfield to be killed in a scene which he thinks to be funny, and Tom burns 'a great many of Bonds and Indentures and Obligations' and other legal records with such merriment that he forgets about the rebellion.[25] In *2 Henry VI* (which was probably produced after *Jack Straw*, though the dates for both plays are conjectural), Shakespeare presents his rebels as simple 'actors' trying to play complicated parts. Their dreams are child-like, but their actions are vicious, always serving to undercut the humour of their lines. After Cade has promised to increase the number of hoops on a three-hooped pot, for example, he betrays the perversion of his values by hanging a clerk who can read and write. His excuse is that literate men fool honest, illiterate craftsmen; his commonwealth will have no learning. Thus the dream of a world in which poor men will not be opposed becomes, in the real world, an excuse for killing an innocent scholar.

The same juxtaposition of inflated dreams and terrible reality appears later when Cade enters London. As usual, Cade is comic in asserting his power: 'Now is Mortimer lord of this city. And here, sitting upon London Stone, I charge and command that, of the city's cost, the pissing-conduit run nothing but claret wine this first year of our reign. And now henceforward it shall be treason for any that calls me other than Lord Mortimer.' By putting the definition of 'treason' beside the offer of a claret, Shakespeare makes them seem equally trivial. But the second order is suddenly made horrible by the appearance of a soldier who does not know it is treason to call Cade by his proper name. At Cade's orders, the mob kills the soldier, and Smith the Weaver comments wittily, 'If this fellow be wise, he'll never call ye Jack Cade more. I think he hath a very fair

<hr>

[25] Dodsley, V, 397, 401.

warning.'[26] Smith and the other craftsmen take the murder of a soldier to be a subject for humour. Child-like in their utopian dreams, they are also child-like in their unthinking cruelty.

In view of the negative portrait of rebels in 1591, it is surprising to find that by contrast the rebels in *Sir Thomas More*, written by Munday, Dekker, Chettle, and Shakespeare in 1595 or thereabouts, are presented with sympathy. Although the play presents rebellion with disapproval, the cause of the rebels is just and the rebels themselves are decent, honourable, outraged people. The grievance that causes the rebellion (the Evil May Day riot in Henry VIII's reign) is the unbearable pride of the Lombard 'strangers' who live and work in London. The audience sees these aliens steal food from an honest carpenter, attempt to drag off his wife, abuse English craftsmen to their faces, and finally run off to the protection of their ambassador, who guards them against English law. The enraged craftsmen, who have suffered this kind of treatment many times before, are all too ready to follow the suggestion of John Lincoln, a broker, that they should deal with the aliens themselves since the traditional channels of complaint are closed to them. The rebellion, then, is made completely understandable, though the craftsmen fail to see that they would be better off to tell the king their problems. Even this omission is laid partly at the door of others: when the commons' restlessness is being discussed at court, a knight tells the Earls of Shrewsbury and Surrey:

> Now, afore God, your honours, pardon me:
> Men of your place and greatness are to blame.
> I tell you true, my lords, in that his majesty
> Is not informed of this base abuse
> And daily wrongs are offered to his subjects;
> For, if he were, I know his gracious wisdom
> Would soon redress it.

The riot, in short, would not have come about if the peers of the realm had done their duty as magistrates.

The fault of the rebels is not brutality, but simplicity. As More says, they are merely 'silly' (simple-minded, innocent) children who do not think of the consequences of their actions. They must be stopped, but they must not be severely punished.

---

[26] *2 Henry VI*, IV, ii, lines 854–110; IV, vi, lines 1–11.

> for silly men
> Plod on they know not how, like a fools pen,
> That, ending, shows not any sentence writ,
> Linked but to common reason or slightest wit:
> These follow for no harm; but yet incur
> Self penalty with those that raised this stir.[27]

Rebels are not vicious upstarts like Jack Straw or Jack Cade; they are men who need to be saved from themselves. More saves them by teaching them the implications of their actions: he reminds them that if a mob can rule, no man will be safe from wicked men who raise mobs to further wicked ends. The rebels agree with him completely and remark upon his sound reasoning. He then shows them how rebellion against the king's peace is rebellion against God, and how xenophobia is a sin against one's neighbour. Impressed again, they agree to 'do as we may be done by', and lay aside their weapons. They have learned his lesson, and like docile schoolboys they walk off to prison, confidently awaiting the pardon More has said the king will give them.

The simplicity of the rebels is tempered with a sturdy, honest spirit – a fact emphasized in their final scene in the play. The king's pardon comes late, and Lincoln is hanged. He is fearless and at the same time repentant:

> I had no ill intent
> But against such as wronged us over much:
> And now I can perceive it was not fit
> That private men should carve out their redress,
> Which way they list.[28]

Lincoln is not a demagogue but a man genuinely concerned with the welfare of simple Londoners. Doll, an Amazonian carpenter's wife who has fought like a man with a sword and buckler in the riot, adds to the pathos by begging to die before her husband does and saying a moving farewell to him from the scaffold. When she and the rest of the rebels are pardoned, the audience is relieved, not horrified that such dangerous people should escape punishment.

By modern standards, the portrayal of the rebels in *More* is hardly inflammatory, and the suggestion that the riot could have

---

[27] *Sir Thomas More*, I, ii, lines 64–70; II, iv, lines 45–50, in *Shakespeare Apocrypha*.
[28] *Ibid.*, III, i, lines 55–9.

been prevented by a diligent aristocracy is mild indeed. By 1595, however, sympathy with rebels and criticism of the aristocracy, however mild, was likely to be censored or severely punished. *More* was written in a year (the second of four) in which the price of grain was high and many poor men were suffering from hunger and poverty; sanction of riot in such circumstances could be taken as a political statement. Thus, when Sir Edmund Tilney, Master of the Revels, read the rebellion scene, he scribbled hastily in the margin of the manuscript: 'Leave out the insurrection wholly and the cause thereof and begin with Sir Thomas More at the mayor's session with a report afterwards of his good service done being Sheriff of London upon a mutiny against the Lombards. Only by a short report and not otherwise *at your own perils*.'[29] The manuscript, which is much worked-over, suggests that the playwrights tried to salvage their play; but it is possible that it was never produced. Like Deloney's 'Ballad on the Want of Corn', its political implications were too dangerous.

Sir Thomas More, interestingly enough, was the last Elizabethan play in which craftsmen were portrayed merely as comic rebels. Heywood's *1 Edward IV* (c. 1599) portrayed craftsmen rebels in the first act (the scene of the siege of London), but this episode was possibly an adaptation of an earlier play, and the corrupt rebels were more than balanced by the valorous London citizens who held the city for their king. The play also contained one of the most notably outspoken 'new' craftsmen of the period, Hobs, the Tanner of Tamworth. By the time the play was produced, the old stereotype of the craftsman rebel had changed a great deal.

After 1595, the craftsman in drama retained many of the surface characteristics of the craftsman clown, but he also gained wisdom and dignity. He remained simple, but his simplicity became a virtue; he remained child-like but his 'innocence' came to resemble that of the child in Andersen's fairy tale who told the truth about the Emperor's new clothes. The first craftsman who had a few characteristics of his later counterparts was Nick Bottom the Weaver of Shakespeare's *A Midsummer Night's Dream*. Bottom and his fellow 'rude mechanicals' were little more intelligent, courageous or learned than the clowns in earlier plays, but they were not gluttons, drunkards, or henpecked husbands. They were amateur actors – not

[29] Irving Ribner, *The English History Play in the Age of Shakespeare* (Princeton, 1957), p. 211; emphasis mine.

good ones, to be sure – but enthusiastic, stage-struck followers of the theatre. Bottom, in particular, was saved from the inferiority of earlier clowns by his intuitive grasp of the imaginative world. Acting, for him, was not just pretence; it was a part of his whole being. Such a characteristic, in a play which is in so many ways about plays, could not fail to appeal to a theatrical audience, Elizabethan or otherwise.

Bottom's link with the earlier clowns studied here is visible from his first entrance. He is officious, and he uses malapropisms by the dozen:

> QUINCE   Is all our company here?
>
> BOTTOM   You were best to call them generally, man by man,
>   according to the scrip.

Quince tries to discuss the play and name the characters, but he is perpetually interrupted by Bottom, who urges him to 'say what the play treats on, then read the names of the actors . . . ', then 'Now, good Peter Quince, call forth your actors by the scroll. Masters, spread yourselves.' The audience soon sees, however, that Bottom's officiousness is the result of his child-like enthusiasm for drama. He is captivated by the possibilities of acting each part in turn; he wants to be the lover, the tyrant, the lady, and even the lion. When Quince tells him sagely he can only play one part, he immediately seizes on the possibilities of costume, 'your straw-colour beard, your orange-tawney beard, your purple-in-grain beard, or your French-crown-colour beard, your perfit yellow'. His imagination extends even to props; it is he who invents Wall, through whose crooked fingers the lovers will whisper.[30]

Bottom is also child-like in the distinctions he cannot make. He is not completely clear about the difference between reality and fantasy. Will the ladies think he is really killing himself on stage? Will they think poor Snug the Joiner is really a lion? To provide against these possible misunderstandings, he insists on putting in a Prologue who will explain that the play is not real, just a play. His confusion is wonderfully comic; but on the other hand, in the world of *A Midsummer Night's Dream* the relationship between the imaginary and the real is extremely complicated, and Bottom's confusion reflects a recognition (however simplified) of a kind of truth. For Bottom, unlike the aristocratic lovers who weep and moan as the

---

[30] *A Midsummer Night's Dream*, II, ii, lines 92–6.

fairies make them players in the 'real' world, plays the ass with the same enthusiasm that inspired his portrayal of the tyrant, lady, lover and lion. When he awakens, he is baffled by his experience, but once more, inspiration dawns – he will become a poet (with help from Peter Quince) and write the saga of 'Bottom's Dream'. Bottom, in short, participates in whatever he sees before him, whether what he sees is real or illusory; with him, art and experience are both real and both fantastic, and he is never sure where the one stops and the other starts. Thus, while the play Bottom and his friends put on for Theseus is a delightful parody of amateur theatre, it is also more than that. As Theseus charitably perceives, 'The best in this kind are but shadows; and the worst are no worse, if imagination amend them.'[31] The imagination that amends Bottom's play is not just that of its spectators, but that of its actors, who reverence the shadows of illusion even though they do not understand the play they produce.

Bottom was such an appealing character that he may well have made playwrights hesitate to create more clowns of his nature. Generally, however, when Elizabethan writers learned of a good character type, they copied it, so the absence of craftsmen clowns after Bottom demands some explanation. It is possible that the craftsman clown took on a new guise because the negative aspects of the clown stereotype were becoming painfully obvious to the popular authors who were beginning to celebrate the achievements of principal citizens. Certainly the 'rude mechanicals' in *More* and *A Midsummer Night's Dream* were different from the earlier clowns of the period, but so long as the craftsman remained a buffoon, his literary development was bound to be limited. Furthermore, the authors who portrayed craftsmen as clowns or rebels could hardly hope to draw real craftsmen to their plays at a time when an unprecedented number of these craftsmen were literate and eager for works that appealed to them.

Two years after the first production of *A Midsummer Night's Dream*, Thomas Deloney offered popular authors a new literary stereotype for the craftsman. This new figure was everything the old craftsman clowns had not been – brave, wise, self-conscious, and content with his lot in life. No longer an unreliable member of 'the fourth sort of people', he was 'a gentle craftsman'. The term orig-

[31] *Ibid.*, V, i, lines 211–16.

inally applied to members of the Cordwainers' Company, but it gradually came to reflect a literary type in both fiction and drama. The adjective in the phrase should lead the social historian to suspect that the new stereotype had little to do with the hard-working, industrious and thrifty craftsman of later centuries. Even the historian who expects something other than bourgeois values to emerge from popular Elizabethan stereotypes, however, may be surprised at the variety of paths the gentle craftsman forced his authors to travel in their attempts to portray their new creation in a way that was neither ridiculous nor radical.

9. *The gentle craftsman in Arcadia*

In the last decade of Elizabeth's reign the audience that witnessed the emergence of the businessman in armour also saw the development of a hero appealing to lesser men of trade – the gentle craftsman. Like the businessman in armour, the gentle craftsman was a replacement for earlier stereotypes of men of his kind. He was a fit companion for kings and princes, not a member of the 'fourth sort of people'; he was a chivalric hero, not a coward or a rebel. No longer a creature of appetite, he became the contented denizen of a golden-age world in which good always triumphed over evil, food and drink were always plentiful, pretty maidens were never coy, and poverty was unknown.

It is ironic that the gentle craftsman appeared just when he did, for the political and economic climate of the 1590s certainly did not warrant the optimism that danced on the surface of his story. To be sure, the expansion of internal trade in Elizabeth's reign had allowed some urban craftsmen to become prosperous, and their prosperity had enabled them to educate their sons. At the same time, rural craftsmen had been able to eke out a more comfortable living than their fathers had enjoyed by putting their wives and children to work spinning, woad-gathering, or stocking-knitting.[1] In Elizabethan England, however, prosperity relied on two elements beyond the control of man – the weather and good health. In the mid-1590s, the combination of four summers of rain and a plague epidemic severely affected the well-being of craftsmen and people of all other estates. The succession of bad years began in 1594, when it rained all summer and many grain growers lost a substantial proportion of their crops. Grain prices rose 30% above their normal level, supply was scarce, and farmers, hoping to stave off a crisis,

[1] Thirsk, *Economic Policy and Projects*, pp. 110–11. See also her 'Industries in the Countryside', in F.J. Fisher, ed., *Essays in the Economic and Social History of Tudor and Stuart England* (Cambridge, 1969), pp. 70–88.

sold or consumed much of their seed corn. But the next summer it rained again, prices rose to 36% above normal, and all the store of seed corn was used up feeding a hungry population. The next two years brought disaster; in 1596 (the year in which *Jack of Newbury* was published), a third wet summer forced prices up to 83% above normal, and peas and beans, the supplement for corn, were also scarce. Nor did the next year bring relief, for the fourth consecutive wet summer drove up prices 65% above normal. Farmers who had previously sold corn were forced to buy it. Magistrates tried to relieve some areas by sending them corn from other counties, only to find that no single county had enough corn to spare its neighbour. The poor – the wandering labourers who could find no work, the cottagers who had had to leave their homes to find employment – starved. Town records began to record the burials of men, women and children who had died 'for want of bread' in the streets.[2]

To a population suffering from inordinately expensive food staples, hunger, and outright starvation, plague brought additional misery and death. The summer of 1598 brought the best harvest in five years, but it also brought plague to the northern towns of Penrith, Carlisle and Kendal. In Staffordshire, the plague had combined with the last bad harvest to inflict heavy mortality in nearly all parishes. This plague was widespread, and though it was not so destructive as the 1603 plague that killed 15% of the inhabitants of London and her suburbs, it was severe enough to spread fear and suffering through a population already weakened by want of food.[3]

Nor were these the only problems Elizabethans faced at the end of the 1590s. The war with Spain dragged on and on, necessitating heavy taxation and a supply of soldiers, and yielding no glorious victory like the Armada's. At court, the queen was ageing, and her familiar assistants had died leaving behind them the increasingly divisive rivalry between Robert Cecil and the Earl of Essex. The queen, badly in need of money, raised it by rewarding courtiers with monopolies on consumer goods, a practice that aroused the irritation of the commons. And finally, the Earl of Essex was sent to Ireland with the most expensive army ever raised by Elizabeth's

---

[2] W.G. Hoskins, 'Harvest Fluctuation in English Economic History, 1480–1619', in *AHR*, 12 (1964), 38; Andrew B. Appleby, 'Disease or Famine?', pp. 419–20.
[3] Appleby, 'Disease or Famine?', p. 419; Palliser, 'Dearth and Disease in Staffordshire', pp. 61–3.

subjects' money, only to let it rot away and return to England in disgrace.

Thus, the era in which the gentle craftsman appeared was coloured by war, famine, plague, and disillusionment with the Elizabethan court. The craftsmen who had achieved a measure of prosperity earlier in the reign found their resources undercut by taxes, bad weather, and the plague. Craftsman literacy, which had begun to rise early in the reign and had reached its peak during the late 1580s, was severely curtailed by England's economic troubles. Cressy has shown that the craftsmen schooled in the last decade of Elizabeth's reign had a substantially lower rate of literacy than their fathers had; this statistic suggests the frustration and disappointment many craftsmen may have felt when they found they could not educate their sons, either because they could not pay for education or because so many teachers were forced to move in times of poverty and plague.[4]

It would be surprising if problems of this magnitude failed to appear in works that appealed to craftsmen. Given the state of Elizabethan censorship, however, it would also be surprising to find disenchantment and disillusionment expressly stated; if a criticism of the aristocracy so mild as that in *Sir Thomas More* could not pass muster, if Deloney was nearly arrested for publishing 'subversive' ballads about the want of corn, popular authors were certainly not free to allow craftsmen to reflect upon their problems. To this one should add that, however outspoken Elizabethan authors could be about the frustrations of the 1590s, none of them harboured a consciously disloyal thought about either England or its sovereign. The works that praised craftsmen were patriotic to the point of chauvinism, and the virtue they all praised most in craftsmen was their loyalty to the crown. Still, Deloney, Dekker and Heywood were thoughtful men who were disturbed by the problems they saw about them. In their praise of craftsmen, they groped for a way of defining the consciousness of men who had hitherto had no rank in society at large; they also looked for a way of communicating the concerns of these men to the Elizabethan audience.

The phrase 'gentle craft' was an old one, attached exclusively to the

[4]Cressy, 'Levels of Illiteracy', 13 (graph), 18–20. Craftsmen were not the only people who suffered in the 1590s; Cressy postulates a general educational slump during the dearth and plague.

Cordwainers' Company. Shoemakers had a long-standing folk tradition of fellowship that made them obvious examples of craftsman virtue and merriment. Robert Greene drew on the tradition for his *Quip for an Upstart Courtier* (1592), by telling how shoemakers had treated Mercury to so much powdered beef and ale that the god accidentally slipped when he asked Jupiter to favour them, and asked that they might forever more 'spend a groat afore they can earn two pence', thus ensuring that shoemakers remained poor but merry. Greene accounted for the name 'the gentle craft' in his play *George à Green, the Pinner of Wakefield* (c. 1587–93). At a merry, ale-drinking party given by the yeoman George, the King of England pledges the shoemakers of Bradford and says they will ever be known as 'the gentle craftsmen'. Thus, when Deloney turned to shoemakers in *The Gentle Craft*, he was not creating but amplifying an image. He achieved this task by drawing on a variety of historical sources and turning various men – craftsmen and otherwise – into shoemakers.[5] In so doing, he did more than praise one craft; he created a stereotype for the craftsman that contradicted the old, negative portrait of the clown, and he developed a structure in which to praise this craftsman.

The structure Deloney used to praise his craftsmen is evident from the very dedication of *The Gentle Craft, Part I*. Addressing 'all the good Yeomen of the Gentle Craft', he begins:

You that the Gentle Craft profess, list to my words
    both more and less;
And I shall tell you many things, of worthy and renowned Kings,
And divers Lords and Knights also, that were Shoemakers long ago;
Some of them in their distress, delighted in this business;
And some, for whom great wait was laid, did save their lives
    by this same trade:
Other some, in sport and game, delighted much to learn the same.

The 'history', in other words, is primarily concerned not with shoemakers, but with 'worthy and renowned Kings, / And divers Lords and Knights also' who became shoemakers in bygone days. True to his promise, Deloney does deal with aristocrats in the first two stories of *The Gentle Craft, Part I* and in the second (and longest) story in *The Gentle Craft, Part II*. He also includes the stories of two

---

[5] Greene, XI, 264–5 (*Quip*); XIV, 178 (*George a Green*). For the 'real' backgrounds of Deloney's heroes in *The Gentle Craft*, see Deloney, *Works*, pp. 522–3, 531–6.

shoemakers who thrived so well in the craft that they became principal citizens – Simon Eyre and Richard Casteler – in Part I and Part II, respectively. These men have in common with the lords and knights the fact that they 'pass through' the world of shoemaking and end up far better off than they began. Immediately, the reader is aware of a vague sense of irony; Deloney is praising men who rose *above* craftsman status, men for whom shoemaking was a temporary vocation. What about men who stay shoemakers? Is there any place for them? Deloney hurries on to explain himself. Knights and lords enjoyed shoemaking, he says,

> For evermore they still did find that shoemakers bore a
>   gallant mind:
> Men they were of high conceit, the which wrought many a
>   merry feat;
> Stout of courage they were still, and in their weapons had
>   great skill . . .

> Wrong they wrought not any man, with reason all things did
>   they scan:
> Good houses kept they evermore, relieving both the sick and poor.
> In law no money would they spend, their quarrels friendly would
>   they end . . .

> Thus in joy they spent their days, with pleasant songs
>   and roundelays,
> And God did bless them with content; sufficient for they He sent;
> And never yet did any know, a Shoemaker a-begging go;
> Kind they are one to another, using each stranger as his brother.[6]

These shoemakers, with their 'gallant minds', their military prowess, their generous housekeeping, their merriment and their wealth, are very 'gentle' indeed; a prince who lives among them can feel entirely at home. But a prince who lives among real craftsmen learns some virtues he may not encounter at court. The two key words in Deloney's closing rhymes are 'brother' and 'content'. Shoemakers look out for each others and for strangers in distress; they are happy with what they have; they are kind as well as cheerful. The fellowship of shoemakers is more than a cheery kind of gild loyalty; it is a state of mind that acknowledges that no man can

[6]Deloney, *Works*, p. 71.

always fend for himself and that every man must look after his fellow mortals. This, as Deloney hints in his introductory poem, is a state of mind far superior to that of men who never forgive offences and spend their lives dragging their neighbours to court – a condition shared by many Elizabethan gentlemen and aristocrats.

The scheme of things Deloney sets up in his dedication outlines the structure of what I would like to call the urban pastoral romance. It is drawn from the pastoral romance proper – the tale of mixed prose and verse that is descended on one side from the idylls of Theocritus, the eclogues of Virgil and the medieval pastoral lyric, descended on the other side from medieval chivalric romance, and born in England in Sidney's *Arcadia*.[7] The hero of pastoral romance is typically a prince who has been forced to leave his realm and who wanders into the world of Arcadia; Deloney has substituted the shop for the pastoral countryside, and peopled his pastoral landscape with shoemakers instead of with shepherds. The hero of pastoral romance falls in love with a shepherdess who turns out to be a princess; the hero of urban pastoral romance either falls in love with a princess who sees through his disguise or falls in love with a city widow. The hero in pastoral romance learns to appreciate the simple life as shepherds live it, and he is instructed in pastoral values by an experienced shepherd; the hero of urban pastoral romance sings and dances with shoemakers and is instructed in the proper use of discipline and power by a master craftsman. The hero of pastoral romance returns to his country a wiser man than he came; the man who leaves the world of the shop in urban pastoral romance has matured, learned a great deal, and come to know his proper duty in life. The urban pastoral romance, in other words, moves Arcadia from the mountains of Greece to the shops of London and surrounding villages; it keeps the basic structure of the pastoral romance intact and uses it to praise the simple life of craftsmen.

The pastoral romance was popular during Elizabeth's reign; Lodge's *Rosalynd*, Greene's *Pandosto*, Sidney's *Arcadia*, Shakespeare's *As You Like It* and a number of lesser plays all appear in our canon of popular literature. When Deloney adapted the pastoral romance to the history of shoemakers, then, he was simply adding one more type of popular literature to his eclectic repertory. In many ways, the adaptation was a natural one: the plot-line was

---

[7]Walter Davis and Richard A. Lanham, *Sidney's Arcadia* (New Haven, 1965), p. 8; Peter Marinelli, *Pastoral* (New York, 1971), Chapter III.

familiar; it was a fine framework for an adventure story; and it permitted reflection upon the simple lives of lowly subjects. On the other hand, the pastoral romance had certainly not been created to deal with social consciousness; it had nothing whatever to do with the social cohesion of shepherds, and it had never been used as anything but a backdrop for the spiritual, amorous, poetic and chivalric exploits of princes in disguise. Thus, the urban pastoral romance posed problems for the popular authors as well as solving them; it enabled them to praise craftsmen, but it limited what they could say.

At its lowest level, the pastoral romance was merely an adventure story in which a disguised prince did great deeds on the battlefield. At this level, the urban pastoral failed miserably in its attempt to praise craftsman heroes. In the second story of Deloney's *The Gentle Craft, Part I*, for example, the story of Crispine and Crispianus is designed to show that shoemakers, unlike the craftsman clown, are brave warriors – but it actually suggests something quite different. Crispine and Crispianus are the sons of the King of Logria; their father has been killed by the Tyrant Maximus, and the two boys have been forced out into the world. They are taken in by merry, kindly shoemakers and apprenticed; in the fullness of time, their master gains such a reputation that he becomes the royal shoemaker to Maximus himself. At court, Crispine becomes the traditional Lover of pastoral romance; he woos and wins Maximus' beautiful daughter. meanwhile, Crispianus has become the traditional warrior.[8] Pressed into the army that is to assist the Prince of Gauls defeat the landing Persians, he appears on the battlefield like 'a second Hector'; he saves the prince's life, and he defeats the Persian general in hand-to-hand combat. The Prince of Gauls is most impressed with Crispianus' power and asks who he is. When he discovers Crispianus is a shoemaker, he says, 'If such fame wait upon Shoemakers, and such magnanimity follow them, it were well for us if all the people in the Kingdom were Shoemakers . . . I find it true, that Magnanimity and knightly Prowess is not always tied within the compass of Noble blood.'[9] But the prince's lesson in democracy is, of course, marred by the fact that Crispianus is merely *disguised* as a shoemaker. Worse still, from the point of view of

[8] Davis points out that in Sidney's *Arcadia*, the two heroes (Pyrocles and Musidorus) split between them the active and contemplative sides of pastoral life (*Sidney's Arcadia*, p. 55).

[9] Deloney, *Works*, p. 101.

craftsman valour, the Persian general Crispianus defeats is the son
of a real shoemaker. He has risen through the ranks because of his
military prowess, and he is the best fighting man the Persians have
– but he is no match for Crispianus' inborn (and untrained) aristocratic valour. The vehicle Deloney has chosen to celebrate the
valour of craftsmen has forced him to undercut himself.

Deloney was not the only popular author to encounter this problem with the pastoral romance. Heywood encountered it too when
he used the motif in his play *The Four Prentices of London* (c. 1600).
The 'prentices' are in fact no city boys, but the sons of the banished
Earl of Boulogne; while their father assures the audience that they
'have no scorn' of civic trades and the boys assure their father that
they are obedient and loyal apprentices, they agree in private that
they are merely marking time until they can prove their own
chivalric talents.

GUY   Brother, if I knew where to go war,
        I would not stay in London one hour longer.
CHARLES An hour! By heaven I would not stay a minute.
EUSTACE A minute, not a moment. Would you put a moment
        Into a thousand parts, the thousandth part
        Would I not linger, might I go to war.
        Why, I would presently run from my Master,
        Did I but hear where were a Drum to follow.

And when the drum beats, they do indeed desert their masters,
stopping only to adopt the insignia of their trades for use on their
shields and banners. To be sure, in the heat of the fighting, the Four
Prentices wish fervently that they had 'many good lads, honest
Prentices, / From Eastcheap, Canwick-street, and London-stone' in
their armies so they would not have to fear 'the doubtful day's
success'.[10] But while this was probably music to the ears of the teen-
aged apprentices in the audience who were aching to express their
virility in some military fashion, the fact remains that the fighting is
left to the earl's sons, while the real apprentices stay in London.[11]

In these works, the structure of the pastoral romance limited the
content of the authors' praise for craftsmen and apprentices. Presumably, the audience was intended to identify with Crispianus or
the Four Prentices; the works certainly implied that craftsmen and

---

[10] Heywood, II, 172–4; 192–3.
[11] On the appeal of these works to adolescent apprentices, see Steven R. Smith, 'The
London Apprentices as Seventeenth-Century Adolescents', in *PP*, 61 (1973), 159.

apprentices would jump at the chance for military glory. Nevertheless, the heroes of these stories were no more bourgeois than the
heroes of chivalric romance; the real message they conveyed was
that service in a trade did not eradicate an aristocrat's superiority.
As a compliment to craftsmen, this was at best indirect.

Why did the authors who wanted to give craftsmen a military
reputation use aristocrats in disguise in these tales? Could they not
simply have invented other stories and made real craftsmen into
heroes? They could not – and for two reasons. First, the world of the
shop and the world of the battlefield sat very uneasily together, and
it was difficult to relate a young man's military fantasies to what a
young apprentice actually did. Richard Johnson had made an
attempt to relate romance to realism in this manner; but the bookstall failure of his *Nine Worthies of London* (1592) seems to have
warned other authors to avoid his mistake. In celebrating the deeds
of his 'worthies', Johnson found himself insisting that the fastest
way to secure business preferment was to become a military hero.
This led him to an awkward mixture of ideas. One of his heroes, for
instance, was Christopher Crocker, whom he described as a man
'carrying in his brows the picture of Mars, and in his manners the
majesty of a prince'. This miniature Hector was in fact a vintner, and
he told his audience sagely that he had spent his youth working diligently so that his 'master's purse might thrive'. Crocker's industry
won him the undying love of his master's daughter; and to make
himself worthy of her love, he gave up trade, went to France with
Edward III, killed hundreds of the enemy, and modestly accepted a
knighthood. Having proved that 'a prentice (though but small
esteemed) / Unto the stoutest never giveth way', he returned to
London, took up his old trade, and married the boss's daughter.[12] It
did not occur to this warlike vintner (or to his creator) that a knighthood might be more than an assertion of virility, and that trade
might not look quite so attractive to a knight as it had to a lowly
apprentice.

The second reason popular authors chose to adopt aristocratic
'craftsman' heroes was that the knights of chivalric (and pastoral)
romance were supposed to defeat their opponents, and the picture
of a real craftsman knocking his social superiors off their horses
would have had serious social implications. Johnson and the authors

[12] *The Nine Worthies of London*, 454–5.

of ballads about valorous apprentices avoided this problem by making their heroes defeat foreign princes; it was surprising to no Elizabethan that one London apprentice could defeat fifty Turkish knights.[13] In stories set in London, however, an author had to be very careful when praising the virility of craftsmen, or he found himself talking about class rivalry.

Deloney encounters this problem in the story of Lusty Peachy, the second central character of *The Gentle Craft, Part II*. Peachy is both a social and a literary hybrid. A 'gentleman-like citizen', in Deloney's phrase, he is both a shoemaker and a retainer of the Duke of Suffolk. A wise denizen of the urban Arcadia in which he lives, he is both a representative of the pastoral world and a courtier – his journeymen serve both as his workers and as his personal retinue. On Sundays, this strange social cross marches to church with forty men at his back, each dressed in Suffolk's livery, 'with each man his sword and buckler, ready at any time, if need required'. Peachy's retinue is like Jack of Newbury's, and it arouses the same resentment. Captains Stukeley and Strangewidge, two famous Elizabethan sea-dogs and courtiers, see Peachy and assume he is 'some Lord at the least', or perhaps 'some Knight of good living'. When they find that Peachy is only a city shoemaker, they are enraged, and they plot to prove that Peachy is unworthy of such a retinue. They enter Peachy's shop and begin to insult him; he orders them out, reminding them, 'I keep forty fellows in my house, that in respect of their manhood may seem to be your equals.' Stukeley finds this egalitarian comparison 'intolerable'; he gives Peachy 'a sound blow on the ear', and shortly thereafter, the two captains meet peachy and one of his men in Lincoln's Inn Fields for a sword-fight. Peachy and his men defeat the two courtiers soundly on this occasion and on many others, until the two men plead for peace and finally get the Duke of Suffolk to end their quarrel. Suffolk does so 'most honourably', and the story of the rivalry adds 'to the great credit of Master Peachy and all his men'.[14]

The Duke's role in calming Peachy's wrath reminds the reader that Peachy is not merely a shoemaker but a courtier as well. By

---

[13] For example, in *The Nine Worthies* (p. 461), Sir Hugh Malveret, grocer, recalls that he 'gave both knights and Princes heavy strokes' when he was an apprentice. But he was fighting the Infidel during the Crusades, so the social implications of his actions are almost nil.

[14] Deloney, *Works*, pp. 170–5.

stressing the duality of Peachy's status, Deloney escapes the problem he encountered in *Jack of Newbury*, for courtiers like Peachy can be expected to have retainers, and they frequently have tiffs with other courtiers. But Peachy is not just a courtier, and he is not a courtier disguised as a shoemaker – he is a real shoemaker, and he arouses antagonism because he is one. Stukeley calls Peachy's foreman 'Goodman Flat-cap', and the foreman, in return, calls him a 'velvet fool' and a 'silken slave'. The rivalry is one of the city and the court, and the shoemaker proves that he can defeat courtiers at their own military game. Once more, Deloney's adaptation of a familiar literary *topos* turns the issue of a story from one of mere praise to a reflection on social power. If shoemakers can be courtiers and defend their right to courtly status successfully, while remaining shoemakers, why are they technically of lower status than the men they defeat? The social implications of the question are disturbing; and Deloney, as usual, leaves them uninvestigated.

The chivalric aspect of pastoral romance, then, adapted poorly to the praise of craftsmen. If the authors wrote about princes disguised as craftsmen, they undercut the praise they wished to bestow. If they dealt with the exploits of real craftsmen, they encountered the obvious fact that preferment in business did not come from apprentice military fervour, but from the drabber virtue of industry. If they dealt with the virility of master craftsmen in military terms, they found themselves dealing with class antagonism. In all these cases, the literary structure the authors chose for their praise of craftsmen raised more problems than it solved.

There were, however, aspects of the pastoral tradition that adapted happily to craftsman self-consciousness. The pastoral romance, when it was more than an adventure story, permitted reflection upon the values of the simple life enjoyed by the denizens of Arcadia. This kind of reflection worked nicely for authors who wanted to show their audience what fine men craftsmen were; they could draw on gild traditions of 'fellowship', combine them with pastoral traditions of singing, dancing and wooing, and dignify craftsmen by showing what a merry and generous group they were.

One of the 'gentle' virtues Deloney mentioned in his Dedication of *The Gentle Craft, Part I* was 'good housekeeping' – the ability to maintain a household in which all residents lived comfortably and happily, and the generosity to relieve the poor, entertain guests, and care for strangers. Craftsmen in the urban pastoral romance are 'good housekeepers' – their servants and apprentices live merrily, are well paid, and have sufficient leisure to enjoy their modest prosperity. It is, in fact, the good housekeeping of master craftsmen that makes their shops into urban Arcadias that attract kings and lords. In these shops, prosperity makes it possible to have wonderful feasts, and as a result, the amount of food and ale in this pastoral landscape is little short of staggering. Greene, we may remember, starts this tradition with his tale of Mercury's slip of the tongue after drinking a great deal of double beer with his powdered beef at a banquet given by shoemakers. Dekker's shoemakers follow this tradition in *The Shoemakers' Holiday*, in which the shoemakers are happy to take 'a villainous pull at a Can of Double Beer' to celebrate the hiring of a new journeyman – before breakfast.[15] In Deloney's works, food is not merely an extension of good fellowship but an expression of love. When two craftsmen and a parson want to marry Jack's mistress in *Jack of Newbury*, for example, they bring her a pig, a goose, a couple of rabbits, a capon, a shoulder of mutton, half a dozen chickens and a gallon of sack – all of which are consumed by five people at one sitting. In *The Gentle Craft, Part I*, Simon Eyre's journeyman John courts a pretty girl by providing capon, cream and pudding pie for her delicate palate; but she does not come to his banquet because John's rival has waylaid her and told her false stories about him while she daintily eats the 'mess of cream' he buys for her. In *The Gentle Craft, Part II*, Long Meg courts the diligent Richard Casteler by bringing him a 'bottle of excellent good Muskadine', to go with 'a dainty piece of powdered beef, and the tender carcass of a cold Capon'. Richard has no sooner done justice to these delicacies than Gillian appears, 'bringing in her apron the corner of a Venison Pasty, and a good deal of Lamb pie'.[16] Here, Deloney skilfully describes the maidens' officious courtship by focussing upon the good they generously force upon the victim of their love.

There is perhaps an element of wish-fulfilment in these episodes dealing with food, for most of them were written at a time when food was scarce and expensive. The fellowship and love expressed by food, however, has a deeper significance in the urban pastoral world. Food to the craftsman clown had merely been food – an

---

[15] *Shoemakers' Holiday*, I, iv, Lines 85–6.
[16] Deloney, *Works*, pp. 12–13 (*Jack of Newbury*); pp. 126, 119–20 (*The Gentle Craft, Part I*); pp. 146, 150 (*The Gentle Craft, Part II*).

aspect of the gluttony of the 'fourth sort of people'. But food gifts in the later tales appear in a completely different context; cans of double beer, capons, powdered beef and cream express both emotions and the financial ability to be generous. Because urban Arcadians are prosperous, they can also be gentle craftsmen who court their maidens with good taste.

In pastoral romance, one of the primary concerns is with the creation of poetry; shepherds and their princely visitors can write poems to their mistresses, engage in writing contests with each other, and sing happily to themselves while they tend their flocks. In the urban pastoral romance, the songs are ballads, not sestinas (a fact which doubtless says more about the talents of the popular authors than about their heroes' literary taste), but most of them deal with love and chivalry, just as one might expect. Singing in the urban pastoral romance, however, has a great deal more to do with content than with either love or poetry. All work is done while sing-ing – although the singing itself has little to do with the value of work. Crispine and Crispianus, for example, are drawn to the shoe-makers in Roman Britain because they hear them singing merrily

> Would God that it were Holiday, hey derry down down derry,
> That with my Love I might to play, with woe my heart is weary:
> My whole delight, is in her sight, would God I had her company,
>   her company,
> Hey derry down, down adown.

Round Robin, Richard Casteler's journeyman, is called to sing for the king with some fellow, because 'divers members of the Nobility' from court

> did many times hear the Shoemakers' journeymen singing; whose sweet voices and pleasant songs was so pleasing in the ears of the hearers, that it caused them to stay about the door and harken thereunto.

It is not, however, just the sweetness of the songs that draws the nobility to shoemakers' doors – it is the content the singing expresses. The happiness of the gentle craftsmen, overheard by courtiers in the evening, has a kind of serenity that is absent from the court. While it is greatly to the honour of gentle craftsmen to perform songs or 'some device, some odd crochets, some morris, or such like, for the honour of the gentle shoemakers' at court, it is not merely the talent of the craftsmen that makes the king enjoy their music.[17] It is the peace of men who are content with their lot in life and ask for no more than work, fellowship and sufficient means to live without grief.

It was the content of the gentle craftsmen that drew aristocrats into their world. Once drawn into the urban pastoral world, these men were deeply affected by it, for they learned a great deal about the most important values in life. Here, then, was the place for a writer like Deloney, Heywood or Dekker to use the pastoral structure to inculcate bourgeois values. For the craftsman did not live all his life courting pretty girls, feasting, dancing and singing. He was expected to work diligently in his calling, like all Elizabethan subjects, and the princes who sojourned with him learned a great deal about diligence while they were craftsmen. 'Diligence', in a pastoral context, however, is not everything the capitalist would expect; it is a peculiar cross between a pastoral virtue and a religious duty, and it has only a little to do with earning a living.

As the preachers applied diligence to men of low status, the virtue was inextricably linked with the duty of obedience. In the elite, magistrates must rule, teachers teach, and preachers preach; in the lower portions of society, servants must obey their masters, thus serving God 'in serving of men'. As William Perkins put it, God ordained all callings and made men to fill each of them: 'Hence we are all taught to walk in our callings with diligence and good conscience. Because they are assigned by God. Hence we are taught to yield obedience to our rulers and teachers' and by extension, masters. Every man, says the 'Exhortation concerning Good Order', has a vocation and a social duty connected with his degree; this applies to kings and subjects, preachers and laymen, masters and servants.[18] Thus, as it applied to men of low status, the doctrine of the calling unfailingly referred to diligence and obedience as parts of the same social duty. As this doctrine appeared in the works of Deloney, Heywood and Johnson, diligence in an inferior calling and obedience (or service) to one's master were very nearly the same thing.

Johnson and Heywood assume that an apprentice's job is to increase his master's well-being by serving him loyally. Godfrey, the eldest of the Four Prentices of London, tells the Earl of Boulogne that he is satisfied with his apprenticeship:

---

[17] *Ibid.*, pp. 91, 167; *Shoemakers' Holiday*, III, ii, lines 145–7.
[18] Perkins, *Works*, I, 126; II, 177; *Certain Sermons*, p. 69.

> Bound must obey: Since I have undertook
> To serve my Master truly for seven years,
> My duty shall both answer that desire,
> And my old Master's profit every way.

In the *Nine Worthies*, William Sevenoak similarly says he did 'refuse no toil nor drudging pain' by which he 'might increase [his] master's gain'. Diligent labour is a form of service; it is not presented as a good in itself. The diligent apprentice clearly helps his master's business prospects; as Deloney points out, masters like the one adopted by Crispine and Crispianus become shoemakers for kings because their shops breed 'the best workmen in the country'. But Deloney praises the diligence of the two princes by saying that they *serve* their master and mistress well, 'refusing nothing that was put to them to do', even washing dishes.[19] Thus, the two princes learn that one of the things that becomes a man is his ability to do whatever his vocation requires him to do, instead of disdaining work that is beneath his dignity.

The most interesting and perceptive use of the pastoral romance in the consideration of diligence appears in the central stories of Deloney's *The Gentle Craft, Part II*. The heroes of the piece are two young men on the brink of taking up the responsibilities of manhood: Harry Neville, son and heir of a gentleman in the country, and William the Apprentice, servant of a city widow, Mistress Farmer. Harry is a prodigal son; he becomes a shoemaker because he has run away from his parents and spent all his money. William, on the other hand, is responsible – like Jack of Newbury, he comes to his mistress's attention because he is so 'diligent and careful about all things committed to his charge'. Both William and Harry want to marry Mistress Farmer; both of them discover, in the course of their courtships, a vital link between diligence, obedience, and success in love and business.

Harry comes to the pastoral world of Lusty Peachy's shop because he is disobedient; he has engaged in 'abominable swearing' and has refused his father's orders to stop. He is too proud to live on the charity of his friends, so he takes up a trade, but his lack of obedience follows him into the pastoral world. Instead of working diligently for Peachy, he runs from his duties and engages in experimental sexual conquests. He first courts Mistress Farmer and loses

[19]Heywood, II, 169; *Nine Worthies*, p. 447; Deloney, *Works*, p. 93.

her to William. When she refuses him, he becomes a goldsmith (only to be fired for seducing his master's daughter), a barber-surgeon (only to be fired for seducing his master's wife), a cook, a comfitmaker, a smith (only to be fired for seducing a maid) and a joiner. In the midst of all these failures, Harry hears that his father is sick; he goes home and makes peace. Having accepted the duty of obedience, he matures and fulfils his responsibilities as a gentle-man. Thematically (and psychologically) Harry's inability to work diligently at any calling is an extension of his refusal to obey. Dis-obedience has robbed him of his place in society; lack of diligent work for his masters makes him unable to find a new place; obedi-ence makes him a diligent gentleman.

William, the diligent apprentice, finds his place in society by marrying Mistress Farmer; but he, too, has to learn the value of obedience before he can mature. Unlike Jack of Newbury, who is content to let his charms speak for themselves, William is not initially content to serve his mistress. He proposes to her, a step that threatens to take him out of his rank and make him, as Mistress Farmer says angrily, 'the master of his mistress'. This is insubordi-nation, and it is clearly unacceptable. Mistress Farmer accuses William of being 'lazy' (which in context means that he refuses to recognize his duty of obedience) and sets him many menial tasks to do. The other apprentices are shocked that he actually does them, for they are far below the tasks that senior apprentices usually do; one friend advises him to seek preferment elsewhere. Mistress Farmer, too, is surprised that he endures so much drudgery without complaining, and at first she reflects upon his obedience as a lack of virility: 'if he bore a man's mind he would never endure it, but being of a base and servile condition, he doth easily endure the yoke of servitude'. But then she thinks again and sees that his obedience is both a token of his love for her and a sign that he is a wise and con-stant man. As she watches him do his jobs, she falls in love with him: 'see, see how neatly he goes through his work, how handsomely he handles everything: and surely well may I suppose that he which is so faithful a servant, would certainly prove a kind husband, for this has been no slender trial of his constant heart'.[20] And so Mistress Farmer learns, as William has learned, that 'some kinds of baseness / Are nobly undergone'.[21] The Diligent Apprentice has won the wealthy widow, and the prodigal Gentleman has failed. And yet, while the social stereotypes in this story lead one to anticipate a capitalistic conclusion (for example, that *all* gentlemen are prodigals and *all* apprentices are diligent, or that William wins Mistress Farmer because he is going to be rich, while Harry loses her because he is no good at trade), no such conclusion is forthcoming. Diligence in this story is not a capitalistic virtue, but a pastoral one; it separates mature, constant, and (hence) sexually attractive men like William from immature, inconstant, and (hence) sexually experimental youths like Harry Neville. In case the reader should miss the point, Deloney has added a third character to the story – Tom Drum, a journeyman shoemaker who has fled in disgrace from many masters because they make him work, and who will not work because he hates to obey. Tom is good company, but he achieves nothing, and to hide this fact, he fills his life with empty bragging: he can make eight score pairs of shoes in a day; women fall all over him when he walks down the street; he kills thousands of enemies in battle. But Tom's bragging suggests his impotence, both as a man and as a worker. Mistress Farmer, who understands what manhood is all about, has him thrown out of her house. Nobody else takes him seriously, because his lies are 'so manifest that he [can] no longer stand in them'. Tom finally flees England altogether; since he will not obey and cannot work, he has no place in society, and his manliness is permanently impaired.[22] Tom is a walking definition of the opposite of diligence – anti-authoritarian behaviour, immaturity (with sexual overtones), and concern with outer show of work rather than the inner state of self-knowledge that dignifies work in every calling.

The diligence that wins a city widow, then, is not a mark of business success, but a mark of 'the pastoral within' – a state of mature, dignified acknowledgement of one's place in society, and a willingness to do the duties that life presents without complaining or rebelling. How different this Elizabethan definition of diligence is from its counterpart in eighteenth-century usage can be seen at a glance at Defoe's advice to the 'Complete English Tradesman'. When Defoe urges this tradesman to be diligent, he is not talking about a

---

[21] Shakespeare, *The Tempest*, III, i, lines 2–3. Ferdinand speaks these lines as he carries wood for Prospero and Miranda.
[22] Deloney, *Works*, pp. 179, 187, 210.

pastoral virtue:

> Nothing can give a greater prospect of thriving to a young Tradesman, than his own diligence; it fills him with hope, and gives him credit to all that know him; without application nothing in this world goes forward as it should do: let the man have the most perfect knowledge of his trade, and the best situation for his shop, yet without application nothing will go on.

Diligence here is 'application' – the industrious pursuit of success. Furthermore, the tradesman who works diligently in Defoe's world leads a very different life from the shoemaker who sings at his work, courts pretty girls and drinks double beer. To Defoe, the tradesman's work:

> is called *Business* very properly, for it is a business *for* life, and ought to be followed as one of the great businesses *of* life; I do not say the chief, but one of the great businesses of life it certainly is: Trade must, I say, be worked at, not played with; he that trades in jest, will certainly break in earnest.

Trade has become the central issue of the tradesman's life. Even the duties of religion 'must be kept in their places'; a man must be sure not to be at his prayers when he should be tending his shop. The tradesman is no pastoral figure; he is a busy, deeply committed capitalist. He cannot teach the elite the lesson of content, for he is ambitious himself; his goal, if it is not to become a gentleman, is at least to join the ranks of those wealthy and industrious tradesmen who are 'at this Time, able to buy the Gentlemen almost in every part of the Kingdom' with the fruits of their diligence.[23]

In Defoe's language, all pastoral overtones have disappeared. The complete tradesman, unlike the gentle craftsman, is an entrepreneur. He is not the companion of the elite, but its competitor. If this tradesman teaches members of the elite anything, it is that they had better become diligent themselves, or they will be bought out by ambitious shopkeepers who take business seriously. In the 1590s this language did not exist; nor did the idea that gentlemen and craftsmen might have different and competing systems of values. Deloney could talk of the rivalry between court and city, but his city shoemaker was praised for his swordsmanship, not his industry. He could compare the suits of an industrious apprentice and a prodigal gentleman, but he praised the apprentice for his maturity and will-

[23] Defoe, *The Complete English Tradesman*, I, 45–6, 48, 50; *A Plan of the English Commerce*, p. 61.

ingness to serve a lady, not for his entrepreneurial activity. In the sixteenth century, the gentle craftsman was a man of gentle values; in the eighteenth century, the complete tradesman was a man of bourgeois values.

The discovery that craftsmen might not have the values of the elite was unlikely to emerge from the structure popular authors used to explore the social consciousness of craftsmen. The function of pastoral romance was to allow analysis of ideas in a moral and aesthetic laboratory, out of the context of everyday occurrences. A shop could serve as a laboratory just as well as the Forest of Arden, but it allowed an author to make only certain kinds of experiments. The Arcadian laboratory was equipped to isolate universal problems pertaining to men of all ranks; one could use it to study problems of time, loss, self-knowledge, forgiveness, love, and poetic experience. It was not equipped, however, to examine concrete problems of social rivalry, economic self-definition, or the application of aristocratic values to craftsmen.[24] Deloney touched upon some of these themes, but he could not examine them closely; his stories were shaped by the limitations of the ideological equipment at his disposal, and there was no new ideology for him to turn to.

It is possible, in fact, that the structure of the pastoral romance actually discouraged authors who wrote about craftsmen from questioning the values of the elite. For the pastoral, as a mode of thought, habitually looked backward to a golden age in which want, ill-health, greed and ambition were unknown, in which land was held in common, in which the earth produced food without cultivation, and in which all men lived in harmony.[25] In the pastoral landscape, capitalism – with its competition, its praise of money-making values, and its emphasis on investment and gain – was not to be thought of. It was, in fact, an attribute of the iron age of contemporary life – the very world which men went to Arcadia to escape. The urban pastoral romance modified this split between the worlds of *otium* and *negotium* to an extent, for craftsmen in all the pastoral stories worked at their callings. But urban pastoral romance looked back to a golden age of its own – the age of gild solidarity, in which masters helped their servants, took care of the lesser men in their companies, and never let a poor man in their gild go hungry. In this age, no man competed with another for a market; no entrepreneurs

[24] On the pastoral as laboratory, see Davis and Lanham, *Sidney's Arcadia*, p. 8.
[25] Marinelli, *Pastoral*, Chapter II.

took over the more lucrative aspects of business and left the less successful men in their companies to fend for themselves; and shoemakers were shoemakers, instead of being tanners, drapers, glovers who simply belonged to the shoemakers' gild. The 'history' of the gentle craft was not history; it was nostalgia. While the gentle craftsman looked forward to the world of capitalism, he looked backward to an idealized medieval economy.

The urban pastoral romance, then, had great limitations as a structure that permitted reflection on the sociological role of craftsmen in Elizabethan society. The very phrases 'urban pastoral romance' and 'gentle craftsman' suggest the nature of the problem facing popular authors who wanted to praise men of trade; both are contradictions in terms that reflect conflicting ideologies. The portrait of the gentle craftsman was, sociologically speaking, a double exposure. On the one hand, it presented men who worked in their shops and made money; on the other, it presented trade as a vocation dominated, like military prowess, by chivalric ideals – courteous, mature, generous fair play. The creation of shop-life Arcadia helped the popular authors disguise their double vision, but it did not really solve the problem of defining craftsman consciousness. As satirists were quick to point out, the gentle craftsman and the bellicose apprentice were inherently ridiculous figures – unrealistic, fantastic, and, for all their military skill, clumsy amalgamations of ideas.

There was one way, however, that the gentle craftsman could be used in Elizabethan literature without invoking satire, and this was as a political critic. There were inherent political tensions in the scheme of things presented by Deloney and balladeers; they emerged in stories like the one of Lusty Peachy, but as we have seen, Deloney did nothing with them. The urban pastoral romance showed craftsmen to be the spiritual and moral equals of the elite, but it also expected them to accept their places in society – places which, in the 1590s, were by no means so full of cakes and ale as the shop-life idealized in prose fiction. The advocation of content was perfectly supportable so long as the elite lived up to its responsibilities in the sociological scheme of things. But towards the end of Elizabeth's reign, during the hardest times any living man could remember, there was reason to believe that England's most powerful men were more interested in their own political advancement than they were in caring for the queen's loyal subjects. The court was torn between selfish factions; courtiers who gained monopolies harassed craftsmen who did not have the queen's special permission to make wares; and while war may have been a source of glory to Raleigh or Essex, it was a source of horrible misery to the common soldier. Elizabethan courtiers *needed* the lessons of Arcadia; and the urban pastoral romance gave popular authors a way of telling them they did. For the pastoral motif, by contrasting the duplicity of the court with the simplicity of the countryside, carried beneath its decorative exterior the seeds of political criticism.[26]

The gentle craftsman appeared as a political critic only on the stage, and, not altogether surprisingly, he was a sophisticated version of the craftsman clown as well as a pastoral figure. While the clown's simplicity had been a matter of appetite, however, the gentle craftsman's simplicity was a virtue. He became the teacher of the elite, and also the teacher of the audience. It was plain to anybody leaving the theatre that kings (or queens) and courtiers would do well to listen to the lessons taught by Bunch the Botcher, Rafe the Shoemaker, or Hobs the Tanner of Tamworth. In fact, it may have been too plain; the weakness of the gentle craftsman on the stage was that he enabled his creators to say too much, not too little, of what they had to say.

Bunch the Botcher is the gentle craftsman clown figure of an anonymous play *The Weakest Goeth to the Wall* (c. 1600). In the tradition of the clown, but also in the upgraded tradition of the gentle craftsman, he is a great admirer of the virtues of ale – 'fresh Ale, firm Ale, nappy Ale, nippitate Ale, irregular, secular Ale, courageous, contagious Ale, alcumistical Ale'. Bunch is also, however, proud of his craft and defends it against men who appear to belittle it. He realizes that botching (mending clothes) is not the most glorious of trades – he calls himself 'the fag end of a tailor' – but he allows nobody to discuss his work ironically but himself. When he thinks a Flemish innkeeper has insulted his trade, he is furious; and when the princely hero of the piece calls him a peasant, he retorts, 'I am no peasant, I am Bunch the Botcher: Peasants be plowmen, I am an Artificial'.[27]

Bunch is thrown into the company of the disguised Duke Lodowick of Boulogne, who has been driven out of his dukedom by

[26] *Ibid.*, p. 12.
[27] *The Weakest Goeth to the Wall*, The Malone Society Reprints, gen. ed., W.W. Greg (Oxford, 1912), lines 222–4 (ale), lines 1220–1.

the treacherous Duke of Anjou. Lodowick and his family are in dire need of Bunch's friendship, for they are quite unable to support themselves. While Bunch sets up his shop and goes to work as soon as they find a place to stay, the duke's family simply laments its fate and stays idle until at last it is hopelessly in debt to their detestable host, a lecherous innkeeper. Finally, at the innkeeper's insistence, Lodowick leaves his wife and daughter 'hostage' at the inn and goes to find work. But long before he finds it, kindly Bunch pays off his debt and leaves the duchess free to seek her husband. The play does not judge harshly; but this scene certainly does compare the help-lessness of the (French) aristocracy and the self-sufficient gener-osity of the sturdy (English) man of trade.

Bunch, while he likes his creature comforts and would like a steady income, will have nothing to do with court favours. When he first meets the duke's disguised family, Lodowick asks him not to say where they are from, and promises to pay him for his silence. Bunch is offended; his favours are not to be bought.

Why what do ye think of me? a horseleach to suck ye? or a trencherfly to blow ye? or a vermin to spoil ye? or a moth to eat through ye? no, I am Barnaby Bunch, the Botcher that never spent any man's goods but my own, I'll labour for my meat, work hard, fare hard, lie hard, for a living, I'll not charge ye a penny, I'll keep your council. And ye shall command me to serve you . . . in the way of honesty, like honest Barnaby.[28]

Here we are given a brief glimpse of the difference between the court and the country. Lodowick is used to paying for service – and for honesty; Bunch is insulted by the implication that he serves Lodowick out of hopes of a reward. The merry man 'that never spent any man's goods but [his] own' and looks out for himself while helping his neighbour is the antithesis of the ambitious Duke of Anjou and the other aristocrats in the play. Bunch is also an example to courtiers in England; for in the waning years of Elizabeth's reign, competition ran very high at court, and the gratuities accepted by Elizabethan courtiers were enormous. While the lesson Bunch's simplicity has to teach the court is tempered by the fact that he is an honest Englishman among quarrelling French-men, an intelligent audience would certainly see that his example should be followed in England as well as on the Continent.

---

[28] *Ibid.*, lines 493–500.

The Weakest Goeth to the Wall is hardly a subversive play; its gentle political message is only part of a long pastoral drama with many characters and a complicated plot. It is interesting, however, because it typifies the Elizabethan plays in which gentle craftsmen appear as teachers; none of them are subversive, and what criticism does appear seems to turn up almost by accident. This is particularly true in Thomas Dekker's play *The Shoemakers' Holiday* (1599), which, despite its implicit criticism of the aristocracy, was produced at court as well as in the popular theatres.

The Shoemakers' Holiday is an adaptation of the Simon Eyre story in Deloney's *Gentle Craft, Part I*. The play centres upon Eyre's shop and its inhabitants, and it turns Eyre into a democratic figure who gives a feast for his king and all the London apprentices at the same time, thus celebrating the fellowship of lord mayors, craftsmen, apprentices, and monarchs. The subplot, however, which was Dekker's own invention, touches upon slightly darker themes of social injustice as it deals with the hardships of Rafe the Shoemaker.

Rafe is one of Eyre's journeymen; he is a good workman married to a pretty girl, Jane. But Rafe has been pressed to fight the French; he is introduced to the audience as Eyre and his wife, Jane, and Eyre's journeymen plead with the captain of the London forces to exempt him from military service. The captain of the London forces is Roland Lacy, nephew and heir of the Earl of Lincoln, and a young man secretly in love with the daughter of the Lord Mayor of London. Lacy insists he cannot let Rafe stay at home ('I cannot change a man'), and so Rafe must go, even though, as one of the journeymen points out, Jane may have to 'beg in the day time' in his absence. Rafe marches off, and all the shoemakers wish him well; Eyre especially reminds him to 'fight for the honour of the Gentle Craft, for the gentleman Shoemakers, the courageous Cordwainers'.[29] But Rafe, unlike Crispianus and Johnson's brave apprentices, performs no chivalric feats. He is seriously wounded, and he comes home permanently lamed. Meanwhile, Jane has disappeared, and none of the shoemakers know where she is. Overcome with grief, the disabled Rafe goes back to work for Eyre.

Roland Lacy, in the meantime, has deserted his command and fled to the pastoral world of Eyre's shop. Ironically, Eyre hires him because he is shorthanded, so Lacy takes Rafe's place in the shop.

---

[29] *Shoemakers' Holiday*, I, i, lines 144–6, 139, 211–16.

Like a true pastoral hero, Lacy has given up Valour for Love; disguised as a shoemaker, he woos and wins the lord mayor's daughter, marries her, and – with Eyre's help – obtains the king's pardon for his desertion. The king, in fact, is so impressed that Lacy stooped to 'bare necessity' in order to court his love that he makes him a knight, to redeem 'the honour which he lost in France'.[30] Thus, the man who refused to exempt Rafe from service because he had newly married Jane is rewarded for desertion and courting a pretty girl. In the heir of an earl, desertion is merely a pastoral episode; in a shoemaker, it would have been a crime punishable by death.

The Shoemakers' Holiday is a romantic comedy, not a social treatise. It draws no conclusions about the contrast between Rafe's treatment and Lacy's; in fact, Lacy remains likeable from beginning to end. Nevertheless, the audience is not allowed to forget that Lacy's pastoral sojourn is an aristocratic privilege; nor is it allowed to forget that if Lacy had excused Rafe as he excused himself, Rafe could have been saved a serious injury.

Nor does Dekker stop there – Rafe gets his wife back only after enduring great insult. In Rafe's absence, Jane has been persuaded to marry one Master Hammon, a gentleman who wins her by showing her a forged casualty list on which Rafe's name appears. Rafe, however, finds out that the wedding is about to take place because Hammon gives him one of Jane's shoes (which Rafe made especially for her before he was sent to France) to determine the size of new shoes for the great event. To make sure Hammon's lady is Jane, Rafe delivers the shoes in person. Jane does not recognize him because he is so altered by his injury, but she does think he is 'somewhat like' her dead husband; because of that, she gives him a gold piece to spend. Nothing could point out more clearly the difference between the betrothed love of a gentleman and the wife of a shoemaker.[31]

In order to prevent his wife from marrying Hammon, Rafe and a band of shoemakers meet the wedding party at the church. Rafe demands his wife, and the shoemakers and Hammon's servants both flourish their weapons. But Hammon, not wishing to risk a street brawl, tries to buy Rafe's cooperation by offering him £20 'in fair gold' for his wife. Rafe is, of course, insulted: 'Sirrah Hammon Hammon, dost thou think a shoemaker is so base, to be a bawd to his own wife for commodity? take thy gold, choke with it: were I not lame, I would make thee eat thy words.' Hammon has no choice but to give in, especially since Jane returns happily to Rafe, saying that he is more valuable to her than all Hammon's wealth.[32] But although it may be flattering for craftsmen to see that Jane will not trade a shoemaker for a gentleman, Dekker has shown that Hammon, like Lacy, can take advantage of his social position – unless, of course, he is stopped from doing so by craftsmen. The shoemakers who accost Hammon at his would-be wedding are a little different from the shoemakers who obediently watched Rafe march off to war. They have learned, through Rafe's experience, that gentlemen cannot be expected or trusted to look out for crafts-men's interests. In this play, it is not the elite (disguised or other-wise) that has been educated in Arcadia, but the Arcadians them-selves. The king, Lacy, and even Hammon (who is genuinely pained at his loss of Jane, not just affronted to lose a bride to a shoemaker) are sympathetic figures – and yet it is the king who is pursuing the war in which common men like Rafe are wounded, Lacy who deserts the army and is rewarded for doing so, and Hammon who offers a man money for his wife. Again, we are looking at a strangely 'double' consciousness; the undercurrents of the play distort the cheerful comedy that seems to flow smoothly to the fifth-act solution. Was this a conscious plan of Dekker's, or did the under-current creep in by accident? It is very difficult to tell.

Heywood's *Edward IV*, unlike the two comedies we have just examined, is a political play, and it is of particular interest to his-torians. It is not, by any manner of means, a good play; it is episodic, bombastic and sentimental by turns. And yet, it contains one of the most open critiques of the court to appear on the Elizabethan stage, all disguised in the pastoral interlude in which Edward IV talks to the most outspoken gentle craftsman of the age, Hobs the Tanner of Tamworth. To begin with, there is the character of Edward IV, about whom Heywood's feelings are extremely ambivalent. He is handsome, charming, kind to those he loves, and personally courageous, but he consistently puts his own convenience above his subjects' welfare. When the Londoners are defending their city against the Bastard Fauconbridge, Edward postpones riding to their aid because he wants to celebrate his wedding feast – so he arrives

[32] *Ibid.*, V, ii, lines 75–7, 82–5, 55–89.

after the battle is over. When he is supposed to reward the lord
mayor by feasting with him, he leaves discourteously because of his
attraction to Jane Shore, whose husband served him valiantly by
defeating Fauconbridge's rebels. In seducing Mistress Shore,
Edward is faithless to his newly wedded wife and to the Londoners
who saved his throne. Even death fails to stir his reflections; when
he hears that Henry VI has died, he is relieved and delighted.

This brave, callous king chances to meet Hobs, the Tanner of
Tamworth, when he is hunting, and the two befriend each other as
Edward laughingly offers to swap horses with the craftsman. The
episode is taken from a popular ballad; Heywood turns it into a pastoral interlude in which the king is forced to see a side of his realm
(and of himself) that he has not seen before.[33] Hobs has traces of the
craftsman clown in his makeup; he uses malapropisms continually,
and he is provincial about matters of culture (he likes the theatre,
but he confuses 'comedy' with 'commodity' – a slip that would
delight a Marxist heart). But Hobs is also an intelligent and sensible
political critic, and Heywood contrasts his deep concern with justice
and his distrust of court faction with Edward's light-hearted pursuit
of his own whims.

Hobs' distaste for faction is apparent before he meets Edward.
Asked by Edward's attendants if he has seen the king hunting, he
asks, 'Which king dost thou ask for?' When the courtiers answer
that they could be looking only for King Edward, Hobs retorts:
'There's another king, and ye could hit on him; one Harry, one
Harry: and by our Lady, they say he's the honester man of the two.'
The shocked courtiers warn him he could be hanged for such
treacherous words. Hobs grumbles: 'I know not when I speak
treason, when I do not. There's such halting betwixt two kings, that
a man cannot go upright, but he shall offend the one of them. I
would God had them both, for me.' Faction is not a matter for common men to meddle with; Hobs knows better than to have lasting
sympathy with Edward or his defeated competitor. When Edward,
who introduces himself to Hobs as Ned, the king's butler, tries
repeatedly to tease the tanner into saying which king he honours
most, Hobs will say only that he is like a windmill: 'If it be Harry, I
can say, Well fare Lancaster. If it be Edward, I can sing, York, York
for my money.' And when news comes that Henry VI is dead,

[33] Francis James Child, ed., *The English and Scottish Popular Ballads* (5 vols., 1882–
90; rpt. New York, 1965), V, 81–3.

Edward inquires anxiously what the common men will think, Hobs reflects sadly, 'Well, God be with good King Henry', and then adds a political answer:

> Faith, the Commons will take it as a common thing.
> Death's an honest man; for he spares not the King.
> For as one comes, another's taken away;
> And seldom comes the better, that's all we say.[34]

The duty of the commoners is to be loyal to the king who rules. Hobs fulfils this duty (he contributes generously to Edward's war with France), but he is well aware that the usurper who ousted Henry VI is a lesser man than his victim.

Hobs' most trenchant criticisms concern the court, not the king. It is important to remember that he thinks Edward is a 'courtnol', for in his half-serious teasing of his friend he criticizes many aspects of the Elizabethan court. Some of his criticisms are merely stock: he wants Edward to marry his pretty daughter, for example, on condition that he will give up the court and become an honest tanner 'for service is no heritage: a young courtier, an old beggar'. Hobs betrays his own provinciality and pride in his trade here – though Edward's actions in the play certainly confirm Hobs' suspicions of courtiers.

Of greater interest is Hobs' comment on the fashionable apparel that Edward and his courtier wear to Tamworth when they have dinner with him: 'Troth I doubt ye ne'er came truly by all these gay rags. 'Tis not your bare wages and thin fees ye have of the King can keep ye thus fine; but either ye must rob the King privily, or his subjects openly, to maintain your probicality.' For all his malapropisms, Hobs has hit upon a sore point – and his target is not Edward's court but Elizabeth's. Like her grandfather, Elizabeth did not pay her officers sufficient fees to enable them to live as the court required; a courtier maintained himself not with his 'bare wages and thin fees' but with his 'fruits of office', the gratuities he received for obtaining the queen's favour for his followers, finding friends minor positions at court or in the country, or for helping suitors out of legal difficulties. Given the small salaries connected with governmental offices in Elizabethan England and the queen's comparative poverty in inflationary times, this political 'gift-giving' was simply a

---

[34] Heywood, I, 40–1, 45, 51.

necessary part of the political world. In the last years of Elizabeth's reign, however, the gratuities given for favour and influence grew greater and greater as faction at court intensified in the struggle for power between the Earl of Essex and Burleigh's son, Robert Cecil. What had been necessary became corrupt, divisive and expensive; and it affected the common people because the Queen frequently expressed her favour by giving courtiers rights to customs duties or monopolies, which raised the prices of everyday goods. These are the abuses Hobs refers to; fancy dress is not bad *per se* – but it reflects the amount of money courtiers take from the king *and his subjects*. Unlike political faction, this is not merely a matter of the court.[35]

Heywood reserves his most trenchant criticism of Elizabethan politics for monopolies, and again, he uses Hobs' sharp tongue to present his views. Edward, who enjoys Hobs' outspoken criticism of his policies, suggests that the tanner should come to court so the king could give him a monopoly on the leather trade by letters patent. Hobs staunchly refuses such favour:

> By the mass and the matins, I like not those patents.
> Sirrah, they that have them do, as the priests did in old
> time, buy and sell the sins of the people. So they make the
> King believe they mend what's amiss, and for money they
> make the thing worse than it is. There's another thing in
> too, the more is the pity.

KING What pity, John Hobs? I prithee say all.

HOBS Faith, 'tis pity that one subject should have in his hands
what might do good to many through the land.[36]

Here Hobs speaks directly to the Elizabethan audience (for Edward's offer of a monopoly is, of course, as anachronistic as Hobs' post-reformation view of indulgences). Letters patent, granting the founder of a 'project' sole rights to produce the good he had contributed to the economy, had come by the 1580s to entangle beneficial projects like ivy choking out a shade tree. Originally, these patents had been designed to permit the founder of a project and his financial backers to profit from their ingenuity without competition (on condition they yield a percentage of their profits to the queen); but gradually, more patents were given to courtiers who

[35]*Ibid.*, I, 50. See J.E. Neale, *Essays in Elizabethan History* (New York, 1958), pp. 61–79.
[36]Heywood, I, 46.

would hire craftsmen to work out the project rather than direct to inventors, and patents became oppressive. A poor inventor had no way to keep his methods secret, so his commercial improvements spread quickly to different towns; a courtier, however, had both power and money enough to ferret out competition, with the result that many small local producers who dealt in the patented good were taxed, fined or harrassed out of business and new industries were not allowed to spread. Many producers avoided detection by moving out of towns into rural areas, taking their skilled workers along with them; others took up other activities. But the hampering of industry and the high prices of monopoly goods aroused anger among the common people. In 1597, popular anger had found its expression in the House of Commons as some members tried to introduce a bill against monopolies. The queen, hard pressed, had promised reform; but at the time Hobs spoke, few (if any) reforms had materialized. Little could be done about the situation until parliament was summoned again, and meanwhile, the problem bred increasing disenchantment with the court.[37]

Hobs' criticism of faction, gratuities and monopolies, then, reflected serious grievances with Elizabeth's political policies. It is surprising that his remarks escaped censorship; certainly no other play of the period contained such plainly put, specific political criticism. Possibly the play was spared because Hobs' situation softened his sharp tongue. The spectacle of a craftsman preaching political wisdom to the king himself, unwittingly worsening his situation at every critical word, is genuinely funny, and it undercuts much of Hobs' frankness. Then too, Hobs is an unquestionably loyal subject; he gives 'twenty angels and a score of hides' to the king for his wars, and his sharp tongue urges his neighbours to be similarly generous.[38] Like other Elizabethans, he may have been allowed to grumble so long as he expressed his loyalty to the monarch with donations of ready cash.

It is more than possible, however, that Hobs was spared because he appeared in a play with the same 'double' aspect as *The Shoemakers' Holiday*. Edward IV is a deeply flawed man, but Heywood never suggests that he is a deeply flawed monarch. The play in many ways is celebratory, and the very scenes in which Hobs criticizes the king are the ones in which Edward comes off looking best, partly

---

[37] Thirsk, *Economic Policy and Projects*, 55, 57–66; Neale, *Elizabeth I and Her Parliaments, 1584–1611* (London, 1957), pp. 352–6.
[38] Heywood, I, 71.

because he is such a good fellow, and partly because he is genuinely interested in what Hobs has to say. *1 Edward IV*, like *The Shoemakers' Holiday*, ends with a comic synthesis; Hobs learns who 'Ned' really is and is sure he will be hanged, but Edward laughs at his fears and pardons his son, who has gotten into trouble with the law. Yet this man who is so magnanimous with Hobs has ruined Shore and seduced his wife, and he is about to embark on a war purely (the play implies) for his own honour. The interlude with Hobs is just that – a pastoral interlude in the king's life of war, seduction, treachery and callousness. Is Edward admirable or not? The play comes down on both sides of the question. Edward certainly bears Hobs no ill-will, but did he listen to his lessons? The play side-steps the issue. The cheerful denouement in the fifth act is merely a prelude to further action; the tension between celebration and criticism is never solved. In *2 Edward IV* the full tragedy of Edward's actions becomes clear, and Master and Mistress Shore die of hunger and sorrow. Hobs, however, does not appear in this play to witness the truth of his perception that courtnols are not to be trusted.

Within a few years of the first productions of *The Weakest Goeth to the Wall*, *The Shoemakers' Holiday*, and *1 Edward IV*, the gentle craftsman disappeared from literature in all but his crudest forms. Hero apprentice ballads continued to appeal to the virility of generations of apprentices, Heywood's *Four Prentices* was revived in 1615 (with its author's apologies for its being so out of fashion), and William Rowley revived the Crispianus story in *A Shoemaker, a Gentleman* in 1608. There were, however, no new creations of craftsmen like Bunch, Hobs, Rafe, or Lusty Peachy; these craftsmen died out at the end of the 1590s. The demise of the gentle craftsman can be attributed partly to Deloney's death in 1600; he had been the prime creator of gentle craftsmen, and when he stopped producing tales from which the playwrights could draw, they turned to other sources. At the same time, literary fashion changed: popular heroics went out of date and were replaced by satirical 'citizen comedy' in which there was little, if any, attention paid to craftsmen at all. Finally, works like *The Knight of the Burning Pestle* ridiculed *The Four Prentices* and bombastic apprentice ballads by calling attention to the absurdity of placing London craftsmen and apprentices in a pastoral, chivalric setting.

Finally, however, the gentle craftsman disappeared because he said at once too much and too little about the social hierarchy. He said too little because the pastoral romance, however it might serve the purposes of an author who wished to reflect upon the values of craftsmen, was a structure that limited new social ideas. Its purpose, as we have seen, was to assert the worth of gentle values, to combat the sin of pride by pointing out how much a hero could learn by living a simple life, and to show how paltry men's ambitions appeared in the context of greater themes of time, love, order and wisdom. As the pastoral romance was applied to craftsmen, it asserted that 'wisdom' consisted in accepting one's place in society and being content with what one had – an idea completely at odds with the spirit of capitalism, which praises the accumulation of resources for the betterment of one's social condition. There was no place in the pastoral ideal for the celebration of diligent work that got a man *out* of a low social position, nothing, in short, that encouraged the energy, skill and drive that had permitted Elizabethan-craftsmen to take advantage of economic change and become prosperous beings who stood out from 'the fourth sort of people'. The structure the popular authors used to praise craftsmen forced them to ignore the complex inter-relationship of money-making and social advancement; ironically, it made them reassert the validity of social ideals that made the *absence* of wealth and social prestige tolerable.

Thus, while the popular authors could turn the values of the elite to their own purposes and appeal to the consciousness of craftsmen by giving them an 'historical' tradition that mirrored the elite's, the very structure and language available to them for this celebration kept them from considering what effect the emergence of the social group they portrayed might have on accepted social ideology. To consider the problems that arose from the laughable unreality of the chivalric apprentices the satirists ridiculed, the authors would have had to jettison the social creed of the preachers, cast aside pastoral romance, and consider the social hierarchy and its values in a completely new context. This context, however, was not available to them – there was not even a language that described capitalistic virtues. And so, in the face of their critics, the creators of the gentle craftsmen were forced to choose between repeating the old themes of pastoral, chivalric service (thus begging for further satire), and ceasing to write about craftsmen altogether. Most of them chose the latter course.

On the other hand, the pastoral motif did, as we have seen, provide the authors a means of reflection on the elite's adherence to their political responsibilities. And here the danger was one of saying too much about the social hierarchy. The gentle craftsman had a lesson to teach his social superiors, and since he was demonstrably their equal in terms of intelligence, bravery and wisdom, he was well equipped to teach it. Hobs and Rafe had something to tell their betters about political and moral responsibility. Deloney's shoemakers taught the knights and lords who lived in their shops to think of their duties first and their personal desires last. Bunch the Botcher showed the Duke of Boulogne that honest service and loyalty was free, if one was not a courtier. Hobs the Tanner taught Edward IV that monopolies, far from bettering the positions of the king's subjects, in fact made them suffer. As a social and political critic, the gentle craftsman emerged as a man whose perceptions were superior to those of the elite.

The insistence that gentlemen, aristocrats and kings could learn about social justice from craftsmen was not necessarily radical. In general, the works that pointed out the failings of the elite were petitions for reform, not challenges of the elite's fundamental right to rule. Nevertheless, the suggestion that men of lowly status could be superior to the elite, accompanied by a hint of the bitter awareness that craftsmen, however intelligent and responsible they might be, had none of the power and privilege of the elite and were in danger of being *exploited* by their social superiors could have very radical implications indeed. These flashes of insight, exposing the roots of injustice inherent in the social order, occasionally appeared in *The Gentle Craft, Part II, 1 Edward IV*, and *The Shoemakers' Holiday*. And while those insights seem almost out of place in works that are basically comic or celebratory, they probably did not appear by accident. These works were written in 1598 and 1599, just after the longest famine England had endured for decades, at a time when the plague was disrupting the economy, and at a time when armies were being levied for war in Ireland and Spain. Furthermore, the authors of these works were the Great Toms of Elizabethan popular literature; men who had concentrated their literary talents on expressing concern for men of middling to lower status. These men had, through their fictive celebrations of craftsmen, begun to reflect upon the social tensions that arose when they abandoned the belief that men of trade were simple, brutish clowns who lived in a world in which the elite had a monopoly on talent, courage and virtue.

The atmosphere of the late 1590s called for this kind of reflection, for if the era saw craftsmen reach a high point of literacy and prosperity, it also saw these gains being eroded by hard times –and by the monopolies of courtiers who made it difficult for craftsmen to benefit from new projects as they had benefited from those of the 1570s and 1580s. The mood of the last three years of Elizabeth's reign, however, was not conducive to the continued consideration of the faults of society. The danger of rebellion – and after 1601, the fact of rebellion – coupled with the knowledge that the queen was ageing rapidly, made it politically inexpedient (and psychologically difficult) to develop any ideas with radical implications. The doctrine of obedience thrust itself into the foreground of political consciousness as the reign drew to an end. The salvation of the state lay in order – the orderly transfer of power to a new monarch, and the willingness of the commons to watch that transfer without interfering in it.

This renewed emphasis on order hastened the demise of the gentle craftsman. If he was to become more than a hybrid figure who bounced from shop to battlefield, something other than a prince in disguise, he had to continue his tentative, fictive inquiry into the tensions between justice and order. There was no other direction in which he could develop, for while his creators could use him to show that courtiers did not live according to the values of their class, they could not use him to question aristocratic values *per se*. Nor could the authors argue that industrious success in trade could solve part of the problem of inequality by making craftsmen wealthy, because the concept of industrious work in an inferior calling was inextricably linked with the ideas of contentation and obedience. They could not praise crafts as callings dignified in themselves, for manual labour in a craft was the very thing that made craftsmen inferior to the elite. The authors could prove that craftsmen were morally superior to the elite, but they could not say that the elite were extravagant, idle parasites while craftsmen were industrious hard-driving capitalists. There was no language in which to express such a dichotomy, and no doctrinal framework that permitted a comparison between gentlemen and craftsmen in these terms.

The gentle craftsman, then, had reached a dead end of social consciousness by 1600. The political ideas he had allowed his creators to develop could no longer bear the scrutiny of fiction; the economic and social issues he raised were beyond the capacity of the explicit social doctrines of his age to handle. And so, while generations of readers continued to enjoy the legendary histories of gentle craftsmen, the hero they admired abandoned his social insights at the end of Elizabeth's reign and quietly disappeared from the popular literature of the seventeenth century.

Appendix A Elizabethan popular literature

I BEST-SELLERS

This list includes all the Elizabethan books (excluding Bibles, textbooks, and translations) that went through three or more editions in the decade immediately following their first appearance. It also includes all books first published 1559–1603 that went through three editions in *any* decade after their first appearance, books whose numerated editions indicate that they went through more editions than presently exist, and books whose early editions (usually recorded in the Stationers' Register) are lost but whose popularity is universally accepted. All the exceptional works have been marked with an asterisk (*).

Foxe's *Acts and Monuments*, whose first three editions spanned thirteen years, is included because it was made available in churches, cathedrals and the halls of merchant companies (see Chapter 9).

The works of Henry Smith and William Perkins were best-sellers individually and in collections. To avoid double counting, I have 'counted' only their collected works in the total of 189 works; but I have listed their popular sermons separately here, so that the reader can assess the independent popularity of each work if he wishes to.

Entries appear as they are listed in the revised edition of the *STC*, but I have not included material that is of purely bibliographical interest.

The following *STC* abbreviations are used:
f.   for
a.   and
aed.   editor

Abbot, George. 24. *A briefe description of the whole worlde*. T. Judson f. J. Browne, 1599. Other editions: 1599, 1600, 1605, 1608, 1617, 1620, 1624, 1634, 1635, 1636, 1642.
Armin, Robert. 772.3. *Foole upon foole, or six sortes of sottes. Written by C. de C. Snuffe* [*pseud.*]. [E. Allde] f. W. Ferbrand, 1600. Other editions: 1604, 1608 (as *A nest of ninnies*).
Ascham, Roger. 832. *The scholemaster or plaine and perfite way of teachyng children, the Latin tong*. J. Daye, 1570. Other editions: 1571, 1573, 1579, 1589.
Babington, Gervase. 1081. *A briefe conference betwixt mans frailtie and*

faith. H. Middleton f. T. Charde, 1583. Other editions: 1584, 1590, 1596, 1602.

1095. *A very fruitfull exposition of the Commaundements by way of questions and answeres.* H. Middleton f. T. Charde, 1583. Other editions: 1586, 1590, 1596.

Bacon, Francis. 1137. *Essayes. Religious meditations. Places of perswasion and disswasion.* [J. Windet] f. H. Hooper, 1597. Other editions: 1597, 1598, 1606, two in 1612; three in 1613; 1614, 1624. (Becomes *Essayes or counsels, civil and morall,* 1625, 1629, 1632, 1639.)

*Bailey, Walter. 1193. *A briefe treatise touching the preservation of the eie sight.* [R. Waldegrave?], 1586. Other editions: 1587–8 (part of 12499), 1602 (6th edn), 1616; 1622 (part of 12499.5), 1626 (part of 24617), 1633 (part of 24618).

Baker, Humphrey. 1209.5. *The well sprynge of sciences.* R. Hall f. J. Rowbothum, 1562. Other editions: 1564, 1568, 1574, 1576, 1580, [1582?], 1583, 1591, 1598, 1602, 1607, 1612, 1617, 1631.

Baldwin, William. 1247. *A myrroure for magistrates.* T. Marshe, 1559. Other editions: 1563, 1571, 1574 ('the laste parte'), 1578.

Balmford, James. 1335. *A short and plaine dialogue concerning the unlawfulnes of playing at cards.* [T. Orwin?] f. R. Boile [1593]. Other editions: [1595], [1600?] (formerly 18324).

Becon, Thomas. 1744. *The pomader of prayer. Whereunto are added Meditations called S. Augustins.* [J. Daye], 1558. Other editions: 1561, 1563, 1565, 1566, [c. 1567], [c. 1570], 1578.

1756.5. *The sycke mannes salue. Newly made.* J. Daye, [c. 1560]. Other editions: 1561, 1565, 1568, 1570, 1572, 1574, 1577, 1579, two in 1582; 1584, 1585, 1587, 1591, 1594, 1597, 1600, 1604, 1607, 1610, 1613, 1619, 1629, 1631, 1632.

Bicknoll, Edmund. 3048. *A swoord agaynst swearyng.* R. Watkins, 1579. Other editions: 1579, [c. 1580], 1599, 1609, 1611, 1618.

Bigges, Walter. 3056. *A summarie and true discourse of Sir Frances Drakes West Indian Voyage.* R. Field, 1589. Other editions: 1589, 1596.

Book. 3294.3 (formerly 2041). *A Booke of Christian questions and answeres.* H. Middleton f. J. Harrison, 1578. Other editions: 1579, 1581.

Bourne, William. 3422. *A regiment for the sea.* [H. Bynneman f.] T. Hacket [1574]. Other editions: 1577, 1580, 1584, 1587, 1592, 1596, 1601, 1611, 1620, 1631.

Bradshaw, William. 3518. *Humble motives for association to maintaine religion established.* [London], 1601. Other editions: two more in 1601.

Brasbridge, Thomas. 3648.5 (formerly 3551). *The poore mans iewell, that is to say, a treatise of the pestilence.* f. G. Bishop, 1578. Other editions: 1578, 1579, 1580, 1592.

Breton, Nicholas. 3694. *A poste with a madde packet of letters [Part I].* [T. Creed] f. J. Smethicke, 1602. Other editions: 1603, [1605?], 1607, 1609, 1620, 1630, 1633 (part of 3692), 1634 (part of 3693).

*3696. *A solemne passion of the soules loue.* [*In verse.*] S. Stafford [in the shop of V. Simmes] f. W. Barley, 1598. Other editions: two in 1622; 1623, [1625?].

*3699. *The soules harmony. Written by N. Breton. [In verse.]* S. Stafford f. P. Bearkes, 1602. Other editions: 6th, 1622; [c. 1630]; 9th, 1637.

3705. *The wil of wit, wits will, or wils wit. Containing fiue discourses.* T. Creed, 1597. Other editions: 1599, 1606.

Browne, John. 3908.4. *The marchants auizo.* R. Field f. W. Norton, 1589. Other editions: 1590, 1591, 1607 (formerly 1049), 1616 (formerly 1050), 1640 (formerly 1051).

Bull, Henry. 4028. [*Christian prayers and holy meditations. Prayers commonly called lydleys prayers, with additions.*] (T. East f. H. Middleton, 1568.) Other editions: 1570, 1574, [1578], 1584, 1596, 1612.

Bullein, William. 4036. [*A dialogue both pleasant and pietifull, against the feuer pestilence.*] [J. Kingston, 1564]. Other editions: 1564, 1573, 1578.

A newe book entituled the government of healthe. J. Day [1558]. Other editions: 1558, 1559, 1595.

Burton, William. 4176. *The rousing of the sluggard, in 7. sermons. By W.B. minister at Reading.* Widow Orwin f. T. Man, 1595. Other editions: 1595, 1598, 1634.

C., T. 4303.5. *An hospitall for the diseased.* T. Man a. W. Hoskins, 1578. Other editions: two in 1579; three [c. 1585], [c. 1597], 1595, 1598, 1610, 1619, 1630, 1638.

Cancellar, James. 4558. *The alphabet of prayers. Newly collected in 1564.* H. Denham, 1565. Other editions: 1570, two in 1573; 1576, 1591, 1601, [c. 1610].

Carlile, Christopher. 4655. *A discourse. Wherein is plainly proued that Peter was neuer at Rome.* T. East a. H. Myddleton f. W. Norton, 1572. Other editions: [1580?], two in 1582.

Cary, Walter. 4730. *A briefe treatise, called Caries farewell to physicke.* H. Denham, 1583. Other editions: 1583, 1587, 1597, 1609, 1611.

4733. *The hammer for the stone.* H. Denham, 1580. Other editions: 1581, 1584, 1586, and reprinted with *Caries farewell* in 1597, 1609, 1611.

Chaderton, Laurence. 4924. *An excellent and godly sermon, preached at Paules Crosse the xxvi day of October, 1578.* C. Barker [1578?]. Other editions: [1578?], 1580.

4926. *A fruitfull sermons, vpon the 3. 4. 5. 6. 7. and 8. verses, of the 12. ch. of the Ep. to the Romanes.* R. Walde-grave, 1584. Other editions: 1584, 1586, 1589, 1618.

*Chamberlaine, Bartholomew. 4946.5. *A sermon preached at S. James, before the lordes of her maiesties priuie councel, the 25. of April, 1580.* Other editions: 1595, 1612, 1613, 1615, 1620, 1623.

Cleaver, Robert. 5382. *A codly [sic] form of householde governement.* T. Creede f. T. Man, 1598. Other editions: 1598, 1600, 1603, 1610, 1612, 1614, 1621, 1630.

Constable, Henry. 5637. *Diana. The praises of his mistres, in certaine sweete sonnets. By H.C.* J. C[harlewood] f. R. Smith, 1592. Other editions: [1594?], [1595?].

Conway, Sir John. 5651. *Meditations and praiers, gathered out of the sacred letters, and vertuous writers.* H. Wykes [1570?]. Other editions: 1571, 1572, [1580?], 1611.

Cooper, Thomas. 5682. *An admonition to the people of England.* Deputies of C. Barker, 1589. Other editions: two more in 1589.

*Coote, Edmund. *The English schoole-maister, teaching all his scholers.* (Widow Orwin f. R. Jackson a. R. Dexter, 1596.) Other editions: 1614, 1621, 1624 ('fifteenth time imprinted'), 1627 ('seventeenth time imprinted'), 1630 ('eighteenth time imprinted'), 1635 ('24th time'), 1636 ('25th time'), 1638, 1640 ('18th time').

Cotton, Roger. 5866. *A direction to the waters of lyfe.* [R. Watkins] f. G. Simson a. W. White, 1590. Other editions: two in 1592; 1610.

Curteys, Richard. 6135. *A sermon preached before the Queenes Maiestie, at Grenewiche.* H. Binneman f. F. Coldocke, 1573. Other editions: 1574, 1579, 1586.

Daniel, Samuel. 6254. *Delia and Rosamond augmented. Cleopatra.* (J. Roberts a. E. Allde) f. S. Waterson, 1594. Other editions: 1595, 1598.

Davies, Sir John. 6355. *Nosce teipsum. This oracle expounded in two elegies.* R. Field f. J. Standish, 1599. Other editions: 1599, 1602, 1608, 1619, 1622 (part of 6359).

Davison, Francis. 6373. *A poetical rapsody containing, diverse sonnets.* V. S[immes] f. J. Baily, 1602. Other editions: 1608, 1611, 1621.

Day, Angel. 6401. *The English secretorie.* R. Walde-graue, solde by R. Jones, 1586. Other editions: 1592, 1595, 1599, 1607, 1614, 1621, 1625, [1635].

Dekker, Thomas. 6476. *The batchelars banquet: or a banquet for batchelars.* T. C[reede], solde by T. P[avier], 1603. Other editions: 1603, 1604, 1630, 1631.

6535. *1603. The wonderfull yeare.* T. Creede [f. N. Ling], 1603. Other editions: two more, [1603?].

*Deloney, Thomas. 6554.5. *The gentle craft. A discourse containing many matters.*M. Flesher f. E. Brewster, 1627 (first extant edition). Other editions: Entered to R. Blore, 19 Oc. 1597, to E. Brewster a R. Bird, 4 Aug. 1626. Also editions in 1637, 1640.

*6555.7. [*The gentle craft. The second part.*] [c. 1598?] (fragments). Other editions: 1639 (first extant complete edition).

6559. *The pleasant history of John Winchcomb, called Jack of Newberie. Now the eight time imprinted.* H. Lownes, 1619 (first extant edition). Other editions: Entered to T. Millington, 7 Mr. 1597, and to H. Lownes, 25 my 1597. Also editions in 1626 ('tenth time'), 1630 ('eleventh time'), 1633 ('ninth time'), 1637 ('tenth time').

6566. *Strange histories, of kings, princes, dukes.* W. Barley, the assigne of T. M[orley], 1602. Other editions: 1607, 1612.

*6569. *Thomas of Reading. Or, the sixe worthy yeomen of the West. Now the fourth time corrected and enlarged.* [R. Blower?] f. T. P[avier],

1612 (first extant edition). Other editions: Assigned from T. Millington to T. Pavier, Ap. 1602. Also editions in 1623, 1632, 1636.

Dent, Arthur. 6625.3. *A plaine exposition of the articles of our faith.* T. Orwin f. W. Yong, a. R. Jackson, 1589. Other editions: 1594, 1603, 1606, 1609, 1616.

6626. *The plaine mans path-way to heaven.* [T. Creede] f. R. Dexter, 1601. Other editions: 1601, 1602, 1603 ('sixth impression'), 1605, 1606, 1607, 1609, 1610, 1612, 1617, 1619, 1622, 1625, 1629, 1631, 1633, 1635, 1637, 1640.

6640. *The ruine of Rome: or an exposition upon the whole Revelation.* f. S. Waterson a. C. Burley, 1603. Other editions: 1607, 1611, 1622, 1628, 1631, 1633.

6649.5 (formerly 6672). *A sermon of repentance . . . preached at Lee in Essex 1581, the 7. day of Marche.* f. R. Sergier, 1582. Other editions: 1582; four in 1583; 1584, 1585, 1586, 1587, 1588, 1589, 1590, 1595, 1598, 1599, 1600, 1602, 1606, 1607; two in 1611; 1613, 1615, 1616, 1620, 1621, 1622, 1626, 1627, two in 1630; 1631, two in 1636; 1637, 1638.

Dering, Edward. 6684.5. *Godlye piruate praiers for householders to meditate vpon and to say in their families.* J. Awdely, 1574. Other editions: 1576; two [c. 1578?]; [c. 1580?], two in 1581, 1593, 1624.

6691. *A lecture or exposition vpon a part of the v. chapter of the epistle to the Hebrues.* J. Awdely, 1573. Other editions: 1574, 1583.

6694. *A sermon preached at the Tower of London, the eleunth day of December. 1569.* J. Daye [1570?]. Other editions: three more [c. 1570]; 1584, 1589.

6699. *A sermon preached before the Quenes maiestie, the 25. day of February. 1569.* J. Awdely [1569?]. Other editions: two [c. 1570?]; three [c. 1574?]; [1575?], 1578, 1580, 1584, 1586, 1589, 1593, 1596, 1600, 1603; also 1590, 1597, 1614 in Dering's *Workes.*

6726. *XXVII. lectures, or readings, vpon part of the Epistle to the Hebrues.* [T. East a. H. Middleton f.] L. Harrison, 1576. Other editions: 1577, 1578, 1583; two in 1590; and 1590, 1597, 1614 in Dering's *Workes.*

Dowland, John. 7091. *The first booke of songes or ayres of fowre partes with tableture for the lute.* P. Short, 1597. Other editions: 1600, 1603, 1606, 1613.

Drant, Thomas. 7171. *Two sermons preached, the one at S. Maries Spittle and the other at the court at Windsor.* J. Daye [1570?]. Other editions: two more [1570].

Drayton, Michael. 7193. *Englands heroicall epistles.* J. R[oberts] f. N. Ling, 1597. Other editions: 1598, 1599, 1600, 1602, 1630 (part of 7224).

Edwards, Richard. 7516. *The paradyse of daynty deuises.* H. Disle, 1576. Other editions: 1578, 1580, 1585, [1590?], 1596, 1600, 1606.

Fenton, Sir Geoffrey. 10794. *Golden epistles, contayning varietie of discourse.* H. Middleton f. R. Newbery, 1575. Other editions: 1577, 1582.

Forde, Emanuel. 11171. *Parismus, the renoumed prince of Bohemia.*

T. Creede f. R. Clive, 1598. Other editions: 1599 (part 2), 1604/5 (both parts), 1608/9, 1615, 1630, 1636.
*Foxe, John. 11222. *Actes and monuments.* J. Day, 1563. Other editions: 1570, 1576, 1583, 1596, 1610, 1631.
11242. *A sermon of Christ crucified.* J. Daye, 1570. Other editions: two more in 1570; 1575, 1577, 1585, 1609.
Fulke, William. 11422. *A comfortable sermon of faith. Preached 1573.* J. Awdeley, 1574. Other editions: [1574?], 1578, 1586, 1611.
11449.5. *A sermon preached at Hampton Court, 12. Nov. 1570.* J. Awdely, 1570. Other editions: 1571, 1572, 1574, 1579.
G., R. 11504. (Begins) 'Salutem in Christo. Good men and euill delite in contraryes.' [J. Day, 1571]. Other editions: three more [c. 1571].
Garden. 11554.4. *A godlie gardeine, out of which most comfortable herbes may be gathered.* W. Griffith, 1569. Other editions: 1574, [1576?], 1581, 1587, 1604, 1607, 1619, 1621, 1629, 1631, 1640.
Gee, Alexander. 11696.4. *The ground of christianitie. Composed in maner of a dialogue.* R. Waldegraue, sold by T. Woodcock [1581?]. Other editions: 1582, 1584, [1588?], 1614.
Gibson, Thomas. 11838.5. *A fruitful sermon [on 1 Cor. ix. 16], preached at Occham.* R. Walde-graue [1584]. Other editions: two more in 1584.
Gifford, George. 11845. *A briefe discourse of certaine points of the religion, which is among the commō sort of christians.* T. Dawson f. T. Cooke, 1581. Other editions: 1581, [1582?], 1582, 1583, 1598, 1612.
11857.5. *Foure sermons vppon the seuen chiefe vertues of faith.* T. D[awson] f. T. Cooke, 1581. Other editions: 1582, 1584.
11860. *A godlie, zealous, and profitable sermon vpon the second chapter of Saint James.* T. East f. T. Cooke, 1582. Other editions: 1582, 1582/3, 1583, 1586.
11862.5. *A sermon on the parable of the sower.* [T. Dawson] f. T. Cooke, 1581. Other editions: [1581?], 1582, 1583, 1584.
Gosson, Stephen. 12097. *The schoole of abuse, conteining a plesaunt ineuctiue against poets, pipers, plaiers, iesters, and such like caterpillars of a cōmonwelth.* [T. Dawson f.] T. Woodecocke, 1579. Other editions: 1579, 1587.
Grafton, Richard. 12148. *An abridgement of the chronicles of England.* In aed. R. Tottyll, 1563 (1562). Other editions: 1564, 1570, 1572.
12153. *A litle treatise, conteyning many proper tables and rules.* In aed. R. Tottelli, 1571. Other editions: 1572, [1573?], 1576, 1579, 1582, 1585, 1591, 1593, 1595, 1596, 1599, 1602, 1608, 1611.
Greene, Robert. 12217. *Arbasto, the anatomie of fortune.* J. Windet a. T. Judson f. H. Jackson, 1584. Other editions: 1589, 1594.
*12224. *Ciceronis amor, Tullies Loue. Wherein is discoursed the prime of Ciceroes youth.* R. Robinson f. T. Newman a. J. Winington, 1589. Other editions: (entered 1 Oc. 1595), 1597, 1601, 1605, 1609, 1611, 1616, 1628, 1639.
12262. *Gwydonius. The carde of fancie.* T. East f. W. Ponsonby, 1584. Other editions: 1587, 1593, 1608.
122279. *A notable discouery of coosenage.* J. Wolfe f. T. Nelson, 1591.

Other editions: two more in 1591; 1592.

*(There was a series of these pamphlets, many editions of which have apparently been lost. The others are:

12281. *The second part of conny-catching.* (1591, 1592).

12283. *The third and last part of conny-catching.* (1592).

12234. *A disputation betweene a hee conny-catcher, and a shee conny-catcher.* (1592, 1615, 1617, 1621, 1637).

Because of the continuous nature of these pamphlets and the problem of lost editions, I have 'counted' the series as one popular work.)

12285. *Pandosto. The triumph of time.* T. Orwin f. T. Cadman, 1588. Other editions: 1592, 1595, 1607, 1609, 1614, 1619, 1629, 1632, [c. 1635], 1636, [c. 1640].

12300. *A quip for an upstart courtier.* J. Wolfe, 1592. Other editions: five more in 1592; 1606, 1620, 1622, 1635.

Greenham, Richard. 12312. *The works . . . examined, corrected and published by H. Holland.* F. Kingston (R. Bradocke) f. R. Dexter, 1599. Other editions: 1599, 1600 (second part); 1601, 1605, 1612 (both parts).

Hall, Joseph. 12716. *Virgidemiarum, sixe bookes. First three books, of tooth-lesse satyrs.* [Anon.] T. Creede f. R. Dexter, 1597. Other editions: 1598, 1602.

Harington, Sir John. 12773. *An apologie. 1. Or rather a retraction.* [R. Field, 1596]. Other editions: four more, all undated, [c. 1596].

A new discourse of a stale subject, called the metamorphosis of Aiax: written by Misacmos, to his friend Philostilpnos. R. Field, 1596. Other editions: three more in 1596.

Harman, Thomas. 12787. *A caveat for commen cursetors. Newly agmented* [*sic*]. W. Gryffith, 1567. Other editions: 1567, 1573, 1592.

Harrison, William. 12866. *Deaths advantage little regarded, and the soules solace ag. sorrow. Preached in two funerall sermons at the buriall of mistris K. Brettergh. The one by W. Harrison, the other by W. Leygh. Whereunto is annexed the life of the said gentlewoman.* The second edition, corrected. (Ent. 16 Dec. 1601) F. Kyngston, 1602. Other editions: 1605, 1612, 1617.

Harvey, Richard. 12910. *An astrological discourse vpon the coniunction of Saturne & Jupiter.* H. Bynneman, with the assent of R. W[atkins], 1563. Other editions: four more in 1563.

Hayward, Sir John. 13003.5. *The sanctuarie of a troubled soule.* [J. Windet f.] J. W[olfe], sold by C. Burby, 1601. Other editions: 1602, 1604.

Hunnis, William. 13975. *Seven sobs of a sorrowfull soule for sinne. Comprehending those psalmes called poenitentiall: reduced into meeter. Whereunto are annexed his handfull of honisuckles.* H. Denham, 1583. Other editions: 1585, 1587, 1589, 1592, 1597, 1600, 1602, 1604, 1609, 1615, 1618, 1621, 1629, 1636.

Jewel, John. 14600. *A defence of the Apologie of the Church of England, an answeare to a certaine book by M. Hardinge.* H. Wykes, 1567. Other editions: 1567, 1570, 1571.

Johnson, Richard. 14677. *The most famous history of the seaven champions of christendome.* [The first part]. [J. Danter] f. C. Burbie, 1596. Other editions: 1597 (second part); both parts, 1608, 1612 [1626], 1639, [c. 1640].

Ker, George. 14937. *A discouerie of the vnnaturall and traiterous conspiracie of Scottish papists.* Edinburgh, W. Waldegaue, [1593]. Other editions: 1593, 1603, 1625.

King, John. 14976. *Lectures vpon Jonas, delivered at Yorke in the yeare of our Lorde 1594.* Oxford, Jos. Barnes, solde [in London by Joan Brome] 1597. Other editions: 1599, 1600, 1611, 1618.

Kingsmill, Andrew. 15000. *A most excellent and comfortable treatise, for all such as are troubled in minde. And also a conference betwixt a Christian & an afflicted consciēce.* C. Barker, 1577. Other editions: 1578, 1585.

15003. *A viewe of mans estate.* H. Bynneman f. L. Harrison a. G. Bishop, 1574. Other editions: 1576, 1580.

Knewstub, John. 15042. *Lectures of . . . vpon the twentith [sic] chapter of Exodus.* J. Harrison, 1577. Other editions: 1578, 1579, 1584.

Lambard, William. 15145. *The duties of constables, borsholders, tithingmen [etc.] 1582.* R. Newberie a. H. Middleton, 1583. Other editions: two more in 1583; 1584, 1587, 1591, two in 1594; 1599, 1601, 1602, 1604, 1605, 1606; four in 1610; 1624, 1626, [1631], [1633], 1640.

15163. *Eirenarcha: or of the office of the justices of peace, in two books.* R. Newbery a. H. Bynneman, by the ass. [assignment] or R. Tot[tell]a. C. Bar[ker], 1581. Other editions: two in 1582; 1583, 1588, 1592, 1594, 1599, 1602, 1607, 1610, 1614, 1619.

Leigh, Richard. 15412. *The copie of a letter sent out of England to don Bernadin Mendoza. Found in the chamber of R. Leigh a seminarie priest . . .* [By W. Cecil.] J. Vautrolier f. R. Field, 1588. Other editions: two more in 1588; 1641.

Lewkenor, Sir Lewis. 15562. *A discourse of the vsage of the English fugitiues, by the Spaniard.* [Anon]. London, T. Scarlet f. J. Drawater, 1595. Other editions: two more in 1595; 1596.

Ling, Nicholas. 15685. *Politeuphia wits common wealth.* J. R[oberts] f. N. Ling, 1597. Other editions: two in 1598; 1608, [1608?], [after 1612], [c. 1615], [1620?], [1626], [1628?], [1630?], [1640].

Lodge, Thomas. 16664. *Rosalynde. Eupheus golden legacie.* T. Orwin f. T. G[ubbin] a. J. Busbie, 1590. Other editions: 1592, 1596, 1598, 1604, 1609, 1612, 1623, 1634.

Lupton, Thomas. 16951. *Siuqila. Too good, to be true: . . . Herein is shewed by waye of dialoge, the wonderful maners of the people of Mauqsun.* H. Bynneman, 1580. Other editions: 1580, 1584, 1587.

*16955. *A thousand notable things, of sundry sortes.* J. Charlewood f. H. Spooner, [1579]. Other editions: 1586, [c. 1590], 1595, 1601, 1612, 1627, 1631.

Lyly, John. 17051. *Euphues. The anatomy of wyt.* [T. East] f. G. Cawood, [1578]. Other editions: two in 1579; two in 1580; two in 1581; 1585, 1587, [1590], [1593], [1597], 1606, 1607, 1613, 1617, 1623, 1631, 1636.

17068. *Euphues and his England. Containing his voyage and adventures.*

(T. East) f. G. Cawood, 1580. Other editions: two in 1580; 1581, 1582, 1584, 1586, 1588, 1592, 1597, 1601, 1605, 1606, 1609(and reprinted with the *Anatomy* from 1617 on).

Malbie, Sir Nicholas. 172099. *A plaine and easie way to remedie a horse is foundered in his feete.* T. Purfoote, 1576. Other editions: 1583, 1586, 1588, 1594.

Markham, Gervase. 17346. *A discourse of horsmanshippe.* J. Charlewood f. R. Smith, 1593. Other editions: 1595, 1596, 1597, 1599, 1606.

Marlowe, Christopher. 17413. *Hero and Leander.* A. Islip f. E. Blunt, 1598. Other editions: 1598, 1600, 1606, 1609, 1613, 1617, 1622, 1629, 1637.

Mascall, Leonard. 17580. *The first booke of cattell.* (The second booke. The third booke.) J. Wolfe, 1587. Other editions: 1591, 1596, 1600, 1605, 1610, 1620, 1627, 1633.

Nash, Thomas. 18371. *Pierce Penilesse his supplication to the diuell.* [J. Charlewood f.] R. Jhones, 1592. Other editions: two more in 1592; 1593, 1595.

Nichols, Josias. 18541. *The plea of the innocent: Wherein is averred; that the ministers & people falslie termed puritanes, are iniuriouslie slaundered.* [J. Windet?], 1602. Other editions: two more in 1602, both printed in Middelburg.

Norden, John. 18616. *A pensiue mans practice very profitable for all personnes.* [Part I]. H. Singleton, 1584. Other editions: 1589, two in 1592; 1598, 1600, 1609, 1610, 1612, 1615, 1620 ('after 40 impressions'), 1624, 1627, 1629, 1635 ('above 41 impressions'), 1632, 1640.

   1862a.1. *The pensiue mans practice. The second part. Or the pensiue mans complaint and comfort.* J. Windet f. J. Oxenbridge, 1594. Other editions: 1599 (and printed with Part III after 1600).

   18626a.3. *A progress of pietie, being the third part of the pensiue mans practice.* V. S[immes] f. J. Oxenbridge, 1598. Other editions: two in 1600; 1608, 1616, 1623, 1633.

Painter, William. 19121. *The palace of pleasure.* [Vol. I.] [J. Kingston a.] H. Denham f. R. Tottell a. W. Jones, 1566. Other editions: 1569, 1575.

   The second tome of the palace of pleasure (19124), was published in 1567 and [1580?].

*Partridge, John. 19425.5. *The treasure of commodious conceits, & hidden secrets, and may be called, the huswiues closet, of healthfull prouision.* R. Jones, 1573. Other editions: 1584 ('the fourth tyme corrected'), 1584 ('now amplified and inlarged'), 1586, 1591, 1596, 1600, 1608, 1627, 1633, 1637.

Perkins, William. 19646. *A golden chain; or, the description of theologie* [with twelve other treatises, on continuous signatures]. J. Legat, Printer to the University of Cambridge, 1600. Other editions: 1603 (02) (this edition contains five additional treatises and is entitled, as are all succeeding editions, *The works of that famous and worthie minister of Christ in the universitie of Cambridge, M.W. Perkins*);

1605, 1608–9, 1612–13, 1616–18. Vol. I was reprinted in 1626 and 1635; Vol. II was reprinted in 1631; Vol. III was reprinted in 1631.

Perkins' sermons and treatises also sold well in independent editions; the following sermons, in addition to the editions recorded, appeared in *The works* as well.

19665. *A case of conscience . . . Whereunto is added a discourse, taken out of H. Zanchius.* Three editions in 1592; 1595.

19685. *A declaration of the true manner of knowing Christ crucified.* 1596, 1597, 1611, 1615, 1621, 1625, [c. 1628].

19688. *A direction for the gouernment of the tongue.* 1593, [1593?], 1595, 1597, 1603, 1611, 1615, 1621, 1625, 1632, 1634, [c. 1638].

19703. *An exposition of the symbole or creed of the apostles.* 1595, 1596, 1597, 1611, 1616, 1631.

19709. *The foundation of christian religion.* 1590, 1591, 1592, 1595, 1597, 1601, 1604, 1606, 1608, 1615, 1616, 1617, 1618, 1627, 1629, 1632, 1633, 1636, 1638.

19724.5 *A graine of musterd-seed.* Two in 1597, 1603, 1607, 1611, 1615, 1621, 1625, [c. 1638].

19728. *How to live, and that well.* 1601, 1603, 1611, 1615, 1621, [1625], [1638].

19735.8. *A reformed catholike: or, a declaration shewing how neere we may come to the present church of Rome.* 1597, 1598, 1604, 1611, 1619, 1634.

19742. *A salue for a sicke man, or, the right manner of dying well.* 1595, 1595 (in *STC Addenda*), 1596, 1597, 1600 (in *STC Addenda*), 1603, 1611, 1615, 1621, 1625, 1632, [c. 1638].

19752. *A treatise tending vnto a declaration whether a man be in the estate of damnation or in the estate of grace.* [1590?], 1591, 1592, two in 1595; 1597, 1600, 1608, 1619.

19758. *Two treatises. I. Of . . . repentance. II. Of the combat of the flesh and spirit.* 1593, two in 1595; 1597, 1600, 1611, 1615, 1619, 1621, 1625, 1632, [c. 1638].

Pettie, George. 19819. *A petite pallace of Pettie his pleasure; conteyning many pretie histories.* R. W[atkins, 1576]. Other editions: [1578?], [c. 1585], [c. 1590], 1608, 1613.

Platt, Sir Hugh. 19977.7. *Delightes for ladies, to adorne their persons, tables, closets, and distillatories.* P. Short, [1600?]. Other editions: 1602, 1603, 1605, 1608, 1609, 1611, 1615, 1617, 1624, 1628, 1630, 1632, 1635, 1636, 1640.

Playfere, Thomas. 20014. *A most excellent and heauenly sermon. Upon the 23. chapter of the gospell of saint Luke.* [J. Orwin] f. A. Wise, 1595. Other editions: two in 1595; 1596, 1597, 1607, 1611, 1616.

Powel, Gabriel. 20150. *The resolved christian, exhorting to resolution.* V. S[immes] f. T. Bushel, 1600. Other editions: 1602, 1603, 1607, 1616, 1623.

Raleigh, Sir Walter. 20634. *The discouerie of the large, rich, and bewtiful empire of Guiana. Performed in the year 1595. by sir W. Ralegh.* R. Robinson, 1596. Other editions: two more in 1596.

Remedies. 20870. *Remedies for diseases in horses. Approued and allowed by diuers very auncient learned mareschalles.* [Often wrongly ascribed to Sir N. Malbie]. T. Purfoote, 1576. Other editions: 1583, 1586, 1588, 1594.

Rice, Richard. 20973. *An inuective againste vices taken for vertue.* J. Kyngston f. H. Kirckham, [c. 1575]. Other editions: 1579, 1581, 1589.

Robson, Simon. 21131.5. *The choise of change: containing the triplicitie of diuinitie, philosophie, and poetrie.* R. Ward, 1585. Other editions: five more in 1585; two in 1598.

Rogers, John. 21181. *The displaying of an horrible secte of grosse and wicked heretiques, naming themselues the Familie of loue.Newely set foorth by I. R[ogers], 1578. Whereunto is annexed a confession of articles, made the 28. of May 1561.* [H. Middleton] f. G. Bishop, [1578]. Other editions: 1578, 1579.

21183. *The summe of christianitie, reduced vnto eight propositions.* [Anon.] [T. Dawson, 1578?]. Other editions: 1679 [1579], [1580?].

Rowlands, Samuel. 21392.7. *The letting of humors blood in the head-vaine.* W. White f. W. F[erbrand], 1600. Other editions: two more in 1600; [1605?], 1607, 1610, 1611, 1613.

*Scoggin, John. 21850.3. *The iestes of Skogyn.* T. Colwell, [c. 1570]. (Entered 1565–6.) Other editions: 1626. (These are the only extant editions.)

Scot, Reginald. 21865. *A perfite platforme of a hoppe garden.* H. Denham, 1574. Other editions: 1575, 1578.

Shakespeare, William. 22345. [*Rape of Lucrece.*] *Lucrece.* R. Field f. J. Harrison, 1594. Other editions: 1598, two in 1600; 1607, 1616, 1624, 1632.

22345. *Venus and Adonis.* R. Field, sold [by J. Harrison], 1593. Other editions: 1594, [1595?], 1596; two in 1599; [1602?], [1607?], [1608?], [1610?], 1617, 1620, 1627, 1630, [1630/6?], 1636.

Shelford, Robert. 22400.5. *Lectures or readings upon the 6. verse of the 22. chapter of the Prouerbs, concerning the vertuous education of youth.* [Anon.] Widdow Orwin f. T. Man, 1596. Other editions: 1602, 1606.

Sidney, Sir Philip. 22536. *Syr P.S. his Astrophel and Stella. To the end of which are added, sundry other rare sonets of diuers gentlemen.* [J. Charlewood] f. T. Newman, 1591. Other editions: 1591, [1597?].

22539. *The countesse of Pembrokes Arcadia.* [Ed. M. Gwinne and F. Greville?] J. Windet f. W. Ponsonbie, 1590. Other editions: 1593, 1594, 1599, 1605, [1617?], two in 1621; 1627, 1633, 1638.

Smith, Henry, 22718. *The sermons of master Henry Smith, gathered into one volume. Printed according to his corrected copies in his life time.* T. Orwin, [R. Robinson, a. T. Scarlet?] f. T. Man, 1592. Other editions: 1593, 1594, 1597, 1599, 1601, 1604, 1607, 1609, 1611, 1614, 1618, 1622, 1628, 1631, 1637.

Smith's sermons appeared individually and in numerous collections; the list below is a summary of the editions of his works.

22660. *The examination of vsury, in two sermons. Taken by characterie, and after examined.* (Three separate editions in 1591; three in 1591, Part III of 22685 (see below); sixteen in *The sermons*, one in *Thirteen sermons*.)

22666. *Gods arrow against atheists.* (1593, 1600, 1607, 1614, 1617, 1622, 1628, 1631, 1632, 1637. Most of the editions after 1600 were bound with *The sermons*.)

22685. *A preparatiue to mariage. The summe whereof was spoken at a contract, and inlarged after. Whereunto is annexed a Treatise of the Lords supper, and another of Vsurie.* (Three editions in 1591; seventeen more of all three treatises in *Thirteen sermons* and *The sermons*.)

22693. *A sermons of the benefite of contentation. Taken by characterie.* (Five editions in 1590, two in 1591. Another edition in 22783.3, *Certain sermons*, 1591; sixteen editions in *The sermons*; thirteen editions in *Three sermons*, 22735ff.)

22697. *The sinfull mans search: or seeking of God. (Maries choise. With prayers.)* (1592, 1593, two in 1594; 1596, 1598 in *Ten* and *Twelve sermons* (22779, 22790); [1595?], 1598 in *The trumpet of the soule* (22727.5); 1629, 1632, 1637 in *Twelve sermons* (22781).

22770.5. *The sinners confession. By Henrie Smith.* (1593, two in 1594; 1595, 1598, 1599 in *The trumpet of the soule* (22747.3ff.); 1596, 1598 in *Ten* and *Twelve sermons* (22779, 22780); nine in *Two sermons* (22765ff.); 1629, 1632, 1637 in *Twelve sermons* (22781ff.)

22701.5. *The sinners conuersion. By Henrie Smith.* (1593, two in 1594. Reprinted in the same collections as 22700.5, above.)

22703. *Three prayers, one for morning, another for the euening: the third for a sick-man. Whereunto is annexed, a godly letter and a comfortable speech.* (Two editions in 1591, 1592; two more, 1591, in *A preparatiue to mariage* (above); 1591 in *Certain sermons* (22783.3); fifteen in *The sermons*.)

22706. *The trumpet of the soule, sounding to iudgement.* (1591, two in 1592; 1593, 1621, 1626, 1630, 1632, 1640; 1592, two in 1594 in *The sermons* (only three of seventeen editions); twelve in *The trumpet of the soule* (22747.3ff.); 1629, 1631, 1637 in *Twelve sermons* (22781ff.)).

22713. *The wedding garment.* (Three editions in 1590, three in 1591; one each in *Foure sermons* (22783.7), *Certain sermons* (22783.3), and *Twelve sermons* (22783); seventeen in *The sermons*.)

22735. *Three sermons made by maister H. Smith.* (1599, 1601, 1604, 1607, 1609, 1611, 1613, 1616, 1619, 1624, 1628, 1632, 1637.)

22747.3. *The trumpet of the soule. By H. Smith.* [4 sermons]. ([1595?], 1598, 1599; merges with four more sermons of which complete work there eds. in 1602, 1605, 1607, 1609, 1612, 1614, 1617, 1620, 1624.)

22775.3. *Six sermons preached by maister H. Smith. With two prayers.* (1592, 1593, two in 1594; 1596, 1598, 1599.)

Smith, Sir Thomas. 22857. *De Republica Anglorum. The maner of gouernement of England.* H. Midleton f. G. Seton, 1583. Other editions: 1584, 1589, 1594, 1601, 1609, 1612, 1621, 1633, 1635, 1640.

Southwell, Robert. 22950. *Marie Magdalens funeral teares*. J. W[olfe] f.
G. C[awood], 1591. Other editions: 1592, 1594, [1596?], 1602, 1609.

22955. *Moeoniae. Or, certaine excellent poems and spirituall hymnes:
omitted in the last impression of Peters Complaint*. V. Sims f.
J. Busbie, 1595. Other editions: two more in 1595.

22955.7. *Saint Peters complaint, with other poemes*. [J. Windet f.
J. Wolfe], 1595. Other editions: two more in 1595; 1597, 1599,
[1600?], 1602, [1609?], 1615.

22968.5. *A short rule of good life. Newly set forth according to the
authours direction before his death*. [Anon.] (*An epistle of a religious
priest vnto his father* [Init. R.S.]) [London? Fr. Garnet's secret press,
1597?]. Other editions: [1597?], [1602–5], [1603–10], 1622.

22971. *The triumphs over death: or, a consolatorie epistle*. [Init. R.S.]
V. S[immes] f. J. Busbie, sold at N. Lings shop, 1595. Other editions:
two in 1596.

Sparke, Thomas. 23021.5. *A sermon preached at Cheanies the 14. of
September, 1585. at the buriall of the right honourable the earle of
Bedford*. Oxford, J. Barnes, [1585]. Other editions: 1585, 1595.

Spenser, Edmund. 23089. *The shepheardes calender conteyning twelve
aeglogues proportionable to the twelve monthes*. H. Singleton, 1579.
Other editions: 1581, 1586, 1591, 1597, 1611, 1617.

Stow, John. 23319. *A summarie of Englyshe chronicles. Collected by
J. Stow, 1565*. In aed. T. Marshi, 1565. Other editions: 1566, [1570],
1575, 1590.

23325.4 (formerly 23320). *The summarie of Englyshe chronicles*. (*Lately
collected and published*) *now abridged and continued tyl March, 1566.
By J. S*(*tow*). T. Marshe [1566]. Other editions: [1567], [1573], 1579,
1587, two in 1598; 1607, 1611, 1618.

*23333. *The chronicles of England, from Brute vnto this present yeares
1580*. H. Bynneman f. R. Newberie, at the assign. of H. Bynneman,
[1580]. Other editions: 1592, [1600], 1615, 1631. (*The Chronicles* was
the first 4° edition of the expanding *Summarie*; Stow published one
more 8° edition of the *Summarie* in 1590, then revised the format.
This revised work, *The Annales of England*, is recorded in the new
STC as the 1592 edition of the *Chronicles*. I have included it because
of its close links with the *Summarie* and *Abridgement* (23325.4ff.).)

*23341. *A survay of London. Contayning the originall, antiquity,
increase, moderne estate, and description of that citie. With an appendix* . . . [J. Windet f.) J. Wolfe, 1598. Other editions: 1599, 1618,
1633. (I have included this work because of its links with the *Summarie* and *Chronicles*; see Chapter VI, notes 2–5.)

Stubbes, Philip. 23376. *The anatomie of abuses: contayning a discouerie, of
vices in a verie famous ilande called Ailgna. Made dialogue-wise*.
J. Kingston f. R. Jones, 1583. Other editions: 1583, 1584, 1595.

23381. *A Christal glasse for christian women. Contayning an excellent
discourse, of the life and death of Katherine Stubbes*. R. Jhones, 1591.
Other editions: 1592, 1600, 1603, 1606, 1608, 1610, 1612, 1618, 1620,

1621, two in 1623; 1624, 1626, 1627, 1629, 1630, 1631, 1632, 1633, 1634, 1635, 1637.

Sutton, Christopher. 23474. *Disce mori. Learn to die. A religious discourse.* [J. Windet f.] J. Wolfe, 1600. Other editions: 1601, 1602, 1604, 1607, 1609, 1613, 1616, 1618, 1626, 1629, 1634.

    23483. *Disce vivere. Learne to live.* J. Windet f. C. Burby, 1602. Other editions: [1604?], 1608, 1611, 1617, 1626, 1629, 1634, with 23474.

T., A., Practitioner in Physic. 23606. *A rich store-house or treasury for the diseased. now set foorth for the benefit of the poorer sort. By A.T.* [T. Purfoot] f. T. Purfoot and R. Blower, 1596. Other editions: 1601, 1607, 1612, 1616, 1630.

*Tarlton, Richard, 23683.3. *Tarltons jests. Drawne into these three parts.* T. Snodham f. J. Pudge, 1613 (first extant edition). Other editions: [c. 1620], [c. 1630], 1638.

    *The sequel, *Tarltons newes out of purgatorie*, had editions in 1590 [c. 1600], and 1630.

*Thomas, Lewis. 24003. *Seauen sermons, or the exercises of seuen Sabbaoths. Together with a short treatise vpon the commaundements.* V. Sims, 1599. Other editions: 4th, 1602; 7th, 1610; 9th, 1615; 10th, 1619; 11th, 1638.

Tilney, Edmund. 24076. [*A brief and pleasant discourse of duties in marriage.*] H. Denham, 1568. Other editions: two more in 1568, 1571, 1573, 1577, 1587.

Timberlake, Henry. 24079. *A true and strange discourse of the travailes of two English pilgrimes: to Jerusalem [etc.].* [R. Bradock] f. T. Archer, 1603. Other editions: 1608, 1609, 1611, 1612, 1616, 1620, 1631.

Topsell, Edward. 24127. *The reward of religion. Delivered in sundrie lectures vpon the booke of Ruth.* J. Windet, 1596. Other editions: 1597, 1601, 1613.

[Treatise]. 24252. *A very proper treatise, wherein is briefly sett forthe the arte of limming.* R. Tottill, 1573. Other editions: 1581, 1583, 1588, 1596, 1605.

Tusser, Thomas. 24375. *Fiue hundreth points of good husbandry vnited to as many of good huswiferie, now lately augmented.* [H. Denham? f.] R. Tottill, 1573. Other editions: two more in 1573; 1574, 1576, 1577, 1580, [1585], 1586, 1590, 1593, 1597, two in 1599; 1604, 1610, 1614, 1620, 1630, 1638.

Udall, John. 24494. *A commentarie vpon the lamentations of Jeremy.* [Anon.] Widdow Orwin f. T. Man, 1593. Other editions: 1595, 1599, 1608, 1637.

    24503. *Peters fall. Two sermons vpon the historie of Peters denying Christ.* [On Matt. xxvi. 34–5, 72–4 and Luke xxii. 54–8, 60–2]. J. Windet a. T. Judson f. N. Lyng, 1584. Other editions: two more in [1588].

    24505. *The state of the church of Englande, laide open in a conference betweene Diotrephes a Bishop, Tertullus a Papist, [etc.* Anon.] [R. Waldegrave, 1588]. Other editions: [c. 1585], [1587?], 1589.

Vaughan, William. 24612. *Naturall and artificial directions for health.* R. Bradocke, 1600. Other editions: 1602, 1607, 1611, 1617, 1626, 1633.

Vicary, Thomas. 24707. *The Englishemans treasure, or treasor for Englishmen: with the true anatomye of mans body. Also the rare treasor of the English bathes, written by W. Turner. Gathered by W. Bremer.* J. Windet f. J. Perin, 1586. Other editions: 1587, 1596, 1599, 1613, 1626, 1633.

Warner, William. 25079. *Albions England. Or historicall map of the same island.* G. Robinson [a. R. Ward] f. T. Cadman, (1586). Other editions: 1589, 1592, 1596, 1602, 1612.

Webbe, Edward. 25151.5. *The rare and most wonderfull things which E. Webbe hath seene in the landes of Jewrie, Egypt, Grecia, Russia, and Prester John.* [J. Wolfe] f. W. Wright, 1590. Other editions: two more in 1590; [1592?], [1600].

Weever, John. 25220. *An agnus Dei.* [Life of Christ. In verse.] V. Sims f. N. Lyng, 1601. Other editions: 1603, 1606, 1610.

West, William. 25267. [Pt. I] Συμβολαιογροία. *Which may be termed the art, description, or image of instruments.* R. Tothill, 1590. Other editions: two in 1592; 1594, 1597, 1598, 1603, 1605, 1610, 1615, 1622, 1632.

    25276.3. [Pt. II of Symbolaeography. Heading Biʳ:] *A treatise concerninge the forms of fines, concords, recoueries, arbirementes and indictments etc., being a parcel of Symbolaeography judiciall.* [R. Totell, 1593]. Other editions: 1594, 1597, 1601,1606, 1611, 1618, 1627.

Whitgift, John. 25427. *An answere to a certen libel intituled, An admonition.* H. Bynneman f. H. Toy, 1572. Other editions: 1572 [1573]; 1573.

Willet, Andrew. 25696. *Synopsis papismi, that is, a generall viewe of papistry; deuided into three hundreds of popish errors.* T. Orwin f. T. Man, 1592. Other editions: 1594, 1600, 1613, 1634.

    25701. *Tetrastylon papisticum, that is, the foure principal pillers of papistrie.* R. Robinson f. T. Man, 1593. Other editions: 1596, 1599.

*Willis, John. 25744a. *The art of stenographie, teaching by plaine and certaine rules, the way of compendious writing. Whereunto is annexed a direction for steganógraphie, or, secret writing.* [Anon.] [W. White] f. C. Burbie, 1602. other editions: 1617; 6th, 1618; 8th, 1623; 9th, 1628; 10th, 1632; 12th, 1638.

*Worship, William. 25987. *The christians mourning garment. The third edition.* f. T. Pavier, 1603. (Entered 7 aug. 1602). Other editions: 1608, 1610, 1618, 1630, 1636.

*Wright, Leonard. 26025. *A display of dutie, dect* [sic] *with sage sayings, pythie sentences, and proper similies.* J. Wolfe, 1589. Other editions: 1602, 1614, 1616, 1621.

    26033.5. *A summons for sleepers. Wherein offenders are cited to repentance. Herevnto is annexed, A patterne for pastors.* [J. Wolfe, sold by E. Aggas], 1589. Other editions: three more in 1589, 1596, 1615, 1637.

[Writing Tables or Tablets.] 26049.2 (formerly 102). *Wryting tables, with a necessarie calender for xxv [yea]res, with all the principall fayres in Englande, the festiuall holydayes, the hie wayes from one towne to another [etc.].* Made by Franke Adams. [H. Singleton f. F. Adams, 1577?]. Other editions: [1579?], 1580, 1581, 1584, 1594, 1598, 1601, [1602?], 1604, 1609, 1611, 1615, 1618, [1625], 1628.

II POPULAR DRAMA

The entries appear in the basic form adopted by Harbage in *Annals of English Drama*: all titles are modernized, and following each title is the year in which the play was first performed (or for those plays with no recorded first performance, the time-span in which the first performance most likely occurred). I have not, however, listed the dramatic companies by which the plays were performed; and I have listed the plays alphabetically by author, or by title if author is unknown, not chronologically. The dates in parentheses are the dates of publication, as they appear in the *STC*, or, if the play was printed after 1640, as recorded by Harbage (who lists the first edition only).

A Larum For London, or The Siege of Antwerp. c. 1598–1600 (1602)
Arden of Feversham. c. 1585–92 (1592, 1599, 1633)
Captain Thomas Stukeley. 1596 (1605)
Chapman, George. *An Humorous Day's Mirth*. 1597 (1599)
    The Blind Beggar of Alexandria. 1596 (1598)
Chettle, Henry. *Hoffman, or Revenge for a Father*. 1602 (1631)
Chettle, Henry and Day, John. *The Blind Beggar of Bednall Green*. 1600 (1659)
Chettle, Henry, Dekker, Thomas and Haughton, William. *Patient Grissil*. 1600 (1603)
Chettle, Henry and Munday, Anthony. *The Death of Robert, Earl of Huntingdon (2 Robin Hood)*. 1598 (1601)
    The Downfall of Robert, Earl of Huntingdon (1 Robin Hood). 1598 (1601)
Clyomon and Clamydes. c. 1570–83 (1599)
Common Conditions. 1576 (1576?)
Dekker, Thomas. *Old Fortunatus*. 1599 (1600)
    The Shoemakers' Holiday, or The Gentle Craft. 1599 (1600, 1610, 1618, 1624, 1631)
Dekker, Thomas, Day, John and Haughton, William. *The Spanish Moor's Tragedy (Lust's Dominion)*. 1600 (1657)
Drayton, Michael, Hathaway, Munday, Anthony and Wilson, Robert. *I Sir John Oldcastle*. 1599 (two in 1600)
Edward III. c. 1590–5 (1596, 1599)
Fair Em, The Miller's Daughter. c. 1589–91 (1593? 1631)
The Fair Maid of the Exchange. c. 1594–1603 (1607, 1625, 1637)
The Famous Victories of Henry V. c. 1583–8 (1598, 1617)
Fulwell, Ulpian. *Like Will to Like*. c. 1562–8 (1568, 1587)

Garter, Thomas. *The Most Virtuous and Godly Susanna*. c. 1563–9 (1578)
Greene, Robert. *Friar Bacon and Friar Bungay*. c. 1589–92 (1594, 1630)
   ? *George à Green, the Pinner of Wakefield*. c. 1587–93 (1599, 1632)
   ? *John of Bordeaux, or The Second Part of Friar Bacon*. c. 1590–4 (Ms.)
   Orlando Furioso. 1588–92 (1594, 1599)
   The Scottish History of James IV. c. 1590–1 (1598)
   ? *I Selimus*. c. 1586–93 (1594, 1638)
Greene, Robert and Lodge, Thomas. *A Looking Glass for London and England*. c. 1587–91 (1594, 1598, 1602, [1605], 1617)
Haughton, William. *The Devil and his Dame* (*Grim, the Collier of Croydon*). 1600 (1662?)
   Englishmen for My Money, or A Woman Will Have Her Will. 1598 (1616, 1626, 1631)
Heywood, Thomas. *1* and *2 Edward IV*. c. 1592–9 (1599, 1600, 1605, 1613, 1619, 1626)
   The Four Prentices of London. c. 1592–1600 (1615, 1630)
   The Royal King and the Loyal Subject. 1602–18 (1637)
   A Woman Killed With Kindness. 1603 (1607, 3rd edn, 1517)
How A Man May Choose a Good Wife From a Bad. c. 1601–2 (1602, 1605, 1608, 1614, 1621, 1630, 1634)
Ingleland, Thomas. *The Disobedient Child*. c. 1559–70 [c. 1569?]
Jack Straw. c. 1590–3 (1593)
Jonson, Ben. *Every Man in His Humour*. 1598 (1601)
   Every Man Out of His Humour. 1599 (three in 1600)
King Darius. 1565 (pub.) (1565)
King Leir. c. 1588–94 (1605)
A Knack to Know a Knave. 1592 (1594)
A Knack to Know an Honest Man. 1594 (1596)
Kyd, Thomas. *The Spanish Tragedy*. c. 1582–92 (c. 1592, 1594, 1599, two in 1602; 1610, 1615, 1618, 1623, 1633)
Locrine. c. 1591–5 (1595)
Lodge, Thomas. *The Wounds of Civil War*. c. 1587–92 (1594)
Look About You. c. 1598–1600 (1600)
Lupton, Thomas. *All For Money*. c. 1559–77 (1578)
Marlowe, Christopher. *Doctor Faustus*. c. 1588–92 (1604, 1609, 1611, 1616, 1619, 1620, 1624, 1628, 1631)
   Edward II. c. 1591–3 (1594, 1598, 1612, 1622)
   The Jew of Malta. c. 1589–90 (1633)
   The Massacre at Paris. 1593 ([1594])
   1 Tamburlaine the Great. c. 1587–8 (1590, 1597 both parts, 1605 *1* only)
   2 Tamburlaine the Great. c. 1587–8 (1590, 1597 both parts, 1607 *2* only)
Merbury, Francis. *A Marriage Between Wit and Wisdom*. 1579 (or 1570) (Ms.)
Mucedorus. c. 1588–98 (1598, 1606, 1610, 1611, 1613, 1615, 1618, 1619, 1621, 1626, 1631, 1634, 1639)
Munday, Anthony. *John à Kent and John à Cumber*. c. 1587–90 (Ms.)
New Custom. c. 1570–3 (1573)

The Peddler's Prophecy. c. 1561–3 (1595)

Peele, George. *The Battle of Alcazar*. c. 1588–9 (1594)
    Edward I. c. 1590–3 (1593, 1599)
    The Old Wives Tale. c.1588–94 (1595)

Phillip, John. *Patient and Meek Grissil*. c. 1558–61 (c. 1566?)

Porter, Henry. *1 The Two Angry Women of Abingdon*. c. 1585–9 (two in 1599)

1 Richard II, or Thomas of Woodstock. c. 1591–5 (Ms.)

Shakespeare, William. *All's Well That Ends Well*. c. 1601–4 (1623, 1632)
    As You Like It. c. 1598–1600(1623, 1632)
    The Comedy of Errors. c. 1590–4 (1623, 1632)
    Hamlet. 1599–1601 (1603, 1604, 1611, 1623, c. 1625, 1632, 1637)
    1 Henry IV. c. 1596–8 (1598, 1599,1604, 1608, 1613, 1622, 1623, 1632, 1632 (2nd folio), 1639)
    2 Henry IV. c. 1597–8 (1600, 1623, 1632)
    Henry V. 1599 (1600, 1602, 1608, 1623, 1632)
    1 Henry VI. 1592 (1623, 1632)
    2 Henry VI. c. 1590–2 (1594, 1600, 1619, 1623, 1632)
    3 Henry VI. c. 1590–2 (1595, 1623, 1632)
    Julius Caesar. c, 1598–1600 (1623, 1632)
    King John. c. 1591–8 (1623, 1632)
    Love's Labour's Lost. c. 1588–97 (1598, 1623, 1631, 1632)
    The Merchant of Venice. c. 1594–7 (1600, 1619,1623, 1632, 1637)
    The Merry Wives of Windsor. c. 1597–1602 (1602, 1619, 1623, 1632, 1637)
    A Midsummer-Night's Dream. c. 1594–8 (two in 1600; 1623, 1632)
    Much Ado About Nothing. c. 1598–1600 (1600, 1623, 1632)
    Richard II. c. 1594–5 (1597, two in 1598; 1608, 1615, 1623, 1632, 1634)
    Richard III. c. 1591–7 (1597, 1598, 1602, 1603, 1612, 1622, 1623, 1629, 1632, 1634)
    Romeo and Juliet. c. 1591–7 (1597, 1599, 1609, 1623, 1632, 1637)
    The Taming of the Shrew. c.1594–8 (1623, 1631, 1632)
    Titus Andronicus. 1594 (1594, 1600, 1611, 1623, 1632)
    Troilus and Cressida. c. 1601–3 (1609, 1623, 1632)
    The Two Gentlemen of Verona. c. 1590–8 (1623, 1632)
    Twelfth Night, or What You Will. c. 1600–2 (1623, 1632)

(All references to editions of 1623 and 1632 are to the First and Second Folios of Shakespeare's works. The other editions are quartos.)

Shakespeare, William, Munday, Anthony, Dekker, Thomas, Chettle, Henry and Heywood, Thomas (?). *Sir Thomas More*. c. 1593–1601 (Ms.)

Thomas Lord Cromwell. c. 1599–1602 (1602, 1613)

The Trial of Chivalry. c. 1599–1603 (1605)

1 and 2 The Troublesome Reign of King John. c. 1587–91 (1591, 1611, 1622)

The True Tragedy of Richard III. c. 1588–94 (1594)

Wager, Lewis. *The Life and Repentance of Mary Magdalen*. c. 1550–66 (1567)

Wager, W. *Enough is as Good as a Feast.* c. 1559–70 ([c. 1565–70])
    The Longer Thou Livest, The More Fool Thou Art. c. 1559–68 ([c. 1569])
    The Trial of Treasure. 1567 (pub.) (1567)
Wapull, George. *The Tide Tarrieth No man.* 1576 (pub.) (1576)
A Warning for Fair Women. c. 1598–9 (1599)
The Weakest Goeth to the Wall. c. 1599–1600 (1600, 1617)
Wilson, Robert. *The Three Ladies of London.* c. 1581 (1584, 1592)
    The Three Lords and Three Ladies of London. c. 1588–90 (1590)
Woodes, Nathaniel. *The Conflict of Conscience.* c. 1570–81 (1581)
Yarington, Robert. *Two Lamentable Tragedies.* c. 1594–8 (1601)

Appendix B The popular authors

The material here is a distillation of the information available in standard biographical references and in biographies of individual authors. It is intended to serve as a brief guide to the status and occupations of the popular authors, not as a study of their lives or a bibliography of the works written about them.

In column 5 I have listed the standard source(s) available for a brief study of each author. An asterisk (*) indicates that a biography of the author exists, either in his collected works or in an individual study. An abbreviated title, other than those listed below, refers to a work referred to in the notes.

The *DNB* is generally reliable when it deals with the university training and professional careers of the authors it treats (with the exception of the article on John Norden, which has been proved wrong by A.W. Pollard); but it is not altogether trustworthy about family backgrounds, since the scholars who compiled it tended to attribute gentle connections to any author of note if it was possible to do so. It is always wise to consult modern biographies when they exist, or to consult the *Alumni Oxonienses* and the *Alumni Cantabrigienses* on matters of background.

The following abbreviations have been used:

AC	John and J.A. Venn, *Alumni Cantabrigienses*, Part I
AO	Joseph Foster, *Alumni Oxonienses*
(Both these works guide the reader to further works on the alumni)	
DNB	*The Dictionary of National Biography*
Chambers	E.K. Chambers, *The Elizabethan Stage*, Vol. III
Lewis	C.S. Lewis, *English Literature in the Sixteenth Century Excluding Drama*
Pollard, 'Unity of J.N.'	A.W. Pollard, 'The Unity of John Norden: Surveyor and Religious Writer', *The Library*, new series 7 (1926–7), 233–52
Porter	H.C. Porter, *Reformation and Reaction in Tudor Cambridge*
+	Biographical material available in prefatory material of the author's work

Name	Family	Training	Occupation	Source
Abbot, G., 1562–1633	s. shearman, of Guildford, Surrey	Oxford: BA, BD, DD	Master of University College, Oxford, bishop	DNB, AO
Armin, R., b. c. 1570		Apprenticed to a goldsmith	Pamphleteer, playwright, actor	DNB, Chambers
Ascham, R., 1515–68	s. John, steward to 7th Baron Scrope, of Yorkshire	Cambridge, BA, MA	Scholar, tutor secretary to Queen Mary, other political figures	DNB, Lewis, *
Babington, G., 1550–1640	s. Bernard, of Nottinghamshire	Cambridge: BA, MA	Chaplain to Earl of Pembroke, bishop	DNB, AC
Bacon, Sir F., 1561–1626	s. Sir Nicholas, statesman	Cambridge: n.d.; Gray's Inn	Scholar, politician	DNB, *
Bailey, W., d. 1593	s. Henry, of Portisham, Dorset, esq.	Oxford: BA, MA, BMed, DMed	Regius Professor of Physic, Oxford; physician to Queen Elizabeth	DNB (Bayley), A
Baker, H., fl. 1562–87	b. London	Apprenticed?	Merchant adventurer?	DNB, +
Baker, J., fl. 1581		Sizar, Cambridge; Oxford, BA, MA	Divine	AC, AO
Baldwin, W., fl. 1547	West Country	Oxford: MA?	Minister, author, printer	DNB, +
Balmford, J., b. 1566	s. poor carpenter		Divine; calls mayor and aldermen of Newcastle-on-Tyne his patrons.	DNB
Becon, T., 1512–67	b. Norfolk, father d.y.	Cambridge: BA, BD	Reformer, Marian exile, beneficed preacher, London	DNB, AC,
Bicknoll, E.	No information available			
Bigges, W., d. c. 1586			Soldier: a 'land-captain' killed on Drake's West Indian voyage	+
Bourne, W., d. 1583	s. William, of Gravesend		Mathematician, minor official. Free of Mercers' Company; innkeeper (?)	DNB
Bradshaw, W., 1571–1618	s. Nicholas, of Bosworth, Leicestershire	Cambridge: BA, MA (sizar)	Puritan divine	DNB, AC

ame	Family	Training	Occupation	Source
rasbridge, T., 1547–1590	Northamptonshire	Oxford: BA, MA	Divine, doctor?; vicar of Banbury	DNB, AO
reton, N., 1545–1626?	s. William, merchant (y. s. of gentle family)	Oxford? n.d.	Poet: Countess of Pembroke's circle	DNB, *
rowne, J., c. 1529–95	s. John, Draper, of Bristol	Apprenticed	Merchant, mayor of Bristol	*Merchants Avizo*
ull, H., d. 1575	Warwickshire	Oxford: BA, MA	Divine	DNB, AO
ullein, H., d. 1576	Ely	Probably took MD abroad	Divine, doctor	Bullen, *Elizabethans*
urton, W., d. 1616	b. in Winchester	Oxford: BA	Puritan divine and teacher, translator of Erasmus	DNB, AO
ancellar, J., fl. 1564			'one of Queen Mary's chapel'	DNB
arlile, C., d. 1588		Cambridge: BA, MA, BD, DD	Fellow, Clare Hall, Cambridge, divine	DNB, AC
ary, W., fl. 1580	Gentle family, Buckinghamshire	Oxford: BA, MA	Doctor	AO
ecil, W., 1520–98	s. groom of the robes, constable of Warwickshire castle	Cambridge: n.d.; Gray's Inn	Statesman	DNB, *
aaderton, L., 1536?–1640	Gentle – disinherited for turning Protestant	Cambridge: BA, MA, BD, DD	Puritan divine; master of Emmanuel College, Camb.	DNB, Porter, AC
aamberlaine, B., b. c. 1545	Oxfordshire gentry	Oxford: BA, MA, BD, DD	Noted preacher in Oxford region	AO
aapman, G., 1559–1634	s. wealthy yeoman of Hitchin, Hertfordshire (mat. grf. gentle)	Oxford?: n.d.	Dramatist, poet	DNB, Chambers, *
aettle, H., d. 1607?	s. Robert, Dyer, of London	Apprenticed to T. East, printer	Printer, later dramatist	DNB, Chambers, *
eaver, R., 1562–1620	'of Oxon., pleb.'	Oxford: BA	Divine, rector of Drayton	AO
onstable, H., 1562–1613	s. Sir Robert, of Newark	Cambridge: BA	Became Catholic, lived in Paris, involved in plots to convert Elizabeth	DNB

Name	Family	Training	Occupation	Source
Conway, Sir J., d. 1603	Heir Sir John, of Warwickshire	No university	Soldier, governor of Ostend	DNB
Cooper, T., 1517?–94	s. poor tailor of Oxford	Oxford: BA, MA, BD, DD	Doctor (during Mary's reign), scholar, bishop	DNB, AO, *
Cotton, R., fl. 1596	5th s. Shropshire gentleman	Probably apprenticed	Draper, of London, patron of Hugh Broughton	DNB
Curteys, R., 1532–82	from Lincolnshire	Cambridge: BA, BD, DD	Bishop	DNB, AC
Daniel, S., 1562–1619	'of Somerset, pleb.'; possibly wealthy family	Oxford: n.d.	Poet, playwright, tutor to daughter of Earl of Cumberland. Court connections	DNB, AO, Lewis, *
Davies, Sir J., 1569–1626	3rd s. John, of Wiltshire, gentleman	Oxford: n.d.; Middle Temple	Attorney General for Ireland	DNB, *
Davison, F., d. c. 1619	Eldest s. William, secretary of state	Gray's Inn	Poet	DNB
Day, A., fl. 1586	s. Thomas, of London, parish clerk	Apprenticed to T. Duxsell stationer	Stationer	DNB
Dekker, T., 1570–1641	London (almost certainly not gentle)	No university	Pamphleteer, dramatist	Jones-Davies, *Thomas Dekker*
Deloney, T., d. 1600	Norwich?	Probably grammar school	Silk-weaver, balladeer, novelist	F.O. Mann, *Works of Thomas Deloney*
Dent, A., 1553–1607	b. Melton, Leicestershire	Pensioner, Cambridge: BA, MA	Rector, S. Shoebury, Essex, Puritan divine, connected with Robert, Lord Rich	DNB, Porter, AC
Dering, E., 1540?–76	Kent, gentle family	Cambridge: BA, MA, BD	Puritan divine	DNB, AC
Dowland, J., 1563?–1626?	(Probably *not* Irish)	Educated abroad	Musician: court Lutenist in Denmark, England	DNB, *
Drant, T., d. 1578?	s. Thomas, of Hagworthingham, Lincolnshire	Pensioner, Cambridge: BA, MA, BD	Divine; chaplain to Grindal, translator of Horace	DNB, AC, Lewis

ame	Family	Training	Occupation	Source
ayton, M., 1563–1631	b. Hartshill, Warwickshire, s. butcher or tanner	Page in service of Sir H. Goodere	Poet, dramatist	DNB, Lewis, *
dwards, R., 1523–1566	Somerset	Oxford: BA, MA	Gentleman of Chapel Royal, Master of Children of the Chapel Royal	DNB, AO, *
nton, Sir G., 1539–1608		No university	Translator; government official in Ireland. Knighted 1589	DNB, Lewis
rde, E., fl. 1585		Sizar, Cambridge: n.d.	Romance writer (no other profession clear)	DNB, AC (Fourd)
xe, J., 1517–87	s. citizen of Boston, Lincolnshire	Oxford: BA, MA	Divine, martyrologist	Mosley, *John Foxe*
lke, W., 1538–89	s. Christopher, wealthy London citizen	Cambridge: BA, MA	Master Pembroke Hall, Cambridge; Puritan polemicist	DNB, AC
well, U., 1546?–86	Gentle, Somerset	Oxford: n.d.	Rector of Nauton, Gloucestershire	DNB, Chambers, AO
rter, T.	No information available			
e, A., fl. 1580–95		Sizar, Cambridge: BA	Rector of Thorpe-on-the-Hill, Lincolnshire	AC
son, T., fl. 1580	s. Thomas, of Lancashire, 'scholar'	Cambridge: BA	Divine	AC
ford, G., fl. 1620	Cambridgeshire?	Cambridge: BA, MA	Puritan divine, active in Presbyterian movement	DNB, AC
sson, S., 1555–1624	Kentish, parents poor	Oxford: BA	Playwright, pamphleteer, by 1584, a divine	DNB, Lewis, *
fton, R., . 1572	b. London	Apprenticed	Grocer, printer	DNB, Stow, *Survey*
ene, R., 560–92	s. Norwich saddler	Sizar, Cambridge: BA, MA	Pamphleteer, playwright	DNB, AC, *

Name	Family	Training	Occupation	Source
Greenham, R., 1535?–94?		Sizar (in his 20s), Cambridge: BA, MA	Rector of Dry Drayton, Cambridgeshire, for 20 years	DNB, Porter
Hall, J., 1574–1656	s. John, deputy to Earl of Huntingdonshire	Pensioner, Cambridge: BA, MA, BD, DD	Satirist, later divine, chaplain to Prince Henry, bishop	DNB, AC, *
Harington, Sir J., 1561?–1612	s. John, courtier and author	Cambridge: BA	Courtier, soldier; translated *Orlando Furioso*	DNB, *
Harman, T., fl. 1567	s. Kentish gentleman, grf. clerk of the crown for Henry VII	No university	Gentleman, pamphleteer	DNB, *
Harrison, W., fl. 1600	(*Not* the topographer – no knowledge of father)	Sizar, Cambridge: BA, MA	Preacher appointed by Elizabeth for Courts Palatine, Lancashire	AC
Harvey, R., 1560–1623	s. master rope-maker, Saffron Walden, Essex	Pensioner, Cambridge: BA, MA	Fellow of Pembroke Hall, Cambridge, astrologer, pamphleteer	DNB, AC
Haughton, W., c. 1575–1605			Playwright for Admiral's Company	Chambers
Hayward, Sir J., 1564?–1627	b. Felixstowe, Suffolk	Cambridge: BA, MA, LLD	Historian, religious pamphleteer. Imprisoned for writing pamphlet on Henry IV and Richard II, dedicated to Essex	DNB, AC
Heywood, T., d. 1650?	s. preacher, of Lincolnshire	Cambridge: n.d.	Playwright, pamphleteer	DNB, Chambers
Hunnis, W., d. 1597		No university	Musician, Master of Children of the Chapel Royal (member Grocers' Company by marriage)	DNB, Bradbrook, *Common Player*
Inglelend, T.		Cambridge: n.d.?		Chambers
Jewel, J., 1522–71	s. yeoman, of Devonshire	Oxford: BA, MA	Marian exile, bishop	DNB, *

ame	Family	Training	Occupation	Source
ohnson, R., 1573–1659	London	Calls himself an apprentice in *Nine Worthies*	Wrote romances (nothing else definite)	DNB, +
onson, B., 1572–1637	s. minister, step-father bricklayer	Apprenticed (not completed)	Dramatist, poet	DNB, *
er, G.	Scottish	No material available		
ing, J., 1558–1621	s. Philip, page to Henry VIII, of Worminghall, Bucks.	Oxford: BA, MA, BD, DD	Bishop	DNB, AO
ingsmill, A., 1538–69	s. John of Sidmonton, Hampshire	Oxford: BCL	Fellow, All Souls, Oxford, lived abroad	DNB, AO
newstub, J., 1544–1624	Westmorland	Cambridge: BA, MA, BD	Rector of Cockfield, Suffolk for 45 years	DNB, AC
d, T., 1558–94	s. Francis, London scrivener	Merchant Taylors' School	Scrivener?, playwright	DNB, Chambers, *
mbard, W., 1536–1601	1st s. John, draper, alderman, sheriff of London	Lincoln's Inn	JP, Master in Chancery, keeper of Tower Records	DNB, *
wkenor, Sir L., d. 1626	s. and heir of Thomas, of Shelley, Suffolk	Cambridge: MA?; Inns of Court	MP, Master of Ceremonies to James I, knighted 1603	AO, AC
ig, N., d. 1597		Probably apprenticed	Printer	Wright, *MCC*
dge, T., 1558?–1625	s. Thomas, grocer, lord mayor of London	Oxford: BA	Pamphleteer, playwright	DNB, *
oton, T., l. 1583	No material available			
y, J., 1554?–1606	s. minor ecclesi-astical official at Canterbury	Oxford: BA	Courtier, author	DNB, Hunter
lbie, Sir N., 530?–84	Yorkshire gentry	No university	Distinguished soldier, various official positions in Ireland	DNB (Malby)
rkham, G., 568?–1637	3rd s. Tobert, Cottam, Nottinghamshire, family gentle	Educated privately	Soldier in Low Countries, Ireland; later, pamphleteer	DNB

Name	Family	Training	Occupation	Source
Marlowe, C., 1564–93	s. John, member shoemakers' and tanners' gilds, Canterbury	Cambridge: BA, MA (pensioner)	Dramatist	DNB, Chambers
Mascall, L., d. 1589	Sussex gentry		Clerk of the kitchen in household of M. Parker	DNB
Merbury, F., fl. 1579	No information available			
Munday, A., 1553–1633	s. Christopher, draper, of London	Apprenticed to J. Alde, stationer (left after 2 yrs)	Messenger of the Chamber, pamphleteer, playwright, draper in later life	DNB, Chambers, J.C. Turner *Anthony Mundy*
Nash, T., 1567–1601	s. William, minister	Cambridge: BA (sizar)	Pamphleteer, playwright	DNB, AC, *
Nichols, J., 1555?–1639		Oxford: BA	Puritan divine; rector of Eastwell, Kent 1580–1603, suspended, 1603	DNB, AO
Norden, J., c. 1548–1623	Somerset	Probably Oxford: BA	Topographer, religious writer attorney	Pollard, 'Unity of J.N.'
Painter, W., 1540?–94	s. citizen and wool-comber of London	Sizar, Cambridge: n.d.	Clerk of Tower of London	DNB, AC
Partridge, J., fl. 1570–80			Known only by his works, possibly a barber surgeon	DNB, +
Peele, G., 1558–97?	s. London salter, author of pamphlet, pageants	Oxford: BA, MA	Dramatist	DNB, Chambers
Perkins, W., 1558–1602	s. Thomas, of Marston Jabbett, Warwickshire	Pensioner, Cambridge: BA, MA	Fellow, Christ's College, Cambridge, lecturer, Gt St Andrew's	DNB, Porter, *
Pettie, G., 1548–89	y. s. of John, esq., of Oxford	Oxford: BA	Soldier, gentleman author	DNB, AO
Phillip, J., fl. 1570–1626?			Member of Queens' College, Cambridge	Chambers
Platt, Sir H., 1552–1608	3rd s. Richard, brewer, sheriff of London	Cambridge: BA, Lincoln's Inn	Scholar of natural science, agriculture	DNB, AC

ame	Family	Training	Occupation	Source
ayfere, T., 1561?–1609	s. William, of London	Pensioner, Cambridge: BA, MA, BD, DD	Various positions at Cambridge, chaplain to James I	DNB, AC
orter, H., fl. 1580s	s. London gentleman?	Poss. B.Mus, Oxford	Musician and dramatist?	Chambers
owell, G., 1573–1611	s. David, Welsh historian, divine	Oxford: BA (possibly BD)	Divine, pamphleteer, chaplain to R. Vaughan, bishop of London	DNB, AO
aleigh, Sir W., 1552–1618	Devonshire gentry	Oxford: n.d.	Poet, courtier, sea-dog	DNB (Raleigh), *
ice, R., fl. 1548–79	s. chaplain to Cardinal Wolsey	Monastery	Abbot of Conway, career unclear after 1537	DNB
obson, S., d. 1617	s. John, of W. Morton, Durham	Pensioner, Cambridge: BA, MA, BD, DD	Various benefices, Dean of Bristol for 20 years	AC
ogers, J., fl. 1560–80		Oxford: BA, MA	Fellow, Queen's College, Oxford, divine	AO
owlands, S., 1570–1630?	London		Pamphleteer, satirist	DNB, *
ot, R., 1538?–99	Kentish gentry	Oxford: n.d.	Minor county official, MP, probably JP, wrote long work on witchcraft	DNB, Lewis
akespeare, W., 1564–1616	s. glover, bailiff of Stratford-upon-Avon	King Edward's Grammar School	Poet, dramatist	DNB, *
elford, R., 1563–1627		Sizar, Cambridge: BA, MA	Divine, benefice in Suffolk, 1599–1627	AC
dney, Sir P., 1554–86	Heir, Sir Henry	Oxford: n.d.	Courtier, soldier, poet	DNB, *
ith, H., 1550?–91	s. Erasmus, of Withcote, Leicestershire	Oxford: BA, MA	'Silver-tongued Smith', popular preacher in London	DNB, AO, *
ith, Sir T., 1513–77	Heir, John of Saffron Walden, Essex (coat of arms 1545)	Cambridge: BA, MA; Padua: DCL	Regius Professor Civil Law, statesman	DNB, AC, *Rep. Ang.*
uthwell, R., 1561–95	Gentle	English College, Rome	Jesuit, poet, martyr	DNB, *

Name	Family	Training	Occupation	Source
Sparke, T., 1548–1616	South Somercotes, Lincolnshire	Oxford: BA, MA, BD, DD	Chaplain to Cooper, rector of Bletchley, Buckinghamshire	DNB, AO
Spenser, E., c. 1552–99	s. John, cloth-maker, of London	Sizar, Cambridge: BA, MA	Secretary to Young, Lord Grey of Wilton, official in Ireland, poet	DNB, *
Stow, J., 1525?–1605	3rd generation London, probably s. of a tailor	Apprenticed	Merchant taylor (yeoman), chronicler	DNB, Stow, *Survey*
Stubbes, P., fl. 1581–93	Probably gentle	Cambridge or Oxford?: n.d.	Gentleman pamphleteer	DNB, *Anatomy*
Sutton, C., 1565?–1629	'of Hants., pleb.'	Oxford: BA, MA, BD, DD	Various benefices, Canon of Westminster, Lincoln	DNB, AO
Thomas, Lewis, 1568–c. 1619	Welsh	Oxford: BA	Divine, benefices in Wales	AO
Tilney, E., d. 1610	Gentle; family related to the Howards	No university	Master of the Revels, 1579–1607	DNB
Timberlake, H., d. 1626		Apprenticed?	Merchant adventurer, worth £1,000 at his death	DNB
Topsell, E., d. 1638?		Cambridge: BA, MA? (records lost)	Divine, amateur zoologist	DNB, AC
Tusser, T., 1524–80	s. William, of Rivenhall, Essex, mother gentle	Cambridge: n.d.	Musician, courtier, farmer	DNB, *
Udall, J., 1560?–92		Sizar, Cambridge: BA, MA	Divine, pamphleteer, involved in Marprelate tracts	DNB, AC
Vaughan, W., 1577–1641	Gentle, related to Earl of Carbery	Oxford: BA, MA; Vienne: LLD	Poet, colonial pioneer to America	DNB, AO
Vicary, T., d. 1561			Master of barber-surgeons 5 times, surgeon to Henry VIII, Elizabeth I, Mary, Elizabeth	DNB
Wager, L., fl. 1560s			Rector of St James Garlickhithe, 1560; 'a corrector of books'	Chambers

me	Family	Training	Occupation	Source
ager, W.	No information available			
apull, G., fl. 1570s			Possibly clerk of the Stationers' Co., 1571–5, went to America, 1584?	Chambers
arner, W., 1558–1809	s. sailor?, London	Probably did *not* attend Oxford	Attorney of Common Pleas, man of letters	Lewis and a +
ebbe, E., b. 1554	s. Richard, master gunner	Trained as gunner at age 12	Ships' gunner, captured by Turks and made galley slave, adventurer	DNB, +
eever, J., 1576–1632	Lancashire	Sizar, Cambridge: n.d.	Poet, antiquarian, wrote epigrams on contemporary literary figures, treatise on funeral monuments	DNB
est, W., b. c. 1550	s. Thomas, of Beeston, Nottinghamshire probably gentle	Inns of Court	Made fortune as lawyer, settled in Yorkshire c. 1590	DNB
hitgift, J., 1530–64	1st s. Henry, merchant of Great Grimsby, Lancashire	Cambridge: BA, BD, DD	Bishop	DNB, AC, *
llet, Andrew, 1562–1641	s. Thomas, notary public, later divine	Pensioner, Cambridge: BA, MA, BD, DD	Rector of Barley, Hertfordshire for 33 years, friend of Perkins	DNB, AC
son, R., fl. 1600		Sizar, Cambridge: n.d.?	Comic actor, playwright	DNB, Bradbrook, *CP*
oodes, N., fl. 1570s		Sizar, Cambridge: BA, MA	Minister in Norwich	Chambers, AC
rship, W., 1575?–1626	Leicestershire	Cambridge: BA MA, BD, DD	Vicar of Crofts, Lincolnshire, chaplain to Earl of Huntingdonshire	AC
ight, L., fl. 1588–91	Bassingbourne, Cambridgeshire		Pamphleteer, defending bishops vs. Marprelate	DNB
rington, R., fl. 1590s	No information available			

Appendix C Topical breakdown of Elizabethan popular literature

The topical breakdown of these works depends, to a certain extent, on the decisions of the person who compiles the filing system. Should Foxe's *Acts and Monuments* be filed under 'religion' or 'history'? Does Southwell's religious poetry belong under 'religion' or 'poetry and fiction'? Are descriptions of Tudor voyages 'essays' or 'history'? In each of these cases, I have opted for the latter choice, but I admit that the placement of such borderline works tends to be arbitrary. For the sake of clarity, then, I have compiled the following brief sketch of my filing system so that the reader can study the choices I have made if he wishes. Works are listed under their author's name only, except in cases where confusion might arise; in these cases, I have given the *STC* number as well. All the works referred to here appear in full in Appendix A.

RELIGION

Babington (2), Baker, Becon (2), Bicknoll, Book, Bradshaw, Bull, Burton, Cancellar, Carlile, Chaderton (2), Chamberlaine, Cleaver, Conway, Cooper, Cotton, Curteys, Dent (4), Dering (5), Drant, Foxe (*STC* 11242), Fulke (2), Garden, Gee, Gibson, Gifford (4), Greenham, Harrison, Hayward, Hunnis, Jewel, Ker, King, Kingsmill (2), Knewstub, Nichols, Norden (3), Perkins, Playfere, Powell, Rice, Rogers, Shelford, Smith, H., Southwell (*STC* 22968.5 and 22971), Sparke, Stubbes (*STC* 23381), Sutton (2), Thomas, Topsell, Udall (3), Weever, Whitgift, Willet (2), Worship, Wright (26033.5)

FICTION AND POETRY

Armin, Breton (*STC* 3696 and 3699), Constable, Daniel, Davies, Davison Dekker (2), Deloney (5), Dowland, Drayton, Edwards, Forde, Greene (6), Harington (2), Harman, Johnson, Lodge, Lyly (2), Marlowe, Nash, Painter, Pettie, Robson, Rowlands, Scoggin, Shakespeare (2), Sidney (2), Southwell (*STC* 22950, 22955, and 22955.7), Spenser, Tarlton, Tusser

HANDBOOKS

Ascham, Baker, H., Bourne, Breton (*STC* 3694), Browne, Coote, Day, Fenton, Grafton (*STC* 12153), Lambard (2), Markham, Partridge, Platt, Scott, Treatise, West (2), Willis, Writing Tables

HISTORY

Abbot, Baldwin, Bigges, Foxe (*STC* 11222), R.G., Grafton (*STC* 12148), Leigh, Lewkenor, Raleigh, Stow (4), Timberlake, Warner, Webbe

ESSAYS AND EPIGRAMS

Bacon, Balmford, Breton (*STC* 3705), Gosson, Hall, Ling, Lupton (2), Smith (Sir Thomas), Stubbes (*STC* 23376), Tilney, Wright (*STC* 26025)

MEDICAL AND SCIENTIFIC STUDIES

Bailey, Brasbridge, Bullein (2), T.C., Cary (2), Harvey, Malbie, Mascall, Remedies, A.T., Vaughan, Vicary

Appendix D Chronological list of popular works in which merchants appear

A work appears on this list if it contains any reference to a principal citizen. The reference is usually a major one, occurring in the text (as in Browne's *Merchant's Avizo*, or plays and stories in which citizens have major roles), but occasionally it is not. If the reference to citizens appears only in the dedication (as in Chaderton's Paul's Cross sermon) or in a discussion of estates of the realm (as in Curteys' sermon), or in a minor dramatic scene, I marked the work with an asterisk (*).

I have listed best-sellers and drama separately. Each play is listed according to the year in which Schoenbaum suggests it was probably first performed, in the revised edition of the *Annals of English Drama*. The reader who wishes to find the range of dates in which each play was probably first performed should turn to Appendix A, Part II.

1558–69

Drama – none

Best-sellers

Humphrey Baker, *The Well Spring of Sciences* (1562)
Richard Grafton, *An Abridgement of the Chronicles of England* (1563)
John Foxe, *Acts and Monuments* (1563)
William Bullein, *A Dialogue Against the Fever Pestilence* (1564)
John Stow, *A Summary of English Chronicles* (1565)
    The Summary of English Chronicles, . . . now Abridged (1566)
John Scoggin, *The Jests of Scoggin* (c. 1565)

1570–80

Drama

George Wapull, *The Tide Tarrieth No Man* (1576)

Best Sellers

John Foxe, *A Sermon of Christ Crucified* (1570)
*Richard Curteys, *A Sermon preached Before the Queen's Majesty* (1573)
William Bourne, *A Regiment For the Sea* (1574)
*Thomas Brasbridge, *The Poor Man's Jewel* (1578)
*Laurence Chaderton, *An Excellent . . . Sermon, Preached at Paul's Cross* (1578)
Thomas Lupton, *Sivqila* (1580)

1581–91

Drama

Robert Wilson, *The Three Ladies of London* (1581)
The Troublesome Reign of King John (1588)
Christopher Marlowe, *The Jew of Malta* (1589)
R. Greene and T. Lodge, *A Looking Glass for London and England* (1590)
Fair Em, the Miller's Daughter (1590)
Arden of Feversham (1591)
Jack Straw (1591)
*George Peele, *Edward I* (1591)

Best-Sellers

Sir Thomas Smith, *De Republica Anglorum* (1583)
Philip Stubbes, *The Anatomy of Abuses* (1583)
John Browne, *The Merchant's Avizo* (1589)
*Roger Cotton, *A Direction to the Waters of Life* (1590)
Edward Webbe, *The Rare and Most Wonderful Things* (1590)
Richard Tarlton, *Tarlton's Jests* (c. 1590)
*Robert Greene, *A Notable Discovery of Cosenage* (1591)

1592–1603

Drama

William Shakespeare, *The Comedy of Errors* (1592)
1 Richard II, or Thomas of Woodstock (1592)
Robert Yarington, *Two Lamentable Tragedies* (1594)
A Knack to Know an Honest Man (1596)
William Shakespeare (?) *et al.*, *Sir Thomas More* (1595)
Captain Thomas Stukeley (1596)
William Shakespeare, *The Merchant of Venice* (1596)
*George Chapman, *The Blind Beggar of Alexandria* (1596)
William Haughton, *Englishmen for my Money* (1598)

Ben Jonson, *Every Man in His Humour* (1598)
Thomas Dekker, *The Shoemakers' Holiday* (1599)
Thomas Heywood, *1 and 2 Edward IV* (1599)
A Larum For London (1599)
A Warning for Fair Women (1599)
Michael Drayton *et al.*, *1 Sir John Oldcastle* (1599)
Thomas Lord Cromwell (1600)
The Weakest Goeth to the Wall (1600)
How a Man May Choose a Good Wife from a Bad (1602)
The Fair Maid of the Exchange (1602)

Best-Sellers

Angel Day, *The English Secretary* (2nd edn, 1592, and all thereafter)
Robert Greene, *A Quip for an Upstart Courtier* (1592)
Thomas Nash, *Piers Penniless* (1592)
John Stow, *The Annals of England* (1592)
Henry Smith, *The Sermons* (1592)
*James Balmford, *A Short and Plain Dialogue* (1593)
*A.T., *A Rich Storehouse . . . for the Diseased* (1596)
Richard Johnson, *The Seven Champions of Christendom* (1596)
*Nicholas Ling, *Politeuphia* (1597)
Thomas Deloney, *Jack of Newbury* (c. 1597)
    The Gentle Craft, Part I (1597)
Joseph Hall, *Virgidemiarum* (1597)
John Stow, *A Survey of London* (1598)
Thomas Deloney, *The Gentle Craft, Part II* (1598)
*Emanuel Forde, *Parismus* (1598)
Thomas Deloney, *Thomas of Reading* (c. 1599)
Richard Greenham, *The Works* (1599)
William Perkins, *A Golden Chain* (1600)
Arthur Dent, *The Plain Man's Pathway to Heaven* (1601)
Nicholas Breton, *A Post With a Mad Packet of Letters* (1602)
Thomas Deloney, *Strange Histories* (1602)
*Henry Timberlake, *The Travels of Two English Pilgrims* (1603)

Index

Past and Present Publications

General Editor: T.H. ASTON, *Corpus Christi College, Oxford*

*Also issued as a paperback

†Co-published with the Maison des Sciences de l'Homme, Paris